CHICAGO'S STREET GUIDE TO THE SUPERNATURAL

A Guide to Haunted and Legendary Places in and near the Windy City

CHICAGO'S STREET GUIDE TO THE SUPERNATURAL

A Guide to Haunted and Legendary Places in and near the Windy City

By

Richard T. Crowe

With Carol Mercado

© Carolando Press, Inc. October, 2000
All rights reserved

3rd Printing, October, 2004

All photos were taken by Richard T. Crowe unless stated otherwise. Archival photos are from Richard T. Crowe's private collection unless otherwise stated.

Cover and artwork enhancements: Dave Andre

Printed in the United States

Carolando Press, Inc.
Oak Park, IL 60302
708.383.6480
800.366.8843
www.carolando.com
info@carolando.com

ISBN 0-940542-06-4

TABLE OF CONTENTS

For my mother, Mrs. Evelyn B. Crowe,

And my grandmother, Mrs. Mary Zarack,

Who told me my first ghost stories.

ACKNOWLEDGMENTS

Besides the many people mentioned throughout the text, I want to especially single out those who have helped in my career and research over the years.

To my mother and sister, Joann, for always being there to run errands, assist with the mailings, etc., especially during the crazy Halloween season.

A hearty thanks to the professional hospitality organizations and their members: the Chicago Convention and Tourism Bureau, the Chicagoland Chamber of Commerce, and the Chicago Chinatown Chamber of Commerce.

For the coach companies, who not only provide transportation but also invaluable drivers superb in their knowledge of local geography and lore: Mid-America, Illinois Coach, and Keeshin Charter Service (Coach USA).

For Bob and Holly Agra of Mercury Cruiselines.

For Tom and Kathy Buckley of Viscom, Charles Lucas of the Rasputin Clipping Service, Bill Helmer of the John Dillinger Died for You Society, and the members of the Merry Gangster Literary Society.

Thanks to Gene Phillips of the Ancient Astronaut Society, Dick Leshuk of the International Fortean Organization (INFO), and Mike Flores of the Psychotronic Film Society.

Special thanks to the Hellenium Group for permission to use material from my video, "The Ghosts of Chicago."

My special appreciation to the many active members of the police community who must remain nameless until retirement.

A deep appreciation for my many friends in the media including Ed "Chicago" Schwartz, Steve King and Johnnie Putman, the crew at Fox Thing in the Morning, Richard Roeper, Jack Higgins, Irv Kupcinet, Frank Mathie, Roz Varon, Eddie and JoBo, Mancow, Kevin Matthews, and many, many others.

For my friends, associates, and fellow travelers: Tom McCarthy and family, Tony Vaci, Dr. Joe Troiani, Bill Karmia, Joe Karmia, Bob Zmuda, Rick King, George Sassoon, Robert Ritholz, Whitey O'Day, Bryan Knudsen, G. D. Paetsch, Bruce Huey, Bob Falkenburg, Mike Johnson, Tom Brennan, the Tito Brothers, Kelly Wong and family, Dr. Karen Eng, Herman and Betty Wong, Julie Dragon, Janet Lee, Renee Champagne, Karen Uchima, Grant Wylie, Sam Maranto, Karen Barrett, Ted Chianakas, Chuck Rusin, Mike Dietz, Paul Palmer, Bill King, Jim Brophy, Jim McCabe, Kevin Morley, John Duda, Bill Grimstad, Ken and Jennifer Rowe, Karen Harsha, Janet Augustine, Deryl Brunner, Rich Hurth, Vince Iacinno III, Bob and Mary Ellen O'Connell, Barbara Crowe Hickey and Pat Hickey, Sam "Billy Goat" Sianis, the management and staff of Hooters Restaurant in Chicago, and the Rockford Ghost Hunter, John Kahl.

A special thank you to G. E. Smith for his wonderful editing skills and encouragement.

In remembrance of the late Ivan T. Sanderson, Chef Louis Szathmary, and my father, Richard H. Crowe.

Thanks for my financial freedom goes to the tens of thousands who have taken my tours and cruises and attended my lectures over the years.

And, of course, a hearty thanks to Chicagoland's ghosts who have made me what I am today!

FOREWORD

August 2000

Chicago, Illinois

Dear Reader,

I have had the pleasure of Richard Crowe's acquaintance for the past twenty-seven years. His knowledge of Chicago history is extensive. We met at a time when we were completing our graduate degrees and starting our careers. Richard was working as a city planner for the City of Chicago conducting research on our city's ethnic neighborhoods. I was producing the local television show, "News of the Psychic World."

After learning more of his research work on Chicago ghosts, I decided to bring him on as a guest. After his appearance and the overwhelming positive response from our viewing audience, he became a regular.

Richard Crowe is extremely captivating with both the spoken and written word. The book is a personally guided tour. As you will see, he brings to the reader the systemic exploration of the ghost phenomena, and yet at the same time, he has the ability to report on the subject with the voice of a true storyteller. His interpretation opens up a window and allows the reader to become part of the story in a tangible Hitchcock fashion.

Being the only full time researcher in this area who has devoted his life to the study and investigation of the paranormal since the early seventies, I would not expect anything less.

So if you cuddle up with this book some evening and happen to hear curious noises, don't let them scare you. It might just be a denizen from these pages.

Joseph E. Troiani, Ph.D.

Beginnings

I am a product of the South Side of Chicago and was shaped by many unique experiences.

As a boy, I vividly remember hearing ghost stories from my mother and my grandmother whose tales of the "old country" brought to life images of Poland and the Austro-Hungarian Empire. Going to Visitation grammar school, Father Charles Carmody, whom I would serve as an altar boy, spun tales of Holy Family Church and other Catholic sites.

I spent three years at Quigley South Preparatory Seminary where my Latin professor Father John J. Nicola was an inspiration. He taught Latin but a major interest was studying the diabolical. As an expert on the possession case that formed the basis for the novel, *The Exorcist*, he was hired by film director Billy Friedkin, to be an advisor on the film adaptation. He also wrote the introduction to *The Amityville Horror*. Although I dropped out of the seminary, Fr. Nicola certainly helped inspire me to continue my studies into the supernatural.

My senior year in high school was spent at Gage Park H. S. at 56th and Rockwell on the South Side. This was the heart of "Resurrection Mary" country, and I began to hear and collect tales of this classic hitchhiking ghost from fellow classmates whose fathers, uncles, and grandfathers claimed encounters with this elusive spirit.

My college days were spent at De Paul University where I earned both a B.A. and M.A. in English literature with a minor in geography. I turned my academic studies into reading Edgar Allen Poe, H. P. Lovecraft, Washington Irving, and Ambrose Bierce while studying exotic and esoteric locales. I earned a reputation around campus as the guy to go to for ghost stories. That background would point me into the direction of a career.

While finishing my Masters at De Paul, I was working full time, first as a teacher at Lourdes High School and then as a city planner at City Hall in Chicago. One day in early 1973, I ran into my old friend, Dr. Richard Houk, head of the geography department. I had already finished all my class work and was getting ready to graduate, but Dr. Houk had an idea he wanted to pitch to me.

The Geographic Society of De Paul sponsored various tours throughout the year. These were usually of textbook topics like local geology or waterways systems. Dr. Houk was, however, asking me if I could put together a tour of the haunted sites around Chicago as a university-sponsored event. I agreed, thinking that it would be a fun thing to do.

On October 27, 1973, the Saturday closest to Halloween, the very first Chicago ghost tour ran. The trip was sold out and had a long waiting list well before tour day. Thanks to Dr. Houk, I found a commercial application for my knowledge and material.

By mid-1979, my tour business had grown to such an extent that I left my position at City Hall, where I was researching neighborhood and ethnic history, and went into the tour business full time. The rest, as they say, is history.

Introduction

To Ghosts, Curses, Jinxes, etc...

The following material is based upon my research into popular Chicagoland folklore and ghostlore. The stories are researched as accurately as possible and often include firsthand accounts. They are, however, based on area legends and supposed supernatural phenomena.

It should be emphasized that ghosts should not be considered harmful or dangerous. It is we, the living, who are usually trespassing into their space, not the other way around.

So, let us examine what is popularly believed to be true about ghosts and hauntings:

A ghost is a paranormal manifestation. It may take the form of a visual apparition, a disembodied voice, the feeling of a cold spot, or a psychic scent not of this world. The key to all of these extrasensory encounters is that they are all believed to be caused by someone dead.

It is thought that many ghosts are caused by someone dying an unnatural death, usually violent, often at a young age. It is also believed that ghosts haunt if the deceased is not given a proper burial, or not buried at all.

It is not uncommon for ghosts to be tied to colorful characters or historical events, particularly violent or traumatic. Murders, disasters, or fatal tragedies seem to create the right atmosphere for classic ghostly encounters.

Ghosts often occur around deaths that are surrounded by secrets, unsolved mysteries, or when the departed may feel that he or she has unfinished work to complete in this world. A ghost may seek human company in an effort to help or complete business important to it.

Ghostly activity can be found at places and locations that are significant to them such as former homes, work places, and even the resting place of the body. It would seem that some ghosts are unaware that they are dead and continue haunting or "living" in a place important to them.

The popularity of ghost stories is universal. In every culture there is some form of belief in the supernatural. Since Chicago is made up of communities representing peoples from all around the globe, we boast local ghost stories of Irish, Polish, Jewish, Italian, Chinese, German, African-American, Filipino, and many other ethnic groups. We should also not forget the animal ghosts encountered here.

Close kin to the ghost story is the supernatural tale of a curse or jinx. Chicago once again has many fascinating examples of this genre of the paranormal. The Stock Yards Curse and the Billy Goat Jinx are two local tales with national significance.

Strange coincidences, prophetic dreams, possession, and many other esoteric topics round out this volume. As far as I am concerned, ghosts are only a jumping-off point into a vast and strange universe of psychic possibilities.

To really know and appreciate Chicago and its history, one needs to delve into its deep ties to the supernatural. The ghostlore and folklore of this city are like the yeast that makes bread rise. This would truly be a flat and tasteless place to live without our local haunts.

I have mined Chicago's literature, social history, geography, and folklore for more than a quarter of a century for the treasures found here. I hope you enjoy these selections and think about those Chicagoans, our spectral neighbors, who have gone on before us.

Now, come with me on a tour of Chicagoland's ghostly and legendary places!

Richard T. Crowe

A GUIDE TO HAUNTED AND LEGENDARY PLACES
IN AND AROUND CHICAGO

CHICAGO DOWNTOWN

		ADDRESSES
1. Cap'n's Orders	Streeterville & Hancock Bldg.	875 N. Michigan Ave.
2. The Ghost in the Tower	Chicago Water Tower	806 N. Michigan Ave.
3. Satan's Skyscraper	Lake Shore Place	680 (666) N. Lake Shore Dr.
4. Spirited Chicken Wings	Hooters Restaurant	660 N. Wells St.
5. A Haunted Nightspot	The Excalibur	632 N. Dearborn St.
6. A Curse on the Chicago Cubs	Billy Goat Tavern	430 N. Michigan Ave.
7. Giant Armchair Fit For A Ghost	Civic Opera House	20 N. Wacker Dr.
8. Eastland Tragedy Returns	Chicago River	Wacker Dr. between Clark and La Salle Sts.
9. Oprah Winfrey's Haunted TV Studio	Harpo Studios	1058 W. Washington Blvd.
10. Asian Fusion, Psychic Confusion	The Red Light Restaurant	820 W. Randolph St.

CHICAGO NORTH

11. Bloody Valentine	CHA private park	2122 N. Clark St.
12. Ghost of John Dillinger	Biograph Theat. & Dillinger's Alley	2400 block Lincoln near Fullerton Ave.
13. A British Pub Haunted	Red Lion Pub	2446 N. Lincoln Ave.
14. The Pub Owner Is A Ghost	The Bucktown Pub	1658 W. Cortland St.
15. Death Personified	Graceland Cemetery (Main Ave.)	4001 N. Clark St.
16. Little Girl Vanishes	Graceland Cemetery (Center Ave.	4001 N. Clark St.
17. The Totem Pole That Came Alive	Kraft Totem Pole	Lake Shore Dr. & Addison
18. A Vodka-Drinking Poltergeist	Ole St. Andrews Pub	5938 N. Broadway
19. The Little Boy Ghost	Rosehill Cemetery Sec. T	5800 N. Ravenswood Ave.
20. Ghost Solves Her Own Murder	Edgewater Medical Center	5700 N. Ashland Ave.
21. Empty Grave for a Ghost	Acacia Park Cemetery	7800 W. Irving Park Rd.
22. The Haunted Indian Burial Ground	Robinson Woods	East River Rd. near Lawrence Ave.
23. Haunted Hotel	O'Hare Hilton	Chicago Int'l O'Hare Airport Term. 2

CHICAGO SOUTH

24. A Church Full of Ghosts	Holy Family Church	Roosevelt Rd. and May
25. Hauntings at Hull House	Hull House	800 S. Halsted St.
26. The Great Chicago Fire	Quinn Fire Academy	558 W. DeKoven (& Jefferson)
27. The 2,700-Year-Old Scream	Field Museum	1400 S. Lake Shore Dr.
28. Block Full of Ghosts	Chinatown	200 W. 22nd Pl.
29. Tito's On The Edge	Tito's Bar	2600 S. Wentworth Ave.
30. Lincoln's Ghostly Funeral Train	South Shore Ill Central Railroad	south from former 12th St. depot
31. Clarence Darrow's Return	Museum of Science and Industry	57th St. and Lake Shore Dr.
32. Lucifer's Last Waltz	Former Kaiser Hall	2988 S. Archer Ave. (& McDermott)
33. Blood Curse of the Stock Yards	Stock Yard Industrial Park	Pershing to 47th, Halsted St. to Ashland Ave.
34. A Debt Beyond The Grave	Visitation Church	843 W. Garfield Blvd. (& Peoria)
35. Ghost Guilt	5501 S. Racine Ave.	also, Longwood Dr. south of 103rd St. and McKinley Pk. area
36. All Soul's Day Apparitions	St. Rita Church	6243 S. Fairfield (63rd. St. & Fairfield Ave.)
37. Ghost Nun	Lourdes High School	4034 W. 56th St.
38. The Priest Who Never Retired	St. Turibius Church	5646 S. Karlov Ave.
39. A Haunted Castle	Beverly Unitarian Church	10244 S. Longwood Dr.
40. The Hungry Fence	Mt. Olivet Cemetery	2755 W. 111th St.
41. The Grinning Phantom	St. Casimir's Cemetery	4401 W. 111th St.

Suburban Chicago North and Northwest | Addresses

42. Seaweed Charlie	Calvary Cemetery	301 Chicago Ave., Evanston
43. Only Tenant for 46 Years	Mayflower Place	405 N. Mayflower Rd., Lake Forest
44. Got the School Spirit	Barat College	700 E. Westleigh Rd., Lake Forest
45. The Soil Cries Murderer	Former house site	8213 Summerdale Ave., Norridge
46. Jet Crash Hauntings	Des Plaines Mobil Home Park	500 W. Touhy Ave., Des Plaines
47. Ghosts Still on the Job	Allstate Arena	6920 North Mannheim Rd., Rosemont
48. Cuba Road Curiosities	Cuba Road area between Rand Rd. & Northwest Hwy.	Lake Zurich to Barrington Hills
49. The House With No Corners	Stickney Mansion	1904 Cherry Valley Rd., Bull Valley
50. Balcony Seat for a Ghost	Woodstock Opera House	121 Van Buren St., Woodstock
51. Road Stop Poltergeists	Al Capone's Hideaway & Steakhouse	35W337 Riverside Dr., St. Charles

Suburban Chicago South and Southwest

52. Emily, The Campus Ghost	Morton College	3800 S. Central Ave., Cicero
53. Restless Gangster	Western side Woodlawn Cemetery	7600 W. Cermak Rd., Forest Park
54. Ghostly Lions, Tigers, Bears...	Woodlawn Cemetery	7600 W. Cermak Rd., Forest Park
55. Flapper Ghost	Melody Mill (replaced by Village Commons)	2401 S. Des Plaines Ave., North Riverside
56. The Bleeding Stop Sign	residential intersection	Riverside Dr. at Olmsted Rd., Riverside
57. Booklover Ghost	La Grange Library	10 W. Cossitt Ave., La Grange.
58. Ghostly Gutter Balls	Alonzi's Villa	8828 Brookfield Rd., Brookfield
59. Flames That Will Not Die	Queen of Heaven Cemetery, Sec. 18	1400 South Wolf Rd., Hillside
60. Scarface is Haunted	Mt. Carmel Cemetery, Sec. 35	1400 S. Wolf Rd., Hillside
61. The Revolving Tombstone	Mt. Carmel Cemetery, Sec. 19	1400 S. Wolf Rd., Hillside
62. The Italian Bride	Mt. Carmel Cemetery, Sec. A	1400 S. Wolf Rd., Hillside
63. A Ghost Just Crossed the Street	Justice Public Library	7641 Oak Grove Ave., Justice
64. The Legend of Resurrection Mary	Resurrection Cemetery	7201 S. Archer Ave., Justice
65. Ballroom Ghost	Willowbrook Ballroom	8900 South Archer Ave., Willow Springs
66. The Legend of Gray-Haired Baby	Sacred Heart Cemetery (nearby woods)	101st St. & Kean Ave., Palos Hills
67. Phantom Horses, Ghostly Riders	Cook County Forest Preserves	95th St. and Kean Ave., Hickory Hills
68. Grave of The Miracle Child	Holy Sepulchre Cemetery, Sec. 7	6001 111th. St., Worth
69. Music From Beyond	Fairmont Hills Cemetery	9100 S. Archer Ave., Willow Springs
70. The Maple Lake Ghost Light	Maple Lake	95th St. E. of Archer Ave., Willow Springs
71. Monks' Castle	St. James Sag Cemetery	107th St. & Archer Ave., Lemont
72. Ghost Car of German Church Rd.	Devil's Creek at German Church Rd.	just east of County Line Rd. Burr Ridge
73. The Soul of a Pet	Hinsdale Animal Cemetery	6400 S. Bentley Ave., Clarendon Hills
74. Ghost is not on the Menu	Country House Restaurant	241 W. 55th St., Clarendon Hills
75. Secrets of Peabody's Tomb	Mayslake	31st St. & Rte. 83, Oak Brook
76. Cold Shoulder From a Saint	Formerly St. Joseph Seminary	St. Jos. Dr. & Midwest Rd., Oak Brook
77. The Glowing Tombstone	Sts. Peter and Paul Cemetery	North & Columbia Sts., Naperville
78. Enigmas of Bachelor Grove	Bachelor Grove Cemetery	Midlothian Turnpike & 143rd St., Midlothian

CHICAGO DOWNTOWN

CHICAGO DOWNTOWN

CAP'N'S ORDERS

STREETERVILLE CURSE

Captain George Wellington Streeter's imagination and strong will forever changed the face and geography of the city. Streeter literally "created" Streeterville, the neighborhood that bears his name. Streeterville is located in one of Chicago's prime real estate areas, beginning around Oak Street Beach and going south to Navy Pier and everything east of Michigan Avenue, roughly forming a triangle of land.

Streeter's colorful career included being a showman, a circus promoter, a Mississippi River steamboat operator, and that of an excursion guide. On July 11, 1886, with the darkening skies threatening and a storm seemed sure and passengers who had traveled to Milwaukee on "Cap'n" Streeter's excursion boat, the *Reutan*, were concerned about her seaworthiness, so instead, they all decided they would take the train back home. Undaunted, the Captain and his wife Maria headed back to Chicago in their homemade wooden steamship. Around 3:00 a.m., the storm-tattered boat rammed into an area called "the Sands." When daybreak came, Streeter found he had run aground on a sandbar that was about 400 feet out from shore. It was in an expensive residential area. He was given permission by one of the owners to remain until he could repair his boat.

But Streeter and his boat stuck around—and for a long time: thirty years. The area encircling his boat rapidly expanded. From nature's impetus came sand that filled in between his boat and the shore. Then contractors obliged by dumping their construction debris near the boat. Streeter's boat became surrounded by 100 acres that had not existed before, which is now around Grand and Michigan Avenues. He renamed his boat, *Mariah the "Squater."*

From 1902 to 1909, Streeter sold off lots of his prime real estate to trusting buyers. His office was set up at the Tremont Hotel. He often traded lots to lawyers in exchange for their legal aid involving property and deed questions and to fight City Hall and the Title and Trust Company.

Finding what he thought was a loophole in the law, Streeter said that his newly created land east of Michigan Avenue was not part of Chicago or Illinois, since the state boundary was delineated on maps as the current shore. He dubbed his land the District of Streeter, akin to the District of Columbia. Of course, "Cap" claimed the right to rule without interference by the city or state. Streeter defended his land with dubious documents and a loaded shotgun. It was said that he had a red-hot temper to match his auburn hair.

It was a noble try, but Streeter was doomed. The money forces were out to get him, and they had many tricks. Streeter served frequent but short stays in jail because of his legal problems. He was in Joliet prison once, framed for a murder. While doing time, his wife Maria was said to have died of exposure and hunger, and for that, Streeter cursed Chicago and City Hall, blaming them for her death.

By 1915, the land actually controlled by the Captain was whittled down to "Fort Streeter," a barbed wire enclosed area where he would have his last stand. On December 11, 1918, agents of the Title and Trust Company, brandishing a legal writ, would forcibly dispossess the old man and his third wife.

After thirty years of standing down the powerful, Streeter watched as his home was burned to the ground.

Streeterville at sundown from Lake Michigan.
Hancock building is on right with twin antennas.

Streeter died in 1921. He was eighty-four. His last words were said to be a, "damn ye," to the "scum of city politicians." His wife carried on his claim of ownership, as did his heirs, however, in 1940, a federal court dismissed the family's final suit.

There was no real thought of a curse on Streeterville for many years. The notion began to be taken seriously only in the early 1970s. Originally, the curse was believed to be just a pitiful old man's raging outburst against progress and change.

The building that forever changed Streeterville was the John Hancock. Built between 1965 and 1969, "Big John" became the tallest building in the world. A giant black monolith, 100 stories tall, with massive twin antennas on top, the Hancock would dwarf other buildings nearby. The John Hancock would later lose its title of being the "world's tallest building" to the Sears Tower.

Symbolically the big, black trapezoid structure reminded some of the mysterious dark monolith in Arthur C. Clarke's movie, "2001: A Space Odyssey," released in 1968. The sci-fi movie was a hit at the same time the Hancock was being completed.

Although a building the size and scope of the Hancock should have been put up at the cost of many construction workers' lives, this was not the case here. According to a John Hancock spokesperson, despite five million hours of labor, there was no loss of life. Once tenants began to move in, however, a series of unusual deaths were noted.

The most notorious death happened in the early hours of August 12, 1971. Lorraine Kowalski was the twenty-nine-year-old girlfriend of affluent Marshall Berlin. Berlin was the vice president of I. S. Berlin Press, a printing company. According to reports, the couple got into a loud argument. He claimed that he retreated into a bathroom. Moments later, the woman plunged to pavement many floors below. She had gone through the window, naked, with her clothing having been left on the floor of the apartment. Although the glass in the double-paned window was capable of taking 280-pounds of pressure per square foot before breaking, the 130-pound woman somehow went through. No charges were brought in the case, but the mystery still remains. Paradoxically, Miss Kowalski entered the record books: hers was the longest fall from any building in the world.

Over the years other deaths would follow. Suicides happened sporadically at Water Tower Place next door or from other buildings along the corridor. There were also celebrity deaths. Comedian and "Saturday Night Live" regular Chris Farley and his brother lived in the Hancock. On December 18, 1997, he would die from an overdose after a wild night of partying.

Although she did not die in Chicago or Streeterville, child-actress Heather O'Rourke has been linked to the Streeterville curse. Followers of "hexed" Hollywood films know that one star in the film died with the release of each of the three "Poltergeist" movies. Portions of "Poltergeist 3" were filmed on location at the John Hancock and Water Tower Place next door.

In 1988, during the production of "Poltergeist 3", little Heather (famous for her line, "They're heeere!") suffered medical complications due to intestinal stenosis and died. Was the actress who played "Carol Anne" in all three "Poltergeist" movies doomed by the "Poltergeist" movie jinx, the Streeterville curse, or conceivably a combination of both? Even Heather's date of death was noteworthy. She died February 1, 1988, the eve of Candlemas, a witches' holiday.

Perhaps the most bizarre piece of trivia involving the Hancock is the fact that Anton LaVey was born at this site on April 11, 1930. LaVey, a former lion tamer and police crime photographer, founded the Church of Satan in 1966. A great deal is made of his birthplace in all published accounts of LaVey, including Blanche Barton's authorized biography.

Even nature itself seems to act strangely at the Hancock. Spiders are found along sky-scrapers as a matter of course, but the Hancock seems to collect more of them than usual. Winds and the building's great height probably have a lot to do with it, but spider webs in the corners of windows do add a Gothic touch to a sleek modern building. The spider colonies are short lived, however, as window washers make a complete circuit every six to eight weeks, and the observation deck windows are washed even more often.

Could there be a connection to the Streeterville curse and to the unusual occurrences or untimely deaths in the area?

Cap Streeter's name lives on in the neighborhood he created, but lost. His decades-old curse seems to be still evolving with the times.

I   John Hancock Building and area

Location:	Streeterville is roughly Oak Street Beach to Navy Pier, everything east of Michigan Avenue, Chicago.
John Hancock Building:	875 North Michigan Avenue
Water Tower Place:	845 North Michigan Avenue
Type of occurrences:	Suicides and strange deaths perhaps due to traditional curse. Strange coincidences and freakish natural behavior also noted.
Characteristics:	A man wronged by society places a curse on those responsible.
Status:	Periodically, deaths usually in a cycle of about two years.

THE GHOST IN THE TOWER

A HANGING MAN HAUNTS THE OLD CHICAGO WATER TOWER

The Old Chicago Water Tower at the Michigan and Chicago Avenues is perhaps the best loved landmark in this city. At the very least, the tower can be credited with inspiring Chicagoans with the "I Will" spirit to rebuild and come back from the ashes after the Great Fire of 1871. As the flames of the fire burned northwards from Mrs. O'Leary's barn on the old West Side, the tower was the only municipal building that remained. Its almost miraculous survival insured that Chicagoans would always have a special place in their hearts for this distinctive stone tower. Its companion structure, the Pumping Station just across the street, on the east side Michigan Avenue, was nearly gutted by the fire.

Designed by the prominent early architect William W. Boyington, the Water Tower and the Pumping Station were constructed in 1869. The stone used in the structures is local limestone, quarried near Lemont, of a beautiful pale yellow hue.

Artistically, the Water Tower is a facsimile of the castellated Gothic style with creative flourishes from Boyington's imaginativeness. The tower became a favorite of Chicagoans and visitors right away.

This ornate tower actually hid a very mundane purpose. The stonework merely camouflaged a 138-foot iron standpipe that provided pressure for water being pumped from Lake Michigan by the Pumping Station. Originally, Michigan Avenue was the shore of Lake Michigan, and water for drinking and other personal use could be pumped from the shoreline with pollution not yet being a hazard.

The Water Tower has the look of a medieval castle and stands out among the more modern structures in the area. The building rises into a tall tower in graduated levels and boasts a crowd of crowned turrets along the way. On the first level, the four sides of the building are identical, with massive arched doors and pointed-arch windows and cylindrical crowned turrets at each corner. The motif continues to the next two levels, with narrow lancet windows and the crowned towers at the four corners; then on to the high tower, with eight small turrets and a copper cupola at its pinnacle. One commentary by a visitor described the Water Tower as, "never were so many cupolas and buttresses, pinnacles and towers grouped together on one spot; none but a true artist could have arranged them in so harmonious a whole."

Apparently, the celebrated Irish wit Oscar Wilde came to a different conclusion. He was quoted during his visit here in 1882, humorously describing the Water Tower as a "castellated monstrosity with salt and pepper boxes stuck all over it," and wondering why anyone would make a water tower masquerade as a miniature medieval castle. He did, however, go on to praise the machinery of the pumping station as "simple, grand and natural." His poignant, oft-repeated observation has become legendary.

Boyington used a similar architectural design for other famous structures that he created, including the Joliet Correction Center and the entrance to Rosehill Cemetery.

In recent years, the tower served as a tourist information center for visitors and shoppers along the Magnificent Mile. It was staffed by the City of Chicago's Department of Cultural Affairs. Those who know a bit more about its background also cherish its folklore and interesting symbolism.

Longtime Water Tower staffer Nancy Caldwell worked in the tourism office for many years. During her years at this location, she remembers many visitors inquiring about the building's haunted reputation. "A lot of people would come in and claim that they saw lights on at the top of the tower at night," Nancy recalls. She reassured people that no offices were in the tower, just on the ground floor, and that there were no lights burning in the high windows.

Although reflections from nearby buildings might account for some of these reports, Nancy finds that one incident still puzzles her.

One night on his day off, a supervisor of the tourism office was visiting a friend at a tall building nearby overlooking the Water Tower. He plainly saw a light on in a high window of the tower, and the window was open also. He called for security. They insisted that there was certainly no light on and no window left open.

After a heated conversation, the security team finally agreed to climb the many stairs up into the tower to check, but only if the supervisor promised them a meal if he was wrong. "He lost the bet and had to buy dinner," Nancy recalls.

Nancy remembers that the supervisor was a very logical type. Even if he was wrong about the light, what about the window's being seen wide open?

I was struck, some years back, with a feeling akin to déjà vu when I realized that Chicago's Water Tower looked a lot like another famous tower. This was not an actual historical tower, but a symbolic one: the tower illustrated in the tarot card deck.

One of the tarot deck picture cards, "The Ruined Tower," depicts a yellow stone tower being set afire by a bolt of lightening. Symbolically it is a visual twin to this historical building that survived the Great Fire of 1871. The dual images, one from the tarot card deck, the other from Chicago's past, involve towers, both stone, both yellow (at least in most tarot card illustrations), and both menaced by flames.

Another tarot card image can be associated with the Water Tower as well. "The Hanging Man" card depicts a man suspended upside down with a rope around one ankle. Curiously, there is a hanging man ghost story connected with the Water Tower.

An early ghost story of the Water Tower involves the shadowy figure of a man with a rope around his neck. This silhouette shape was seen in a window of the tower on various occasions. No real documentation exists to explain why such an image was seen here, and there have been no confirmed reports of sightings since the early 1900s.

Although the hanging victim ghost was not seen upside down, as is the illustration on the tarot card, the imagery is quite close. The coincidence that a "hanging man" ghost haunts Chicago's once fire-threatened water tower should cause the curious to pay close attention to this site, just in case other tarot symbols manifest themselves. Are other tarot-inspired images already here, as yet unnoticed?

Chicago Water Tower, haunted survivor of Great Fire of 1871

2 Water Tower Square

Location:	Michigan Avenue at Chicago Avenue, Chicago.
Type of occurrence:	Traditional apparition seen in window. Mystery lights.
Characteristics:	Shadowy figure of a man hanging from a rope around his neck.
Status:	Apparition not encountered for years. Strange lights in windows are the only current activity.

SATAN'S SKYSCRAPER

NUMBER 666

The American Furniture Mart was conceived when Chicago was the center of the wholesale furniture business. Fronting the lake, the building is actually two structural styles joined together as one bipolar work of architecture. The east end of the building, finished in 1924, is a sixteen-story reinforced concrete structure, while the west end, completed in 1927, is a twenty-story steel-framed skyscraper. Crowning the top of a thirty-story tower is an imaginative pyramidal cap inspired by England's House of Parliament building, which glows with an eerie blue light by night.

As Chicago began to lose its grip on the wholesale furniture market, many of the showrooms began to close or relocate. By the 1980s, the building was reborn as a mixed-use building for commercial businesses and offices, condominiums, and parking. When condominiums here became fashionable, ghost stories suddenly began to circulate about the building. I was having lunch one day at the Omni Ambassador East Hotel's famous Pump Room. A waitress recognized me and began to describe her former haunted apartment and its poltergeist activity. When I asked her where it was, she told me, "the Furniture Mart. You know, 666!" One common thread in all of the prevailing weird tales about this building is the belief the ominous address "666" on the property had something to do with it all.

Perhaps the most notoriously unlucky number in Western tradition, 666 is the sign of the Beast, The Anti-Christ's designation in the last book of the Bible, "Revelations" ("Apocalypse" in the Catholic Bible). For some, the number signifies evil and taints all associated with it.

Numerology can take its toll. Any building that dares to use 666 as its address will attract attention. Around Chicago, there are numerous buildings that could actually have this beastly designation, but only a tiny fraction use the satanic address.

Curiously, the American Furniture Mart used this devilish address for many years, drawing little attention. For six decades the address here was 666 North Lake Shore Drive. Then, in 1984, a dramatic change took place.

New owners, Lohan Associates, acquired the 666 building and announced that it would now be called Lake Shore Place. Furthermore, they would renumber the building as 680 North Lake Shore Drive.

It was said that Playboy Enterprises, who moved there in 1984, insisted on the number change, although there seems to be no concrete evidence to back up the rumor.

New owners, a new name, and a new address, but was it as simple as all that?

The address change was challenged by others who lived and worked in the building. They wanted to keep "666." A new address would not only cause potential confusion for mail deliveries; it would necessitate reprinting stationery, literature, catalogs, business forms, and more. Residents would need new drivers licenses and other identification. The objections were overruled, however, and the change went through.

The dates of the address changeover were somewhat prophetic. The last day for 666 North Lake Shore Drive was on April 30. The first day for the new address of 680 was May 1.

South entrance of Lake Shore Place, "Satan's Skyscraper," originally sported two 666 addresses.

Note: The date of April 30th is exactly halfway to Halloween, the second most evil night of the year in the occult calendar. May 1st is Beltane (May Day), a witches' sabbat (Sabbath). Coincidence?

Before the changeover, I visited the building once again to photograph it from all sides. The four-sided building has one entrance on each side. Three of the four sides have large steel canopies over the doorways. And on each canopy, the address was portrayed twice. There were six sets of 666. The north door bears no canopy and was unmarked. Another coincidence?

When I finished my photography, I phoned the office of the building and asked if I could purchase a set of the 666 numerals for my Chicagoiana collection once they were replaced. The manager's office generously offered to give me a set and told me to drop by after May 1 and pick it up. When I contacted them a few weeks later, I was told that the numbers "had been lost."

Among the businesses located here are a number of small recording studios. I have recorded ghost stories for in-flight airline listening on a few occasions at a studio here. One day, a security guard introduced himself to me and offered to show me something interesting.

On the main floor, he pointed out a "devil's head" carved in stone over an elevator door. The medieval grotesque "green man" seemed fitting for a building with many arcane associations.

Lake Shore Place has not been branded by 666 in well over a decade. But in the collective memory of Chicagoans, this building still remains "Satan's Skyscraper."

3 Lake Shore Place (formerly American Furniture Mart)

Location:	680 North Lake Shore Drive, Chicago.
Type of occurrence:	Traditionally strange site.
Characteristics:	Legends involving devilish or satanic ties due to "unlucky" address.
Status:	Ongoing popularity of tales.

Spirited Chicken Wings

A Haunted Hooters Restaurant

The successful restaurant chain, Hooters, began in Clearwater, Florida, in 1983. In just under twenty years, the number of Hooters Restaurants around the world is close to 200. Their signature item is Buffalo-style chicken wings with sauces that range from mild to 911. Their waitresses, wearing trademarked orange shorts and tank tops, offer friendly service and southern-style hospitality.

Hooters Restaurants decided to invade Yankee land. The Midwest was targeted, so Chicago was a natural choice. Real estate scouts found a corner location at Erie and Wells, and just before Halloween in 1991, the new Hooters opened its doors in the fast-expanding River North area.

The restaurant had certainly found a choice area. They were located on the edge of the sprawling Ontario and Clark nightlife area, ground zero for tourism on the Near North Side. Popular attractions include the Hard Rock Cafe, the Rock 'N Roll McDonald's, the Excalibur Club, the Rain Forest Cafe, and many more.

Hooters opened in an area with a strange track record of commercial failures. For some reason, a four-block stretch of Erie Street straddling Wells has been a bad luck area for many an aspiring business. Perhaps, it is a sort of psychic residue that dates back to 1871 when the Great Chicago Fire decimated this area. It is possible that over 100 or more people were killed in this very area, so the speculation is plausible.

Planet Hollywood, Walter Payton's America's Bar, Oprah Winfrey's Eccentric Restaurant, The International Cinema Museum, The Top Shelf Gentleman's Club, The Won Ton Club, and other endeavors on Erie failed, usually in a relatively short period of time. When Chicago's Hooters opened, the location they acquired had previously been home to some five failed stores during the 1980s. The average life of a business in this building was two years, usually less.

But Hooters broke the jinx and became a roaring success. Management decided to celebrate in a unique way. Symbolic tombstones were painted on the front of the building with the names of the doomed ventures that had financially floundered there. Eventually, the family of an earlier business owner complained, and the mural was painted over.

Hooters may have conquered the ill luck that dogged many of the other local businesses, but the discovery was made that the building was haunted. A number of employees and management have had experiences, auditory and tactile, that can only be explained as psychic in nature.

The popular local TV show, "Fox Thing in the Morning," does a live remote from a haunted spot around Chicagoland every Halloween season with me. On Tuesday, October 26, 1999, the location featured was Hooters. Show anchors Bob Sirott and Marianne Murciano interviewed me along with Hooters' employees about the happenings.

Bartender and waitress, Fawn Doucette, claimed a number of ghostly events, primarily in the storage room in the building's basement. "I was down in the basement," Fawn related, "I was getting stock, and I kept hearing somebody calling my name. Then I felt somebody touch my shoulder. I turned around and nobody was there."

The haunted Hooters restaurant

Fawn has had a number of similar experiences while working here over the years, and they still continue.

Manager Kerri Rury confirmed coworker Fawn's claims and described some encounters of her own. "As managers, we have to go into the basement storeroom quite a bit, and one day, I was walking down the stairs, and I heard someone running up behind me. I thought it was someone coming to get my keys, so I turned around, but no one was there," Kerri said.

"Everything seems to involve the basement," Kerri continued. "We had just had a phone installed down there, and one day, three of us were doing inventory. I was up in the office when suddenly all of our three phone lines on different floors started ringing at once, going nuts for no reason. When we answered, we all found no one was on the line. We called Ameritech and they came out. They claimed that nothing was wrong with the phones and that the phone lines were perfectly fine."

Kerri added, "I now tell my kitchen help that they are not leaving me alone in this building anymore."

The phone difficulties are not the only mechanical or electrical problems that pop up from time to time at Hooters. The jukeboxes go on and off with no explanation and other electrical equipment is also affected periodically.

As I collected the personal experiences from the witnesses, I came to the conclusion that these were not just cases of over active imaginations. Hooters really was haunted.

With its lively, energetic "beach" type atmosphere, Hooters has found its niche on the culinary scene with its American cuisine that offers chicken wings, seafood, sandwiches, salads, and plenty of cold beer. But in Chicago at least, that order of wings and curly fries and beer may be served up with a poltergeist on the side.

4 HOOTERS RESTAURANT

Location: 660 North Wells Street, Chicago.
Type of occurrence: Sound of phantom footsteps, as if running behind you; a mysterious voice calling your name; electroacoustic interferences with telephones and jukeboxes and more.
Characteristics: Restaurant staff encounters various ghostly activities, usually in storage area in basement, but sometime in other parts of building. Nothing seems threatening, but is almost mischievous in nature.
Status: Ongoing.

A HAUNTED NIGHTSPOT

GHOST TALES OF THE EXCALIBUR CLUB

T he popular nightspot, The Excalibur Club, is situated in what has become one of Chicago's hottest tourist areas. It is directly across the street from the Hard Rock Cafe and very close to the Rock 'N Roll McDonald's. Visitors from around the world flock to this near north side area.

Sometimes a building just looks as if it should be haunted. The building that houses The Excalibur Club is one of these. Often referred to as "the Castle," this granite Romanesque Revival building has two conical turrets at its entrance. The granite has a strange property of changing color during the day. Depending on the amount of sunlight, the stone changes in color from shades of gray to an almost dried blood color. Despite many interior changes, over the front door, a carved relief remains bearing a depiction of explorers Marquette and Joliet. On the cornerstone is a monogram "C.H.S."

Built in 1892 as a home for the Chicago Historical Society, this location was not exactly lucky for the Society. Founded in 1856, the Historical Society purchased this site in 1865 at the close of the Civil War. Their first building was destroyed in 1871 during the Great Fire. From 1892 until 1931, the collections of the Society were housed at this location until they moved to their current home in Lincoln Park.

Since then, the building has been home to a variety of tenants including, the Loyal Order of Moose, the WPA, the Illinois Institute of Technology, and even *Gallery* magazine. More recently, it has been a nightclub, first the Limelight in 1985, then The Excalibur Club.

It is often difficult, if not impossible, to discover just how or why a haunting starts. Obviously if a documented death, tragedy, or crime took place at a site, the researcher has a head start. In the case of the hauntings at the Excalibur Club, there really isn't any documented historical reason. Nonetheless, the ghosts are alive and well.

Just after the Limelight opened in Chicago with a flurry of publicity, stories began to spread privately about "the Castle" being haunted. At first, there were little events witnessed by the staff after hours, then eventually some customers noticed unusual things also.

Tom Doody was a special events and public events director for the Limelight for most of its three and a half years. He rapidly became a believer that the building was haunted. Upon taking his job, Doody recalls, "Almost immediately, I was told not to go up to the third floor after closing time. I was told that some very strange things manifested themselves there. Of course, I went right on up anyway." Doody confirmed poltergeist type activity. "Things would move around late at night on their own volition. Glasses would often fall and break by themselves."

Doody witnessed considerable activity around the VIP lounge and the pool tables. "There was one instance when a pool table was set up, racked and ready for play. Then the balls began rolling all over the table. It was like someone had just broken, but nobody was there."

During the very early hours of the morning, after the customers had all gone home, employees putting the club to bed would sometimes hear their name being called. When they went to check, they would find that no one was there. It was mysterious because the voice that

Excalibur Club, former home of Chicago Historical Society

they were hearing often sounded like the voice of someone they knew, but someone who would have been miles away at that time and could have not possibly been there.

The voice phenomena was reported a number of times by the VIP room host, B. J. Murray. He had started work at the Limelight two months before the opening night, while the club was under construction. He quickly decided the place had unusual vibes.

"The building itself, the whole shape and design, looked like something out of a Vincent Price movie," Murray said. "There was a dark side to that place. It was eerie."

Scraping or dragging type sounds are often endemic to haunted sites. At the Limelight, such sounds in the downstairs storage room were sometimes plainly heard. It sounded as if heavy boxes and crates were being pushed about, but when the room was unlocked and entered, no one was there and nothing seemed disturbed. The room had only one door, only one way in or out.

Publicist Cindy De Marko worked at the Limelight for two years and remembers one particular incident involving a part-time receptionist. "The beer room was right off the reception area," Cindy recalled. "This girl kept hearing the sounds of someone picking up the cases and dragging them across the floor again and again."

Since she would have seen anyone enter the storage room's only door, she asked other staff people about the noises. Cindy said that the young woman was visible shaken when she learned that there was a ghostly explanation for the sounds.

During the Limelight years, I was hired to host a number of special events at the club, based on psychic themes. One event, an audience participation "ghost hunt," featured teams of patrons prowling the massive club's three floors, trying photographic experiments and feeling for psychic cold spots.

The basement area proved very productive that night as my team of twenty or so found some very distinct cold spots in front of the women's washroom. These were actually much more than "spots." The cold areas were as large as an area that would be occupied by a human body. You could actually stick your hand into a well-defined cold zone and roughly make out its shape. We followed the cold spot into the large powder room searching the area in front of the enormous make up mirrors and the sinks trying to find where it went. We found it. It entered into a wall at one point and came out a short distance away. The cold spot then disappeared.

Clearly, there was no chance this cold feeling could have been caused by cold water pipes or frozen ground, nothing so fixed. The cold spot could be felt, and it was moving. Apparently, the ghost did not linger long enough to primp.

In 1989, the Limelight closed and new owners opened The Excalibur Club. Millions of dollars were spent by the new owners to turn this century-old building into a posh nightclub. Despite the name change and a more Generation X clientele, the haunted traditions remained. Excaliber's corporate supervisor, Billy McFall, in a 1996 interview with the *Chicago Sun Times* told of a number of unexplained events he witnessed. Although motion detectors are turned on after hours, McFall claimed that somehow beer glasses were found scattered across the bar, and bottles were opened and contents missing. Every day, for one week straight when he opened the club, McFall said he found the bar in the Dome Room in disarray. McFall also claims to have encountered something visual at the club. In early 1996, he observed a light-blue shape running up the stairs. Soon afterward, he saw the same phenomenon in reverse, running down the stairs. A cold breeze passed through the room at the same time.

On a 1997 episode of the popular TV series, "Sightings," interviews were conducted with a number of current employees. Somehow the *Eastland* steamship tragedy was blamed for the hauntings, even though no bodies from that disaster were ever brought to the building.

The possibility exists that some lives were lost when the previous building burned during the Great Fire of 1871. Although undocumented, those deaths remain a possibility, since fatality records from that inferno are very sketchy.

At Excalibur, the ghosts are as unflappable as ever. They are capable of interacting with us at certain times for reasons and motivations known only to them. Ghosts are quite stubborn; they just don't go away.

5 EXCALIBUR CLUB

Location:	632 North Dearborn, Chicago.
Type of occurrence:	Poltergeist-type cold spots, voices, moving of objects.
Characteristics:	Various activity happens to staff (usually), and after hours (for the most part).
Status:	Ongoing.

A Curse on the Chicago Cubs
The Billy Goat Tavern Hex

The Billy Goat Tavern and Grill sits on Lower Michigan Avenue. To enter, you have to venture into "underground Chicago" near the loading docks of the Tribune Tower and the boat docks along the Chicago River. But this is no ordinary tavern. As you walk down the stairs, one more flight down from subterranean Michigan Avenue, you are greeted with a shout of "cheezborger, cheezborger, no fry, cheep, no pep, coke" (translation: "cheeseburger, cheeseburger, no french fries, potato chips, no Pepsi, Coke.") Yes, this bar was the inspiration for the many "Saturday Night Live" skits by John Belushi and Dan Ackroyd, who were lunchtime regulars here before becoming famous. The Billy Goat burgers are so famous that during the annual "Taste of Chicago," more than 5,000 are sold daily.

On any given day, you might rub elbows with celebrities at Billy Goat Tavern. Photos line the walls showing many of the famous visitors from the past and present. There are politicians from both political persuasions: the two Mayor Daleys and President George Bush, Hillary Clinton (twice), former Vice President Agnew, and presidential hopeful Hubert Humphrey. Scores of autographed photos from entertainers include Sean Connery, Anthony Quinn, Kirk Douglas, and Roy Rogers, along with many others.

The bar is also a favorite hangout of local journalists, writers and photographers. The offices of both the *Chicago Tribune* and the *Sun Times* are nearby. The late Mike Royko, political columnist, was a regular. Current customers include Jack Higgins, Pulitzer prize-winning cartoonist; Richard Roeper, *Sun Times* columnist and TV movie critic; and Rick Kogan from the *Tribune*. Or you might see Fr. Andrew Greeley, the priest, sociologist, and novelist; or Jim Agnew (no relation to the other Agnew), true-crime researcher and publisher; or maybe a tour-boat captain or an undercover police decoy. But for the purist, the main reason to come here is not to drink, eat, or celebrity watch. The big draw is the memorabilia on display relating to the celebrated "curse on the Cubs."

The curse dates back to the original founder of the Billy Goat Tavern, a Greek immigrant named William Sianis. In 1934, he opened a bar and grill on Madison Street near the old Chicago Stadium. A larger than life character, Sianis often traveled with his trademark, a pet goat, thus he was bestowed with the nickname, "Billy Goat." He was often seen at public events, from wrestling matches to political conventions, with his goat in tow.

In 1945, the Chicago Cubs were playing the Detroit Tigers in the World Series. It was game three, and Sianis had two tickets for the game at Wrigley Field. When he showed up at the ballpark with his guest, Billy the goat, the ushers refused to allow him inside. Owner P. K. Wrigley had sent word down from his private box: "Don't bring that goat in here. That goat smells."

Billy Goat left the ballpark and went back to his bar to listen to the game on radio. When the Cubs lost, he sent Wrigley a pointed telegram: "Who stinks now?"

Billy Goat Tavern, shrine to the 1945 curse on the Chicago Cubs

The Cubs proceeded to lose the series and have never made it back to a World Series since.

Sam Sianis now owns the Billy Goat Tavern. A nephew of "Billy Goat" William Sianis, Sam came to America in 1955 and to Chicago in 1960. He keeps the curse story alive at the bar with a priceless collection of photos, news clippings, and other memorabilia. He opened the Michigan Avenue location in 1964.

I asked Sam just exactly what words constituted the curse. He told me that his uncle told Wrigley, "You refused the help of the goat to win the World Series and you insulted the goat. Now, the goat got mad, and he's going to put the hex on you and the Cubs, not to win any pennants and any World Series."

As the losing years dragged by, it seemed that the Cubs were forever to be a second-rate team. Then in 1969, things began to look brighter. As Sam recalls, "the Cubs were ahead and it looked for sure that they would win the pennant. Billy Goat was down here laughing, saying, 'They're not going to win.' And they lost!"

Patriarch Sianis died in 1970. During his lifetime, he never tried to take back the curse. Nephew Sam has tried, however. He feels that as the new official "Billy Goat," by virtue of owning the tavern, he has the right. Try as he has, it seems the family curse is still firmly in place.

Sam first tried to take off the curse in 1973. He tried returning to Wrigley Field with a goat, but the goat was refused admission.

By 1984, things began to change. Cub's officials invited Sam to bring the goat to the opening day festivities that year. The Cub's luck partially changed, enough for them to win the division title. Billy Goat was again invited back in 1989.

Sign at Billy Goat

The Billy Goat Curse is America's most famous sports jinx. Film crews from Germany, Mexico, Australia, and Ireland have all visited the tavern for the story. The British TV series, "Arthur C. Clarke's Strange Universe", featured the Billy Goat in its episode on famous curses. In 1997, "Old Style" filmed a nationally run TV beer commercial here at the bar.

And what about the original goat from that day in 1945? After his death, Billy was mounted by a taxidermist and kept at the original bar on Madison Street for many years. During the 1968 riots following the assassination of Martin Luther King, the Madison Street tavern burned down and the stuffed goat was destroyed. Today, a stand-in stuffed goat head hangs over the bar at the Michigan Avenue location.

6 BILLY GOAT TAVERN

Location:	430 North Michigan Avenue, Chicago.
Type of occurrence:	Curse or hex.
Characteristics:	Bad luck of baseball team seems tied to insult of 1945 and resulting curse.
Status:	Despite attempts to "lift" curse, it seems to still be in place, hopefully, not forever.

GIANT ARMCHAIR
FIT FOR A GHOST
MR. SAMUEL INSULL PREPARED A THRONE FOR HIS RETURN

Coming from humble beginnings, Samuel Insull lived a classic American rags-to-riches success story. He emigrated from England in 1881 to the United States where he took a position with Thomas Edison as his secretary. Insull had intuitive skills for grasping the principles of technical problems and systematizing complex business affairs. He eventually became Edison's financial advisor.

In the twelve years Insull was with Edison, he acquired the business acumen he would use to create his own multi-billion dollar empire in the Midwest. He came to Chicago in 1892 to be the Director of Chicago Edison, which later consolidated with Commonwealth Electric to become Commonwealth Edison.

Insull became a public utilities tycoon who controlled holding companies, not only for electric, but also gas and transportation services. Ironically, Insull's name is now obscure, but his accomplishments were notable: He was responsible for centralizing electric service, organizing the predecessor to the General Electric Company; he devised cost accounting techniques; he worked out a model of national product distribution which was copied nation wide; and he also helped popularize mass production and "selling at the lowest price." He pioneered successful welfare programs years before most businesses, or labor or government groups took steps in that direction. His commitment to social reform apparently had been instilled in him by his father. He helped facilitate the growth of important labor unions, believing it was a matter of good business. He devised methods of marketing securities that allowed modern corporations to become gigantic.

Insull's great wealth was balanced by his charitable works, and the list of his philanthropic causes was long. At his peak of financial success in the late 1920s, Insull planned and built a lavish opera house that would showcase his ideas, his interpretation as to what opera was all about. Inside and outside, the Civic Opera House bore the stamp of Insull. Opera was for the people, he believed. He was an opera buff since his childhood in England, and it was said that as a boy he went hungry to save sixpence to attend the London opera, even though he was relegated to an upper gallery seat. His opera house was designed so there were no prominent boxes accentuating class differences; the rich and not so rich sat together. His democratic ideas shocked some but found great support with others.

He did make enemies along the way, and he never forgot the ones who tried to destroy his personal empire. Among those would be numbered Chicago aldermen, and especially, the Eastern establishment bankers. Insull had a Populist's dread of New York financiers.

The location and design of his opera house allowed him to snub these opponents in a dramatic fashion. Set on the bank of the Chicago River, the forty-two-story building was actually a gigantic office built around a 3,500-seat opera house with a 900-seat theater. The intent was that the office rent would act as income to finance the performances of the grand operas staged below. Twenty-million-dollars in stock would set up the nonprofit Chicago Music Foun-

Civic Opera House,
called the "armchair building"

dation to make Chicago the musical capital of the world. The general plans were made public, but the interior of the theater was kept secret until opening night.

The Civic Opera Building was presented as a gift to Chicago from Samuel Insull in 1929. Only one problem arose in Insull's project: The first opera held was in the fall of 1929, just ten days after Black Friday, the October collapse of the stock market.

The Depression of 1929 turned Insull's holdings into "the biggest business failure in the history of the world." His opponents were ready for revenge.

Insull left America and eventually went to Greece. He set up that country's electrical system. He was brought back to Chicago to stand trial for his financial misdeeds, but he was found innocent of any wrong doing.

The shape and location of the Civic Opera House building are not by chance. Above the thirteenth floor, there is a deep setback on the side facing the Chicago River. Architectural guides have described this Art Deco and French Renaissance styled building as being "shaped like a throne." The sheer upright chair or throne incorporated into the design of the building facade facing west looks over the river, away from the downtown. Insull defiantly turned the chair's back on City Hall to the east, as well as the East Coast bankers in distant New York City.

Insull's last symbolic gesture, made possible by his Opera House's unique design, was a ghostly one. He is reported to have said he would return as a ghost and sit in the massive armchair facing west, looking out over his beloved Chicago while snubbing his various adversaries to the east. It seems he was determined not to allow them to triumph after all.

No one yet has claimed that Insull has returned, although his chair sits ever ready, acknowledging his great gift to the city, while its style and form espouses his political and philosophical views.

To really see downtown Chicago, you must take a narrated boat tour. As you cruise past towering buildings and beneath dozens of bridges and view the buildings from the Chicago River, an entirely different perspective of the city emerges.

For years, local cruise line guides have pointed out the Civic Opera House on Wacker Drive as the "armchair" building with its back, armrests, and seat formed in stone and glass.

Looking up at this forty-two-story edifice from its riverside, you do, in fact, see it as a giant's idea of what a chair should be.

7 KEMPER INSURANCE BUILDING/CIVIC OPERA BUILDING

Location:	20 North Wacker Drive, Chicago.
Type of Occurrence:	Traditional ghost story.
Characteristics:	A variation on the promise to return from the dead motif.
Status:	Legend still current. Original premise may be based on a symbolic gesture.

EASTLAND TRAGEDY RETURNS

GHOSTS AT THE EASTLAND DOCK SITE

Saturday morning, July 24, 1915, an excited unsuspecting crowd of about 2,500 people began to board the *Eastland* steamer at her pier between La Salle and Clark Streets. It was a special outing for the employees of Western Electric Company, and their families and friends. Five steamers had been hired by the company to take the approximately 7,000 people. The *Eastland* was the first of the fleet scheduled to depart.

Many were early, and all were jockeying for best positions aboard the boat for a leisurely cruise on Lake Michigan and a picnic across the lake at Michigan City, Indiana. Passengers were moving to the left side of the boat as other steamers drew up the river toward the wharf. The time set for sailing was 7:40 a.m.

A tug was hitched to the *Eastland*, and ropes were ordered cast off. The steamer's engines started, but the *Eastland* did not budge. Instead, the overloaded boat began to list slowly but steadily toward the dockside. Righting herself temporarily, she began to list again in the opposite direction. People began to panic. Cargo slid to the sinking side and water began to enter the lower portholes.

Rolling completely onto her side, the *Eastland* tossed those on her upper deck into the waters of the Chicago River and trapped hundreds of others below deck. Cries came from children and shrieks rang from adults. Then there was a plunge and a sigh of air escaping from the hold. It was over in a matter of minutes. Victims beneath the water line drowned or were crushed by the weight of others scrambling for safety. The surface of the river was thick with people struggling to survive. Whistles from tugs and excursion boats rang the alarms. Barrels and crates were tossed into the river where they were seized by the drowning.

Some did escape. But hundreds of men and women and children, in a frenzied battle for life, churned the water then drowned, perishing in the sight of the thousands who were crowding the shores and bridges.

Fireboats and tugs spread out around the death ship and began the work of taking away the bodies. The body count rose rapidly, and in some cases, entire families were wiped out. Reportedly, a total of 880 bodies were taken to the morgues. To this day a totally accurate account is not known. The count could be much higher.

The *Eastland* was the greatest inland waterway disaster in American peacetime history and the worst disaster in Chicago history. This loss was greater than the Chicago Fire, the Iroquois Theater Fire, or the crash of Flight 191.

Even though for years the location of the tragedy was neglected or forgotten by officialdom, the legends lingered on. Over the decades since the incident, stories of ghostly sounds and sights have been passed on.

Cries are often said to be heard here at night. Passersby on Wacker Drive hear sounds—sounds they attribute to the "drowned souls of the *Eastland* Tragedy."

S.S. Eastland, after disaster – Chicago River.

Eastland disaster, historic scene

Illinois National Guard Armory used as morgue after Eastland tragedy, historic scene

Plaque was missing in 2000

Others say they can see luminescent forms and nebulous shapes as they peer down into the river from the sidewalk or the nearby bridge.

Sounds will carry at night, particularly over the water; and lights from many new buildings towering above may explain most of the reflections in the water, but the sheer number of dead in the *Eastland* disaster seems to demand that we pause and listen and look and wonder.

The City of Chicago and the federal government have yet to recognize the historical significance of this tragedy. However, in 1989 many decades later, the State of Illinois finally paid homage to the departed. It erected a plaque at the former dock site of the Eastland disaster. I attended the ceremony. The one surviving passenger was present to observe the dedication of the fateful anniversary.

This plaque was stolen from the site in May of 2000.

8 EASTLAND DOCK SITE

Location:	Wacker between Clark and La Salle Streets
Type of occurrence:	Reported auditory and visual activity, due to unsettled dead.
Characteristics:	This scene of great tragedy and disaster seems haunted by generic psychic activity fitting the history; reported disembodied cries and visual beings in the form of luminescent silhouettes and nebulous shapes in the water.
Status:	Believed to be ongoing, year-round, nighttime only.

OPRAH WINFREY'S HAUNTED TV STUDIO

HUNDREDS OF GHOSTS OCCUPY FORMER MORGUE

Eastland Disaster continues—

When the *Eastland* boat tragedy struck at its Chicago River dock, the recovery of bodies of victims began within minutes. As the number of bodies grew larger and larger, it became obvious that a central location would be necessary to facilitate the identification of the many dead.

The first bodies were taken to the nearby Reid-Murdoch Building, now the home of Chicago's Traffic Court, or sent directly to mortuaries in the area. The only public building nearby that was large enough and suitable for use as a makeshift morgue was a short distance to the west and the south, the Second Regiment Illinois National Guard Armory on Carpenter Street between Randolph Street and Washington Boulevard. It was a one-block-long building just outside the Loop on the Near West Side.

Bodies of victims arrived for hours at the armory. They were laid out in rows of eighty-five, assigned numbers, and any personal possessions were placed in envelopes docketed with their numbers. The sad task of identifying bodies took place as loved ones and family members searched the rows of the dead. There were twenty-two cases where entire families perished.

The screams and cries of the distraught echoed time and again that weekend within the walls of the armory. The Red Cross treated thirty women for hysteria and exhaustion.

The overworked Coroner's office resorted to making up a rubber stamp reading: "Drowned. July 24, 1915, from Steamer EASTLAND, Chicago River at Clark Street." This designation was stamped onto death certificates in a frenzied pace to keep the identification process moving along. Most of the people actually died of suffocation, not drowning.

It was not until Friday, July 30, that the last of the bodies at the armory was finally identified. A seven-year-old boy, number 396, was identified as little Willie Novotny of Cicero. There was no one left in his immediate family to identify him as both his parents and his older sister also perished on the *Eastland*. The searching was finally over.

As the years went by, the need for an armory on the edge of the Loop passed. Threats to public order, such as the Haymarket affair of 1886 were long past. The Government closed the facility and sold the building to the private sector. The complex has been used at various times as a stable, bowling alley and a film studio. With the proliferation of TV stations and film production companies in Chicago, the near west side area became home to a number of new studios. Harpo Studios was established here in 1989 by TV talk show queen, Oprah Winfrey. Cleverly, Oprah spelled backwards is "Harpo."

For many years, the former Second Regiment Armory on the west end of central Chicago's produce market area was known to harbor multiple hauntings. Even though the building was given a face-lift when remodeled in 1989 by Nagle, Hartray & Associates, the block-long Art Deco Revival office/studio complex beneath the new stucco facade and fancy glass-block windows remained the same, and it seems, so have its occupants.

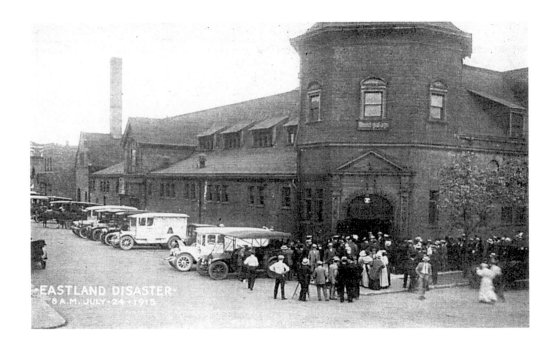

Armory where mourners wait to see the dead from the Eastland disaster. The same site now houses Oprah's Harpo Studio (below)

In early 1993, longtime Chicago free-lance reporter, Denny Johnson, called me to ask my opinion about ghostly activity being reported by night security guards at the Harpo Studios.

Denny described how a number of the security staff claimed to have witnessed activity ranging from hearing sounds to encountering antique perfume scents and even spotting a ghostly woman in attire of the late 1800s to the early 1900s. Given the history of the building with its *Eastland* associations, connecting the activity to the old disaster certainly seemed logical.

In October of 1996, Ms. Winfrey dedicated an episode of Oprah to the unusual history of certain homes and buildings. Oprah told how her studio was housed in a building that years before was a temporary morgue for over 800 victims of the *Eastland* steamship disaster of 1915. She admitted she thought her studio was haunted and that she might not want to be there after hours. Oprah's public announcement was not news to some Chicagoans.

Perhaps it is no accident that unusual activity flared up at Harpo Studios just after Oprah opened the complex in 1989. The structural and extensive cosmetic changes may have caused the stirring up of dormant ghosts. Very often ghostly activity begins after some physical change to property, as if the long dead tenants object or are riled.

Former security guard Robin Hocott worked the night shift at Harpo Studios for three years. She began hearing loud crashing sounds after hours throughout the studio. Searches were made, but she found nothing out of the ordinary to explain the sounds.

The situation began to intensify. "Then things started happening three times a week," Hocott said. After midnight one morning, Hocott's phone rang, and a producer working late in another part of the building claimed she heard the sounds of laughing people just outside her office. Hocott ran to investigate and found a shaken producer locked in her office in fear. The producer explained how she had entered the hallway to find it empty, even though the laughing sounds still continued.

Later when Hocott talked with other security personnel, she learned that many had the same or rather similar experiences.

One particular lobby staircase often echoed with the sounds of the tramping feet of dozens, perhaps hundreds of people. "It was as if Oprah's audience was leaving," Hocott said, "but this happened after midnight, hours after the crowds were gone."

Hocott also encountered a strong psychic scent of perfume one evening. "It was a strong odor of violets," Hocott recalled, "like a cologne your grandmother would wear." As the scent filled the area, she heard a sobbing sound. A cold chill ran through her body.

Perhaps the most interesting manifestation at Harpo Studios is the apparition of a ghost known as the "Gray Lady." A woman in a long flowing vintage dress and large rimmed fancy hat has been seen wandering the halls on security cameras. The gray-shadowy figure doesn't exactly walk, but floats. Security guards have run after her to no avail: There was never anyone there.

Many of the auditory encounters reported in the studio exactly fit the activities taking place on the *Eastland* at the moment of the tragedy. The sounds of glasses are heard clinking together as if people were partying and drinking. Invisible children are heard laughing, running, and playing. Doors are heard opening and closing by themselves. These are just the sorts of sounds that would have been heard on the decks of the *Eastland* in preparation to setting sail.

The immensity of the *Eastland* tragedy seems to guarantee that hauntings will continue into the future. Fueled by the psychic turmoil, produced by hundreds of deaths and thousands of grieving family members and friends, the old armory building seems destined to hold onto its no longer secret past for sometime longer. It could be said that Oprah Winfrey's popular TV show has a ghostly audience, too.

9 HARPO STUDIOS

Location: 1058 West Washington Boulevard, Chicago.
Type of occurrences: Apparition of woman, psychic perfumes, eerie sounds of marching feet, sobbing, muffled voices, etc.
Characteristics: Sights, sounds, and smells fit aspects of the *Eastland* disaster.
Status: Ongoing for many years.

Asian Fusion
Psychic Confusion
The Red Light: A Haunted Restaurant

For well over 100 years, food and produce markets have clustered along West Randolph Street on the Near West Side. Downtown restaurants and hotels have been serviced by these wholesalers for generations. But starting in the 1980s, there has been an encroachment of new businesses into this area.

One relative newcomer to the strip is a fashionable Southeast Asian restaurant called the Red Light. Here patrons can dine and drink from a menu inspired by Vietnam, Thailand, China, Singapore, and other exotic venues.

The Red Light opened in September of 1996 in an old building that had previously been a florist shop. After much rehabbing and a face-lift, the old building was transformed. The kitchen is open, so patrons can watch as their delicacies are being prepared. The main floor sports two bar areas and a splendid vintage '30s wooden bar. The hardwood floors are a rich black walnut, and in one room, an elaborate dragon mosaic inlay catches one's attention.

Although the vast majority of people who patronize the Red Light are oblivious to any paranormal manifestation, the staff knows that things unusual can take place here. They know because they have had experiences with things otherworldly.

Many restaurants reputed to be haunted claim that things take place after hours, or when it gets slow. That is not so with the Red Light. The ghostly events here can be witnessed anytime, but especially during peak crowds.

Cynde Grant was a manager at the Red Light. She is not only convinced it is haunted, but has racked up many personal encounters. In a 1998 interview, she gave me the fascinating details.

"I think it is a friendly ghost," said Cynde, undaunted. "There were times when I would walk into the dining room, and I would hear somebody call my name. I'd turn around, and nobody was there," Cynde declared. "It seemed like a familiar voice, but I couldn't pinpoint it."

Cynde noted, "This happened to other people as well. I know of five other people who have had experiences."

Upon asking some of the staff about their thoughts, I found a number of others who also were believers because of personal experience.

According to Cynde, this voice phenomenon has a mimicking, but reassuring quality to it. However, these hauntings are not just relegated to auditory experiences. Along with other activities, doors have opened on their own volition or were found locked when no one with a key was present. Electrical disturbances have taken place throughout the restaurant, often around the antique wooden bar from the 1930s. The bar lights, on a dimmer switch, seemed to be able to dim or brighten on their own.

Apparently the supernatural unrest has quieted to a whimper in 2000. Manager Andrew Anderson summed up the situation. "Things are quiet here psychically for the time being," he said.

The Red Light Restaurant

Apparently, it seems there have been ongoing attempts to keep the "Feng Shui" of the business in sync with Asian astrological beliefs.

"Just to be on the safe side, chopstick placement will no longer have the sharp ends pointing at a diner," Anderson said.

This is considered poor form and bad luck. Even though, there was no "Feng Shui" master assisting when they opened the restaurant, they are taking ancient customs seriously.

I asked Anderson if the use of the "888" in the restaurant's phone number was on purpose, since eight is an auspicious number representing abundance in the Far East. He told me that the number was given to the business randomly by the phone company. A cosmic coincidence?

The hauntings at the Red Light were subtle, yet very convincing to those who witnessed them. There definitely was "something" present at the Red Light during its first years of operation, but now things are tranquil. Perhaps the spirits once active here find the use of the property to their liking. Only time will tell if the hauntings resume.

Unless, or until, more is discovered about the building's early history, we may never know why the curious hauntings took place here. Meanwhile, although the ghosts are dormant, the food and drink, one might say, continues to be "a triple eight."

10 Red Light Restaurant

Location:	820 West Randolph, Chicago.
Type of occurrences:	Poltergeist tricks and psychic calling of names.
Characteristics:	Old building seemed to continue producing paranormal events because of its past history yet to be discovered.
Status:	Dormant for now.

CHICAGO NORTH

Chicago North

BLOODY VALENTINE

GHOSTS OF THE ST. VALENTINE'S DAY MASSACRE

Chicago's personal day of infamy was February 14, St. Valentine's Day, 1929. A multiple homicide of Beer War soldiers would forever link this city to gangland violence and with the name of Al Capone.

At the SMC Cartage Company Garage at 2122 North Clark Street, seven members of the George "Bugs" Moran gang were surprised at their north side headquarters by what at first appeared to be a Chicago Police raiding party. Lined up against the garage wall, the Moran men soon found out that the police were bogus: Machine gun fire and shotgun blasts cut them down. Never before had that many people been killed in a single Prohibition shooting.

No one was ever put on trial for the murders. Officially, they are still unsolved. Perhaps Bugs Moran's comment at the time (his late arrival at the garage saved his life) echoed the obvious: "Only Capone kills like that."

The incident was not just local news but national and international. It wasn't long before the morbid and curious were coming here, trying to get into the garage to gawk at the gory scene. The building had achieved a cult following of sorts. The notoriety of the site clung for years after Prohibition ended. Gangsters and their hangouts had become part of our pop culture.

People never seem to tire of the tales of the twenty-year-long Prohibition gangster era, but not everyone enjoyed gangland chic. In an attempt to have Chicago shed its mobster image, Mayor Richard J. Daley slated the notorious garage and some adjacent buildings for demolition. In 1967, a quarter of the block was razed for a Chicago Housing Authority senior citizen's development. Change had come, but it wasn't what some people anticipated. There were unexpected consequences.

If the City Fathers believed that tearing down the garage would stop Chicagoans from visiting the site or talking about it, they were dead wrong. The precise death spot was now located in the center of a grassy yard on the south end of the new building. Now there was accessibility, and the curious could walk over and stand directly on top of the site. It didn't take too long before some claimed to have psychic encounters here.

The double lot has a parking area for visitors in the rear, while the front portion is a park-like landscape with five maple trees. The trees are spaced as if they were the five spots on a playing card. Immediately behind the middle tree in the center of the yard is the site where the infamous seven were shot down. There is no sign or marker to alert passersby of the unique history of this site. It seems calm and serene most of the time, but sometimes things change.

Commonly reported were strange sobbing and moaning sounds at night, of course attributed to the dead gangsters. Skeptics tried to write these sounds off as merely overactive imaginations. But something unusual was afoot. It was found that when some people walked their dogs past this yard or into it, the dogs would often act up, staring and growling at something invisible, leaving their masters perplexed. I even talked to a K-9 police dog handler who witnessed such incidents with her highly trained animal.

Residents of the apartment complex also claimed psychic contacts. This was especially true with those who lived in apartments on the south side of the building, facing the massacre site. One compelling account I uncovered was featured on Canadian television in the 1980s and brought fifteen minutes of fame to senior citizen Madeline Bushbaum.

There was always a wait for an apartment in the CHA's 2140 North Clark Street complex due to its popularity and great location. Mrs. Bushbaum was happy to finally get an apartment in the building. Her apartment was on the fourth floor, looking out over the little park.

Soon Mrs. Bushbaum learned that something was amiss with her room. She couldn't get any rest, she claimed, "because the ghosts kept me up all night long." She confided to her neighbors that she was being bothered by strange sounds, mystery knocks, and voices.

Eventually she complained to the building's management. Even though the staff thought her ghost stories were just fantasies, she was assigned another room, but this time not at the south end of the building.

Mrs. Bushbaum was content after her move. She no longer had any psychic problems troubling her sleep. But her old room proved still to be haunted.

The new tenant assigned to Mrs. Bushbaum's old room was Mrs. Katherine McBride. Again, the new tenant verified the room's haunted nature. Mrs. McBride experienced a number of auditory phenomena. The proverbial three knocks were heard at her door, but no one was ever there when she answered.

St. Valentine's Day Massacre site,
CHA building on Clark, actual site of killings,
is now a small grassy park.

The hauntings eventually crested in an apparition. One night, Mrs. McBride briefly saw a dark shadowy figure of a man wearing an old style hat, like a fedora. "It was as if the image had stepped out of the late 1920s," Mrs. McBride was heard to say.

Mrs. McBride was apparently able to endure more than Mrs. Bushbaum. She continued to live in the haunted apartment and seemed to reach détente with the ghosts. Psychic activity, at least for her, waned.

You don't have to actually visit the site of the garage to achieve contact with the dead Moran gangsters. All it takes is a relic of the tragedy, a brick from the massacre wall.

In 1967 even as the building was being prepared for demolition, collectors of gangland souvenirs were on the ready. One large portion of the back room's north wall, the actual crime scene, was sold to a local antique dealer. These 414 bricks were carefully numbered and removed for preservation. This was a section six-feet-high by ten-feet-wide. After the bulk of the massacre section was removed, many other locals moved in for souvenirs. Later some became sorry that they did.

Gangster buff George Patey of Vancouver, British Columbia, obtained the largest holding of bricks. The businessman paid a small fortune to have the 414 prime location bricks shipped to his banjo bar where they would become part of an exhibit. Wax museum-style figures of victims and shooters as well as taped narration and sound effects completed the diorama. Despite this unique attraction, Patey's venture closed. The bricks were placed in storage.

In the late 1990s , Patey offered the complete collection of bricks for sale, advertising in Chicago newspapers. There were no takers. In 2000, Patey placed individual bricks for sale on the Internet auction, eBay. The bricks were mounted with a plaque and encased in acrylic. The high reserve was over $200 and bidders were few.

Did Patey's banjo bar close merely because musical tastes were changing, or did, as some have suggested, the bricks jinx his venture? As bricks were bought and sold, primarily around Chicago, and wound up in the hands of many collectors, rumors spread that having a brick, especially multiple bricks, could bring personal misfortune. Some local collectors may have fallen victim. At least their personal tales of bad luck seem to indicate something more than chance is at work.

Jan Gabriel is a well-known radio disc jockey, commercial announcer, and video producer among many other talents. I first met Jan when he was broadcasting on WJOB radio, Hammond. He is perhaps best known as the voice of US 30 Dragstrip commercials with the high volume introduction "Sunday! Sunday! Sunday!" His documentary production, "Great American Mystery Cars" was nominated for two Emmy Awards.

I knew that Jan was a gangland history buff and that he had obtained a few hundred bricks from the St. Valentine's Day Massacre wall. Not all the prime bricks wound up in Patey's bar. Jan acquired a number of choice bricks where the bullet holes were plugged with corks.

After taking possession of the bricks, Jan suffered a number of personal setbacks.

Jan divorced three times and also suffered some major health problems. "I'm not ready to believe that these bricks are casting a spell on me," Jan said, "but ever since I've had them, I've had a kidney transplant, a four-way heart bypass, and had my gall bladder out. I'm an organ donor, but everything in me is used!"

Similar problems were experienced by Mike Johnson, curator of the Underground Comix Hall of Fame. I met Mike at an auction of Chicago historical and gangland memorabilia one night, and we became good friends. His valuable Chicago autograph and literature collections have items lacking in the Newberry Library or Chicago Historical Society holdings. Portions of Johnson's collections are on display in a Bucktown locale.

When discussing our collections, Mike volunteered that he owned about thirty bricks. He, too, obtained bricks at the site in 1967. Mike was unaware of the belief that bad luck was attached to those who owned these relics, so I explained what I already knew.

Mike then admitted that over thirty some years; " I went through two messy divorces, lost a million dollars in cash and property, have a stag horn kidney stone in one kidney, am awaiting a heart transplant, and am a recovering alcoholic."

As psychic insurance, Mike has decided to sell his bricks at a discount. Although the going rate in area antique shops is around $200 per brick (if you can find one), Mike is wholesaling his at $150 each to liquidate.

The SMC Cartage Company Garage may be gone, but the ghosts obviously don't know that. For us, the living, the spot is a pleasant little park; but as far as the dead men know, it is a greasy, grimy garage floor where they spilled their life's blood.

And for us, the living, time marches on, but for the seven murdered men, February 14, 1929, their moment of doom is always St. Valentine's Day.

II St. Valentine's Day Massacre Site

Location:	2122 North Clark Street, Chicago. (Now an empty lot.)
Type of occurrences:	Primarily auditory, but other phenomena. Hauntings also involve bricks from massacre building.
Characteristics:	Site of the most vicious multiple murder of the Prohibition Era is haunted by sounds and sights of the event.
Status:	Still active.

GHOST OF JOHN DILLINGER
HAUNTINGS AT THE BIOGRAPH THEATER

John Dillinger was an Indiana born outlaw and desperado. Back in the Depression Era he would knock off many a small town bank with cohorts as did his brothers in crime, Pretty Boy Floyd and Baby Face Nelson. Dillinger's war on "banksters" insured him a certain amount of public support. It is well documented that he was generous with the money he stole, often buying cars and other expensive gifts for relatives and friends.

Caught by authorities, he made a famous escape from the "escape proof" Crown Point, Indiana jail in March of 1934. He would, however, have only a few more months to live.

The FBI was now on the fugitive's trail, and they suspected he would eventually come back to Chicago. Dillinger had many personal ties to the North Side where he would be protected by crooked police and paid-off authorities.

During his Chicago days, Dillinger underwent plastic surgery to alter his looks and acid treatment of his fingertips to mutilate his fingerprints. The differences were not very significant, and Dillinger did not alter his lifestyle all that much. He was known to often frequent north side bars, poolrooms and restaurants.

Dillinger was dating a woman named Polly Hamilton, who lived at a rooming house owned by a Rumanian immigrant named Anna Sage. Although he used the alias of "Jimmy Lawrence," the ruse didn't fool many. "Jimmy" had too much money, wore fine clothes, didn't seem to work for a living, and, after all, this was the Depression and hard times.

Sage saw this discovery as an answer to her problems. Facing deportation to her native land as an undesirable for brothel-keeping convictions, Sage sought to cut a deal with the FBI. She offered to give the G-Men Dillinger, if they would see to it that the Immigrations Department would allow her to stay in America. The FBI agreed to the deal, but Anna was deported later.

The summer of 1934 was one of record-breaking heat. Refuge from the high temperatures in those days before home air conditioners could be found in neighborhood "air-cooled" motion picture theaters. The Biograph on Lincoln Avenue offered not only soothing cold air, but a gangster flick, "Manhattan Melodrama," with top stars Clark Gable, William Powell, and Myrna Loy. Dillinger loved gangster movies.

Sunday, July 22, was another scorcher; the temperature was in the nineties for much of the day. "Jimmy" invited Polly to go to the movies, and Anna was invited also. Now knowing Dillinger's plan for later that day, the brothel keeper informed the FBI, and Dillinger's fate was sealed.

The FBI decided to catch Dillinger as he exited the theater that night. As Anna, Polly, and John watched cartoons, newsreels and the feature inside, the G-Men were in position outside on the street. All gangways and alleys were covered. Dillinger would be trapped.

When the theater emptied out that night, it was just past 10:30 p.m. Dillinger and the women came through the front doors of the building and under the bright lights of the mar-

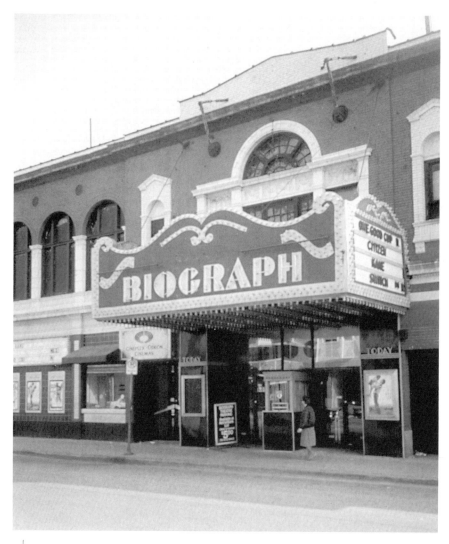

Biograph, theater where John Dillinger was murdered.

quee, Anna's dress glowed scarlet as the Feds rushed toward their wanted man, guns drawn. The flashy dress allowed the Feds from a distance to spot Anna and their mark.

Anna went down in Chicago legend and lore as the "woman in red" that night, Dillinger's betrayer. The dress, actually an orange-red, looked blood red.

He didn't have a chance, but Dillinger died game. He ran south toward an alley connecting Lincoln and Halsted. Bullets tore into him as he took two steps, then crumpled. Dillinger bled to death next to a utility pole. Two innocent bystanders were hit by FBI slugs, but Dillinger never fired a shot. There is evidence that he didn't even have a gun that night.

For all of the notoriety Dillinger received, his career was short, not lasting more than a year and a half. The impact on our pop culture was tremendous. The bank robber's mystique has lived on. John Dillinger joined the pantheon of other historical anti-heroes including Jesse and Frank James, Cole Younger, and Butch Cassidy.

There is no sign or historical plaque marking this site today, but neighborhood people all seem to know its significance. This location is usually referred to locally as "Dillinger's Alley." Dillinger may have died here physically, but psychically many believe that he is still around. There have been a number of reports of mysterious happenings here.

In the early 1970s while I was attending classes at nearby De Paul University, I spent much time along Lincoln Avenue, especially around the Biograph Theater. Even after almost forty years, Dillinger tales of his life and death were still being rehashed around the neighborhood. His last moments at the Biograph, his death spot, and his favorite bars and pool halls in the area were topics commonly discussed.

I began to collect accounts from local shopkeepers and residents. At that time, Sonny Scapini and Pat Clemens of the Rocky Mountain Trading Company were the first to tell me of a ghost seen in the alley.

This manifestation was described as a bluish-gray, manlike silhouette seen running, tripping, and falling down in the alley at the site where Dillinger died decades before. It seems to be a psychic replay of Dillinger's desperate bid for freedom. The vision lasts mere seconds, then melts away, sinking into the pavement.

The story had a great deal of support, I would find out, but no one has claimed to have seen the ghost in recent years. The visual haunting may be over but other things still occur here.

The triple intersection of Lincoln, Halsted, and Fullerton is quite congested most of the time. Not only is car, truck, and bus traffic heavy, but the number of pedestrians is also very high. Locals not only use sidewalks, but also take alleys as shortcuts and thoroughfares. "Dillinger's Alley" is a very short one, a zigzag cut between Lincoln Avenue and Halsted Street. Observing this alley for years, I have noticed something very odd about it. Relatively clean and rat free by north side standards, it is still seldom used.

A good nine times out of ten, no one is in the alley as I pass by. In the Lakeview area, other similar alleys are in constant use. Why should this one alley be empty?

After noticing this ongoing and obvious underuse, I began to make inquiries. Many local people don't know why they don't use the alley, and until I posed the question, they never realized they avoided it. They then realized that for some unconscious reason, they stayed away from the spot.

Some people do admit that they sense an unexplainable presence in the alley; they call it a "vibe," a cold spot, or an impression.

"Something's in the alley," they say. It's something they don't want to be near, that scares them and convinces them to walk down the street and around the corner rather than take the shortcut down the alley.

Brandi Morrison became a believer in 1993. "I was walking down the alley on the anniversary of Dillinger's death," Brandi remembered, "and there was an area of cold that I could feel." The area where the cold was manifesting itself was near the utility pole where Dillinger fell mortally wounded. The night Brandi had her experience was stifling hot, much like that night in 1934.

Ghosts are not just encountered visually, and the Dillinger hauntings prove that. With the passage of time, the apparition may be gone but other feelings and sensations indicate that there is still much psychic unrest here.

Dillinger alleyway near the Biograph. Death spot by the pole.

The reason for this long-lived haunting may have been uncovered by J. Robert Nash, an author of two books on John Dillinger and a well-known Chicago crime buff. Nash hypothesizes that the real Dillinger did not die here, but that a patsy, a look-alike, died in his place. With a corpse identified as "John Dillinger," the real outlaw got away. If Nash's theory is correct, there might be a more compelling reason for a haunting here: the man wrongly killed would feel he needs to protest from the grave, wanting the truth to finally come out.

12 BIOGRAPH THEATER

Location:	Theater and alley on 2400 block of Lincoln Avenue, Chicago.
Type of occurrence:	One time apparition reports, now strange feelings of chills and related uneasy sensations.
Characteristics:	Early reports of bluish-gray silhouette form now totally replaced by typical "haunted" feeling at site where Dillinger fell mortally wounded. Reported by both those who know the history of the spot and those who learn significance of site later.
Status:	Ongoing, year round; more frequent in warmer months, probably anniversary connection to Dillinger's death.

A BRITISH PUB HAUNTED
THE RED LION PUB NO SHABBY COUSIN

S tanding for strength and agility, the lion, king of all beasts, is a frequently used symbol. Spanning all cultures, it has been depicted on the Royal Family of England's coat of arms, starting with Richard I at around 1189. Since the 16th Century, the most popular name in England for a pub has been the "Red Lion." There are thousands of pubs with this name throughout all parts of Britain.

When the late Chicago architect John Cordwell was looking for a name for his new business venture, a British pub, he chose a name that he thought would have great appeal, "The Red Lion Pub." English born, Cordwell's idea was to create a cheery oasis for food and drink that, as far as possible, would have a true public house atmosphere. He opened the pub, assisted by his son Colin and son-in-law Joe Heinen.

Cordwell was well known in Chicago. He was involved with both Sandburg Village and Presidential Towers. He also served on the city of Chicago's Planning Commission.

The Red Lion Pub is located near De Paul University's Lincoln Park Campus. Although the pub opened in 1984, the two-story frame building that houses the bar dates back to about 1882. Over the years, the building was put to many different uses: among them were a Greek green grocery, for a while, an illegal betting parlor, and a country and western bar. The top floor was originally used for apartments.

Even before any manifestations began for the Cordwells and Heinen, neighbors told them that the place was known locally for hauntings. Colin Cordwell heard from the video storeowner across the street that when the place was a country western bar, the proprietor used to talk about his "invisible friends."

Though any notion that their pub might be haunted did not enter their minds at first, before very long, personal experiences made converts out of them and many others. Staff and patrons soon attested to ghostly antics.

My personal involvement began in 1986, shortly after hearing from friends that the pub was potentially haunted. Most believe that there are multiple ghosts present.

There are some confirmed deaths on the property. Lou Demas, whose family once owned the building, still lives in the neighborhood. He remembers a young woman named Sharon who died upstairs. Later, her elderly parents also died on the second floor. No other unusual deaths or tragedies are on record, but something is strangely awry here.

The first floor of the pub consists of a long bar and there are booths and tables for dining. The wall space is covered with authentic posters, vintage prints, and literary portraits. The TV is not obtrusive and is used mainly for historical and military videos. Once the first floor was unable to contain the growing customer base, the second-floor apartments were remodeled to make more dining space and a small bar. When the top floor was altered, ghostly manifestations began in earnest.

The most common event involves a series of heavy, phantom footsteps crossing the top floor from west to east. Staff as well as patrons on the first floor plainly hear the racket at a time when it is apparent no one is upstairs. When someone runs up the stairs to check, the person finds an empty room.

45

Red lion, symbol of strength and agility

In true European fashion, there is even a best time for the ghost to take a walk. At Red Lion Pub, the preferred time is Sundays between 5:00 and 5:30 p.m., during colder weather. This ghost not only has its timing down; it has an agenda.

Another frequent Red Lion haunting is a floral psychic scent, an old fashioned, overly-sweet lavender or lilac woman's perfume. Perfume scents are usually an indication of a feminine presence. This olfactory event happened to me on a Sunday night in October of 1986. I was sitting at a second-floor table with Colin Cordwell, working out details of a luncheon party I was hosting at the pub. No one else was in the room, so there was plenty of privacy. We both realized at the same time that we were in the midst of an aura of very heavy perfume. We looked at each other puzzled. It took a second or two for it to sink in that this must be something paranormal. We searched the top floor and even the first floor for a source of such a perfume and found nothing. The scent lasted less than ten minutes, then disappeared.

Co-owner Joe Heinen has experienced this scent many times. His experiences, also on the second floor, are mainly in the early morning hours after closing when he has the day's receipts spread out for counting. Alluding to the betting parlor, Joe believes that money may have played a part in a woman's death, and displaying it attracts her spirit.

Many have felt a cold spot on the top of the stairwell to the second floor. Just as someone takes the first step into the small bar area, there is a temperature anomaly that no draft or air-conditioning duct can explain. Before remodeling, this room was the bedroom of the young girl who died long before. Once anyone enters her bedroom area, her personal space, even more things are possible.

When lively sing-alongs take place on the second floor around the piano, the piano player has sometimes been tapped on the shoulder by a ghostly hand. Pianist Brenda Varda experienced this and remarked that she at first thought someone was trying to get her attention to compliment her or to request a song. When she turned around no one was there.

At the end of the small bar upstairs, still in the old bedroom area, a number of patrons and staff have felt a dizzy or lightheaded sensation.

The most dramatic unexplained event that happens here is the bloodcurdling woman's scream that can be heard coming from what is now the upstairs women's washroom. On the evening of November 11, 1990, I witnessed this firsthand while leading a private bus tour for a group from Cunningham's Pizza in suburban Worth. I was only a few feet away from the washroom door when a horrific cry came from that direction.

I was the first one to the door, banging at it and asking if everything was all right. There was no reply from inside, so I tried the door handle, only to find that the door was locked from the inside.

A woman in the group identified herself as a police officer and took control. She was unable to get a response from inside the room. With a quick kick, she broke the door open. We all checked inside. The washroom door had been locked from the inside, and the lock, now broken, proved that; but there was no one inside. The only way out, other than the door, was a tiny window, which was too small to climb through. Although rare, this disembodied scream is heard at the Red Lion from time to time.

Often patrons on the first floor are enjoying the pub's hospitality when they hear a racket overhead. Sometimes it is tables and chairs being overturned or moved about. Or it might be certain fixtures being tampered with. No one is on the second floor.

One night, the people on the first floor heard a loud crash. Something upstairs had fallen down. Colin ran up to the top floor but found no one present. As he searched the area, he spotted a cricket bat lying on the floor about twenty feet from the wall where it had recently been hanging.

A few days after hearing about this incident, I visited the Red Lion to investigate. Colin and I went through a re-enactment. I held the cricket bat up over my head against the wall at its original location. Despite a number of drops from the same height, Colin and I could never get the bat to bounce as far away as when it first "fell." We concluded that it must have been flung across the room, poltergeist fashion.

Red Lion Pub

One of the rare reports of a ghost sighting at the Red Lion was claimed by a Michigan florist and psychic Sheila Bitely. Sheila described an image of a cowboy in his twenties, unshaven, in boots and cowboy gear. It was her first time at the Red Lion, and she did not know that the previous use of the building was that of a country and western bar.

By far, the events described at the Red Lion are mischievous or nonthreatening, and John Cordwell took delight telling all who would listen. But he may have had a brush with one evil entity. When going up the stairs one day, he felt an intense push against his chest that forced him back down the stairs. This violence was totally out of character with the various other odd happenings at the restaurant. John always suspected that the ghostly culprit he encountered was the hard-drinking saloonkeeper and previous owner who Cordwell actually had to evict when he bought the building. The man swore revenge and later died.

The vast majority of happenings are on the top floor of the pub or on the stairwell. Several ghosts, several choices: The building was a betting parlor, so the sight of money may parlay one spirit into action. Neighbors speculate an obvious choice for at least one of the ghosts is the young woman, Sharon, who died in an upstairs apartment decades ago.

For some, the pick of the draw is a young cowboy, who perhaps is returning to the bar in a jealous rage to take back his girl. Others vote for Dan Danforth, surmising he is returning to stir things up. He formerly owned the building, and it is where he ran his country western bar, "Dirty Dan's." It was said he had the reputation to match the name. Around the neighborhood, he was known as a perennial troublemaker, and he did swear to avenge his eviction from the premises.

Still, the ghost could have come from a great distance to haunt this cozy site, maybe England. John Cordwell had thought that his own father, who loved pubs and to whom the pub is dedicated, was probably one of the ghosts, although he is buried in England. "My father never wanted a headstone on his grave," Cordwell stated. "He couldn't bear the thought of a weight being put on top of his body." A pub was a more fitting tribute than a mere grave marker. A commemorative plaque and a stained glass window were installed at the stairwell landing on the second floor. Curiously, Colin Cordwell related the story that his grandfather had promised that, if possible, he would come back and give a sign from the grave.

Both customers and future witnesses to the ongoing ghostly events at this traditional pub can draw their own conclusions.

Most British pubs can sport at least one ghost story, and Chicago's Red Lion is no shabby American cousin.

13 RED LION PUB

Location:	2446 North Lincoln Avenue, Chicago.
Type of occurrences:	Apparitions are very rare but poltergeist-type activity, phantom footsteps and screams, and psychic scents are fairly common.
Characteristics:	This typical English pub in Chicago somehow manifests classic British pub hauntings.
Status:	Ongoing, year-round.

THE PUB OWNER IS A GHOST

THE HAUNTED BUCKTOWN PUB

True to its name, Bucktown around the 1830s was a rural area on the outskirts of Chicago, where residents kept goats. The Bucktown neighborhood these days roughly encompasses a triangular area just of west of the Kennedy Expressway, down to Milwaukee Avenue and north of North Avenue.

The homes and storefronts still maintain a flavor and uniqueness, but the move of the yuppies into the neighborhood is pushing out many of the old-time residents because the restorations have increased the tax base.

At first glance, it's just another corner bar in the now oh-so-trendy Bucktown. Krystine Palmer's Bucktown Pub is a good mix of old-fashioned neighborhood bar with a generous wallop of sixties and seventies nostalgia that is only amplified when you hear about the local ghosts still present. This bar serves as a home for an eclectic crew of locals and a ghost who just won't go away.

Walk into the pub, and you find yourself in a pop museum. The decor includes original poster art, musical and political from the 1960s and early 1970s, framed autographs of famous figures of the period, and treasures of underground comic book art. This great material on display has been lovingly collected over many years by Chicago archivist Mike Johnson, and seems right at home in this vintage tavern with the tin-top ceiling and twenty one beers on tap. His collection, the Underground Comix Hall of Fame, is often visited by comix illustrators and pop artists. Comedy legend, Steve Allen, and Playboy founder and editor, Hugh Hefner, are among the regulars when in town.

The ghost, long thought to haunt the bar, however, is not connected with the memorabilia on display, but before his untimely death, was the owner and bartender here years ago .

Wally was a cantankerous, old-fashioned bar owner who was opinionated and loud. From his corner stool, he directed the bar's operations, shouting out orders to his employees. Older neighborhood folk still talk about the tavern when parakeets flew wildly around the bar.

Wally lived upstairs with his wife Annie until the tragic day that he put a gun to his head and committed suicide in 1986. He died in his bedroom on the second floor, over the bar.

The bar stood empty for a while until Krystine Palmer bought the business from Wally's widow in 1991. The transformation was dramatic. The entire look of the bar changed, but Wally would remain.

When the new bar was first set up, it seems someone objected. Every bar owner has his or her personal style. Certain bottles are lined up one way in one bar, and a different way in another. It's not that one way is right or wrong; it's just a personal preference. The morning after the bar was set up at the Bucktown Pub, the bottles were all rearranged and changed. Wally obviously took charge and wanted the bar back to the way it was when he was the owner.

Similar rearrangements were made involving coasters, napkins, and other bar paraphernalia. Poltergeist interventions were surely Wally's. During the night, things were being moved and changed.

Bucktown Pub

Mike Johnson remembers the first days of the new bar well. "There was immediate poltergeist activity," he recalled. "There were also times you could almost see someone in your peripheral vision to the side. You could also hear someone nearby, but no one was there."

Wally, from an older generation, had an apparent dislike for much of the new music on the jukebox. Tunes would be rejected for no reason. The entire jukebox could be turned on or off according to Wally's whims. Sometimes, it began to play automatically.

The ghostly activity involves staff for the most part. Bartenders have reported many unusual antics that they attribute to Wally. One incident, still talked about years afterwards, concerns a new employee who started work at the Bucktown. A total nonbeliever, the young woman loudly denied the possibility of ghosts and began to personally dare Wally, if he did exist, to prove himself. Suddenly, from high on the wall at the back of the bar, a large plaster Rolling Rock statuette crashed down, narrowly missing the "heretic's" head. It wasn't that Wally intended real harm, but he did get her attention. She never knocked Wally out loud again.

Although, Wally is the obvious choice as the prime mover behind the Bucktown Pub's hauntings, he might not be doing the haunting alone at his former bar. There could be under-lying auras left from the early days of this location.

There has been a documented bar operating here since 1933, but before that time, this location was almost certainly a speakeasy, illegally operating until the election of Franklin Roosevelt in 1932 and the end of prohibition a year later. There are many known gangster sites in the neighborhood, and the odds are great that some beer-running activities took place here. The St. Valentine's Day Massacre took place just east of here, and the car that was used by the killers that day was discovered in a "chop shop" nearby.

Strangely, the basement has been largely filled in with dirt. No one seems to know the reason, or just when this took place. What mysteries worthy of a segment on "Geraldo" lie buried beneath? A weird feeling has been described by almost everyone who has gone down there, from beer deliverymen to exterminators.

This cozy and friendly neighborhood bar seems able to hold some of its customers for eternity.

14 THE BUCKTOWN PUB

Location:	1658 West Cortland Street, Chicago.
Type of occurrence:	Nonvisual poltergeist activity, always around the bar.
Characteristics:	Interference with bar paraphernalia is fairly constant, especially when new bartenders are being broken in. Bottles, bar decorations, coasters, and more are moved or sometimes violently tossed across the room.
Status:	Definitely ongoing.

DEATH PERSONIFIED
Eternal Silence

Graceland Cemetery is a Victorian Valhalla for cemetery buffs. Starting at Irving Park Road, Graceland Cemetery runs along Clark Street, totally surrounded by a high wall of red brick and topped with wire. Graceland is nonsectarian. On the other side of Irving at Clark, are Jewish Graceland and Wunder, a Protestant cemetery.

Thousands come here yearly to take organized or self-guided tours of the ornamental tombs and sculptures and obelisks. The winding roads through the cemetery are marked off as avenues. Maps of the most noteworthy graves and artworks are available at the cemetery office building, and most visitors start their walking tour with a visit to the Dexter Graves plot a short distance away.

Dexter Graves brought a colony of settlers from Ohio to the wilds of Chicago in 1831, two years before the City of Chicago began. Although not exactly a superrich Chicago family in the same league as some of our captains of commerce and industry to be found buried here, the Graves family was quite prosperous. The family fortune was based upon hotel ownership, a very lucrative business in the early pioneering days.

The attraction at the Graves family site is the magnificent bronze statue, "Eternal Silence," by noted sculptor Larado Taft. Many who come to visit the cemetery ask to see the "Statue of Death," by which it is perhaps better known. The irony of the family's last name may have spurred the Graves family to immortalize their burial plot. If so, they succeeded beyond their wildest dreams.

Taft was commissioned to produce this allegorical image by the Graves' descendants long after the death of their patriarch, Dexter Graves (1789-1844). It was completed in 1909 and was immediately recognized as a great work of art. No visit would be complete without a visit to this monument, and many come here just for this memorial. Year after year, it is the most popular.

Although veiled or robed personifications of death are commonly found in many late Nineteenth Century cemeteries, this representation is known internationally and has a following that even some rock stars would envy.

I first began to hear legends about this imposing statue in the 1970s. It was commonly believed that one could not photograph the statue. According to a number of my informants, whenever some people attempted to photograph the statue, their cameras malfunctioned. Sometimes they thought they had successfully taken a photo, only to find that upon developing the film that particular frame on the negatives would be blank.

Eventually, after hearing a number of accounts like this, I decided to try my own luck photographing "Death." My color slides came out beautifully. The now-weathered jade-green bronze statue showed up perfectly. So, it was pure folklore that the statue of death could not be photographed.

But this made me wonder why this legend evolved and continued to persist, and how it became entrenched in the minds of so many people. I had thought of the statue as an object, not an icon. It then dawned on me how totally daunting this figure with its ominous face peering out from the hooded folds of the shroud could be to others, and how differently the

Eternal Silence

meaning of this statue could be interpreted. I thought that maybe to some people the empty pictures signify death. Death itself is the great unknown. These people may have a preconception, some subliminal belief, the statue could not be photographed, because any human attempt to define death would be doomed to failure. Eternity could not be scientifically measured, weighed, or pictured by mere mortals. To me, it was pure Carl Jung.

Carl Gustav Jung, the famed Swiss psychiatrist, developed theories, which he termed "analytical psychology." His work included a description of psychological types, "extrovert/introvert," the exploration into what he called "collective unconscious," and the concept of the psyche as a "self-regulating system."

Dr. Jung was quoted as saying that his work regarding the human mind was, "in pursuit of the psyche or the ghost in the machine."

He also had an interest in symbolism, mythology, and religion and made in-depth studies into the symbolism of the picture cards in the tarot deck. He might have been able to appreciate the symbolism of the "Statue of Death," since it looks as if it could have stepped from a tarot card.

Revisiting "Eternal Silence" over the years, I have noticed a new superstitious gesture that has been taking place. On any given visit, a number of coins can be found placed symbolically at the foot of the figure at the statue's base. The denominations vary, but most are copper pennies.

Are these votive offerings to Charon, the ferrymen, who transported the dead to Hades over the River Styx? Greek mythology tells that when a soul of the dead is brought to the sulky old ferryman, he must be paid a coin, an obolus, for passage to the underworld. If payment cannot be made, or Charon refuses, the soul is doomed to wander the banks of the Styx for a period of 100 years.

Are certain Graceland pilgrims prepaying for their last boat ride into eternity? Is "Eternal Silence" accepting their bestowal's graciously, or are their sometimes-paltry offerings to him an insult, since precious metal coins were the proper fare of ancient times?

Sage advice might be, "Don't cheat the ferryman."

15 GRACELAND CEMETERY (STATUE ON CENTER AVENUE)

Location:	4001 North Clark Street, Chicago.
Type of occurrence:	Legends of strange happenings at memorial. Curious customs taking place here, also.
Characteristics:	Reported camera failure when attempts are made to photograph statue. Superstitious offerings left at site.
Status:	Offerings still bestowed.

LITTLE GIRL VANISHES
THE MYSTERIOUS MONUMENT

Inez Clark (1873-1880) died a beautiful little girl of only six years of age. Although we basically know nothing about her, Inez's fond memory is preserved at Graceland Cemetery with her unique memorial.

Unlike the garish tombs of the millionaires, regal columns, and the multitudes of stately obelisks at Graceland, Inez's gravesite is marked by an exquisitely sculpted life-sized statue of the child sitting on a chair with a fancy hat resting on her shoulder, and her left hand holding a parasol. The work of art is protected by a glass case.

The statue is so wonderfully wrought that the cemetery office is constantly asked about it. For years, one of the stories relating to Inez is that she was tragically struck by lightning while on a family picnic, and her grieving parents commissioned this work of art to remember her.

Today, the cemetery admits that they have no information on how she really died. But act of nature, childhood illness, or whatever way death stole innocent Inez away, it is obvious that her parents loved her dearly.

Little Inez is the sweetheart of everyone who visits Graceland. One visit here and you want to know more about this enigmatic child. Not only are the circumstances of her death shrouded in mystery, but also, there are numerous legends surrounding her extraordinary monument.

In the early 1980s, one of my bus drivers, who worked part-time in security, told me a curious tale. He said that while making the rounds at Graceland Cemetery, after hours, he would sometimes come upon the Inez Clark grave only to find the statue appeared to be missing from inside its glass case. The first time this happened, he was ready to report the statue stolen to his superiors, but on making another swing past the spot on his beat, the statue was back. Of course, he doubted himself at first, but after witnessing this inexplicable event on other nights, he was convinced something strange was going on.

One night a different security guard was on duty. He had heard about the so-called "vanishing statue" but was a nonbeliever. Making his rounds, he found the statue missing and promptly fled the cemetery, afraid to continue his patrol. The next morning, as usual, the statue of little Inez was back.

The only reports I had of anything unusual here were from the security personnel, who noticed Inez's statue acting up. A number of times during the 1980s and 1990s, the topic of Inez Clark's monument became the grist of radio talk show calls. I related the security guards' stories over the airwaves, and the legends spread. I presumed that only those working inside the cemetery by night, security watchmen, would ever be witnesses, then recently, I came up with a report of several experiences from a local resident.

Suzy Rothberg, after meeting me on a bus tour, volunteered some remarkable information. A native of Texas, she moved into the area near Graceland in May of 1997. She had never heard any tales about the Inez Clark's unique statue, but she told me she had personally had witnessed an odd phenomenon.

*Inez Clark
Memorial*

One day, while walking down Clark Street past the cemetery, she noticed a glass-encased monument just visible inside the fence. She asked her friend Linda about the reason for the glass enclosure. "Linda just told me that it was because people were stealing the statue," Suzy remembered. At first, it did not arouse any real curiosity in her. From 1997 to 1999, if she happened to be walking past the cemetery, she would gaze at the statue. "It was almost like acknowledging a neighbor," she said.

"I was walking home late one night by the cemetery, and I paused to look at the monument. It was mild. It was late spring or early summer and it was not foggy out, but inside the glass case was a solid dense white cloud. In an upper corner of the case, the mist was swirling," Suzy stated definitely. She described the mist as being similar to a billow of thick cigar smoke. "The case was never completely filled with smoke," Suzy added. "There was always a clear portion or spotty section somewhere."

Suzy says she had three or four encounters. She laments, "I felt sad, a sadness for those who died.

"I'm not a psychic," Suzy says, " but I do have good insight. I wondered if my visits were disturbing me so much that they were somehow subconsciously inducing this sentiment."

When Suzy first told me of her sightings, I was excited to find new evidence concerning Inez Clark's grave. Then, the more I weighed the matter, the more puzzling it became. Graceland is surrounded by a tall, red brick wall. There are no openings, no gaps, in the wall, so how did Suzy see the Clark monument while walking by?

Further research and questioning of Suzy led me to the discovery that she was actually walking past the twin cemeteries of Wunder and Jewish Graceland on the south side of Irving Park. What appeared to Suzy as one long cemetery, was actually three different ones abutting each other. She had observed a glass-encased monument at an entirely different gravesite. South of Graceland, the cemeteries are protected by a wire mesh fence, not a wall, so there is visibility.

It seems that Inez has spectral company when it comes to ghostly possibilities. My work is now to unravel the facts of yet another supernatural event. Ghost hunting often is full of surprises.

From researcher Helen Sclair, who is a noted authority on Chicago area cemeteries and lecturer at Newberry Library on the subject, comes an even more fascinating, enigmatic perspective on the Inez Clark story. She dispels any notion of psychic theories, but says, however, Inez Clark is not even buried at the Graceland cemetery site; it is a little boy by the name of Amos Briggs. She believes the statue was an advertising piece, perhaps donated to the family from a sculptor by the name of A. Gagel, who also created a similar monument at Rosehill Cemetery for the gravesite of another little girl, Lulu Fellows. She has been unable to uncover any reasoning why the statue was placed at his gravesite, or where little Inez is buried.

Could the disappearing statue be trying to tell us something?

The living Inez Clark has been gone from this world for over five generations. But with the ever-growing popularity of cemetery walking tours, tombstone art, and local history, her name is certainly better known now than it was during her lifetime.

16 GRACELAND CEMETERY (STATUE ON MAIN AVENUE)

Location:	4001 North Clark Street, Chicago.
Type of occurrences:	Tales of the statue at the grave disappearing on certain night or the glass case enclosing it filling with white smoke or fog.
Characteristics:	Fabulously detailed grave marker seems to have a life of its own. Statue can disappear for hours, then return, under mysterious circumstances.
Status:	Seems to be on a continuing basis.

THE TOTEM POLE THAT CAME ALIVE

THE KRAFT TOTEM POLE

A genuine Native American totem pole stands at Addison and Lake Shore Drive, a silent guard, as thousands of motorists pass by daily.

The saga of the totem pole in Chicago dates from the twenties. James L. Kraft, founder of Kraft, Inc., made his fortune with cheeses and other fare. A wealthy collector of art, Kraft acquired the totem pole in 1926 while on a buying trip to the Pacific Northwest. The pole originally came from Alert Bay, Vancouver, British Columbia. In 1929, the totem pole was placed on Park District property facing the constant flow of Lake Shore Drive traffic. It was dedicated to the children of Chicago

All totem poles are carved and painted to depict a story of mythical or historical incidents, and this sculpted piece of Kwakiutl Indian art is no exception. It visually describes the saga of a whale hunt.

Central to the story and taking up most of the forty feet of elaborately carved red cedar sculpture is a whale, facing nose down. Sitting on top of the whale's tale at the highest point of the totem pole is a thunderbird. Riding high upon the whale's back with harpoon in hand is the intrepid hunter poised for the kill, and at the bottom, is the intimidating masked sea monster face. The artwork is painted in the traditional colors of green, red, black and white.

As a familiar sight to Chicagoans on the North Side, many picnics and family gatherings took place around the pole. Snapshots often included the totem pole as a backdrop in the family photo albums.

After the passage of years, some of the people who had tucked away those family photographs would later compare them with ones they had taken more recently. They made an unusual discovery. Something had changed from photo to photo.

The figure of the warrior about halfway up the totem pole seemed to change position in these photos. Sometimes the warrior held his arms and spear one way, then sometimes another. He also seemed to vary his stance from time to time, or twist from side to side.

It was presumed by those viewing the photos that the changing movements were only the result of the time of day, or the way the shadows fell upon the figure, or the position and perspective of the photographer, but to others, the movements appeared more radical, and they believed there was cause for explanation.

Some tried to explain the changes as the result of tampering with the arms and legs by unknown parties, conjecture being that they had been sawed off, reattached and repainted, but such tampering could hardly have been done without telltale traces and witnesses.

Could the explanation be the supernatural?

The warrior may have been possessed by a totem spirit, so this was what accounted for this supernatural animation. "Possession" of inanimate objects is still believed by many native peoples and has a long tradition ranging from the Pacific Northwest totem poles to the kachina dolls of the American Southwest.

Totem pole at Addison and Lake Shore Drive

This psychic manifestation has also been introduced into popular culture, such as in a made-for-TV movie aired in 1975, "Trilogy of Terror."

The story is that a young woman is given a Zuni kachina doll as a gift, and when a chain falls off the doll's waist, unstoppable, sinister magic is unleashed. The doll comes alive to stalk and eventually destroy the hapless heroine.

It should be noted that the *Chicago Tribune* had published a story relating the unusual happenings at the Totem Pole prior to the first showing of the TV movie.

Perhaps, more mystifying than the special effects produced in the movie is that magic is believed to occur at this Chicago landmark.

The story of the Kraft Totem Pole continues to take a number of twists. In 1985, then Mayor of Chicago Harold Washington gave the totem pole back to Canada with reasons ranging from conservation needs of the deteriorating wood to concerns about the plight of Native Americans.

However, Chicago would not be long without a totem pole. The Kraft Company commissioned Tony Hunt, a Native American artist, to replicate the original totem pole. It was erected and dedicated at the same location in 1986.

Yet, similar magic seems to surround the successor.

Shortly after being erected, vandalism struck the new work of art, twice. An unknown gunman shot the totem pole six times at seemingly close range. Then the right arm of the warrior and the spear were broken off and stolen.

The Park District has repaired the arm and spear, but these outrages seem to have stimulated some latent powers. Although only here a few years, the new totem pole strangely aged to look like its predecessor. The vivid colors faded and massive cracks ran down the length of the cedar pole, making it look decades older. Ironically, the current totem pole has been repaired and repainted twice.

Photographs now taken of the second-generation totem pole sometimes show mysterious smoke or fog around the figure of the warrior. This ectoplasm is not visible to the human eye, but registers on the photograph negative.

Skeptics have tried unsuccessfully over the years to downplay the totem pole stories. They insist that the alleged movements of the warrior were purely the result of overactive imaginations.

Cub fans often point out the curious positioning of the Totem Pole. The pole stands exactly at Addison and Lake Shore Drive. The warrior's steely eyes steadfastly gaze down Addison toward Wrigley Field.

Taking a trip past the totem pole might answer some of these perplexing questions.

17 Kraft Totem Pole

Location:	Lake Shore Drive (east side) at Addison (3600 North), Chicago.
Type of occurrence:	Reported supernatural animation of inanimate object on original totem pole. Currently unusual photographs reported.
Characteristics:	In early reports, the portion of this totem pole carved and painted as a warrior or hunter seemed to change position on occasion from 1929 to 1985. Replacement totem pole produces photographic anomalies, "ectoplasm" on film.
Status:	Current totem pole still produces strange activity.

A VODKA-DRINKING POLTERGEIST

A HAUNTED SCOTTISH PUB

There are at least three Scottish-theme pubs in Chicago, but the longest established is the Ole St. Andrew's Inn (formerly called the Edinburgh Castle Pub) on North Broadway. It has operated as a Scottish bar since 1961, but before that time, it was just a neighborhood tavern owned by a Norwegian-American named Frank Giff with his wife Edna.

According to neighborhood folk who remember him, Frank was a colorful character who looked and acted like W. C. Fields. He ran his bar his own way, and if you didn't like it, "you could take a hike." Like Fields, Frank was fond of drink, vodka particularly.

Frank regularly partook of his vodka stock each evening. One night in 1959 at the age of fifty-nine, he tipped back a few more than usual. Early the next morning, Edna found her husband dead on the floor behind the counter in the rear of the bar.

After giving Frank a proper funeral, Edna took to running the bar by herself. But it wasn't the same without Frank, and Edna decided to put the bar up for sale. The establishment was purchased in 1961 by a customer named Jane McDougall, a native of Glasgow.

Jane had dreams of transforming the neighborhood tavern into something special, a Scottish pub. She brought in a tartan carpet, Scottish memorabilia to hang along the walls, and a line of Scottish ales and whiskies to sell at the bar, and named it Edinburgh Castle Pub.

As time went by, large quantities of vodka began to disappear in the bar. At first, she naturally suspected her bartenders of helping themselves to her stock. Trying to catch the culprit, she began to secretly mark the level of liquid in the bottles with a crayon. To her amazement, she learned that the level of vodka dropped considerably in the middle of the night when the bar was closed and no one was there.

Jane was not originally a believer in ghosts, but because the vodka continued to disappear, she concluded her bar must be haunted.

"Never let anyone tell you that ghosts don't exist," she was fond of telling patrons. "They do, and mine drinks to excess."

Since Jane had known Frank and his fondness for vodka, she began to surmise it was Frank who was the spirit on the premises and responsible for the thefts. It seems he never really left.

I first learned about the Edinburgh Castle Pub and its hauntings in 1980 when the Chicago Chemists Club hired me to give a slide lecture for their meeting there. When they told me they had selected a haunted site for the talk, I decided to go there beforehand and research the site.

There I was one night, at the bar having a beer when suddenly two long-stemmed glasses hanging upside down from a rack over the cash register crashed to the floor. The bartender ran up to me and said, "Did you see that? The ghost just knocked the glasses down."

"Wait a minute," I replied, trying to be rational, "couldn't the glasses have been knocked to the ground by the vibrations of the heavy traffic just outside the door on Broadway?"

*Ole St. Andrew's
Scottish Pub*

The bartender gave me an odd look and picked up the bases of the broken glasses from the floor. He showed me that the bases of the glasses had been taped down and that whatever had knocked the glasses down had done so with such force that the tape had been ripped away.

"Explain this, wise guy!" was all that he had to say.

A few months later, I was walking into the pub one night around 8:00 p.m. when I saw Margaret, a regular patron, sitting halfway down the bar. Right before my eyes I saw a heavy glass ashtray fly off the counter top and crash to the floor breaking into a number of pieces. It was obvious Margaret was extremely frightened and jumped backwards off the barstool screaming, "I never touched it!" I could certainly confirm that her hands were nowhere near the ashtray.

Margaret was so frightened by that event that she stayed away from her favorite pub for months afterwards, fearful of what Frank might do next.

Besides being a vodka-drinking ghost, Frank is also a typical poltergeist, a "pelting ghost," one who likes to break or trash things to attract attention to himself.

Actually witnessing poltergeist activity in action is quite rare. These are the only two times in my career as a ghost hunter that I actually saw events happen before my eyes that I feel I can honestly attribute to telekinesis. These objects moved without apparent cause.

Hauntings often seem to be "stirred up" when change or disruption takes place at a location. Frank Giff's ghost seems overly protective of his former property and shows his dislike of change by causing some sort of a psychic disturbance. The overhanging rack for long-stem glasses had to be removed after glasses continued to be broken. New electronic cash registers, or anything electronic, such as the icemaker, tended to be broken or played with when first introduced.

The bar has been remodeled to a greater or lesser extent seven or eight times since 1961. Every time that change has occurred, Frank has objected.

A bizarre incident involved Jane McDougall's enclosing the entrance of the building. The front windows were stuccoed over and a large sheet metal heraldic lion was mounted to the wall, a tribute to Scotland. These changes caused almost immediate reaction.

A vertical crack appeared in the stucco for no apparent reason. One morning, McDougall found the lion's legs and even the tongue bent and twisted out of shape. It did not seem possible that vandals could have accomplished the damage without at least removing the heavy artifact from the wall. Jane McDougall had to admit defeat. The misshapen lion was removed and placed in the basement and the front of the building was remodeled again with windows put back in place.

The most active location in the bar is the spot where Frank Giff died decades ago. Currently, after a number of remodelings, the death spot can be found along the left wall in the dining area of the pub. Sit in a booth beneath a light, next to an electronic bowling game, and you are right on top of the site. For some who have sat here, Frank has made himself known.

On the floor there is often a cold spot that affects your toes and feet, sometimes climbing up your legs. It can begin like a slight numbness or sensation as if your foot is falling asleep. It usually only affects one side of your body.

But there had been times when someone has gotten something extra special. Some women have reported that an icy, clammy hand may grasp their shoulder or knee, or other parts of their anatomy. They describe the sensation as being exactly like a hand squeezing or sometimes just a brushing against their skin. Perhaps the sensation could be explained in some cases as imagination. But there is a pattern here that certainly seems to rule out chance. The vast majority of women who claimed these additional contacts are invariably blondes or redheads.

The probability was put forward by Jane McDougall some years ago: Since Edna Giff was a strawberry blond, it is a possibility that her husband Frank was still looking for her at the site where he died. Ghosts don't realize that the years are passing them by, and perhaps Frank was still reliving his moment of death, reaching out for Edna who was not there in his time of need. Perhaps the vodka-sodden ghost of Frank has been mistaking modern-day strawberry blondes for his dear Edna.

It seems Frank must have made the mistake with writer Carol Carlson, for Carol is a strawberry blonde. In 1991, she and her friend Elsie decided they would have a party "out of the ordinary." Sixty people were invited, and they would have dinner at the pub and take my Supernatural Tour. A problem arose. The chef had gotten sick so Carol and Elsie decided they would use the pub's facilities and make a boiled dinner for everyone. Carol said to Elsie, "You know what we forgot, Irish soda bread. Why don't you go to the grocery, and if you can't get it, just get some rye."

This left Carol alone in the kitchen peeling vegetables, but feeling uncomfortable because she "just felt a presence." Carol kept glancing behind and looking at her watch, thinking where is she? Her uneasiness was exacerbated when the ice machine started acting up, making repeated hideously loud sounds. Carol was extremely relieved when Elsie got back.

The dinner went well, and everyone enjoyed the Supernatural Tour. When Carol and her family and some of the group returned to the pub, she was confronted by the man whom she had hired to act as waiter and clean up.

"If you are ever going to use this place again, don't call me!" he stated incensed. "Something is wrong with the kitchen and that ice machine is really weird. There are really strange things going on in this place."

Carol and Elsie began straightening up. Carol had set several bags of leftovers she was going to take home on a table near Frank's booth. All of a sudden, one bag slid to the edge of the table, momentarily hung in midair as though it were being held, then crashed to the floor. Carol and Elsie looked at each other stunned. Carol asked cautiously, "Did you really see that?" Elsie replied, "I think it's time we leave."

That was experience enough to convince Carol Carlson and her friends that Frank was in their midst.

Jane McDougall retired from the bar business and died in 1996. Her legacy of a Scottish pub lives on, but under the current name of the Ole St. Andrews Inn.

While other customers come and go, one regular remains constant. The ghost of Frank Giff now seems just like a member of the extended family of bar patrons. However, his story should also be a cautionary tale for us, the living: Do not leave this world intoxicated, or your soul, too, may be earthbound for a very long time.

18 OLE St. ANDREWS INN

Location:	5938 North Broadway, Chicago.
Type of occurrence:	Various poltergeist happenings ranging from a traditional cold spot to random trashing of bar items and consumption of liquor. Touching. Electrical malfunctions.
Characteristics:	Activity centers around the death spot of a previous owner and the bar area, which was his main concern in life. Dying while intoxicated no doubt is a major reason for the various types of events.
Status:	One of the most haunted sites around Chicago.

THE LITTLE BOY GHOST

MURDER VICTIM, BOBBY FRANKS HAUNTS HIS BURIAL GROUND

The tragedy of the Bobby Franks murder in 1924 would reach far from the South Side of Chicago and would make an indelible mark on American popular culture forever. The crime was a national sensation that fostered novels, movies and radio and television dramas. For decades, questions about the case and its deposition would resurface, and until the Lindberg kidnapping, it was the "crime of the century."

The murderers were eighteen-year-old Nathan Leopold and seventeen-year-old Richard Loeb. They were the sons of affluent families with time and money on their hands. They lived in the Kenwood District on Chicago's South Side near the University of Chicago

Leopold was enamored with Fredrich Neitsche's concept of a "superman." Brilliant, but sadistic, Leopold and Loeb thought they could prove their superiority and attain super status. They contrived a plan to commit the "perfect crime," a kidnapping and murder. Part of the plan was to make the crime look like a kidnapping for money to deflect any suspicion from themselves.

After committing a series of lesser crimes as a stepping stone to murder, they felt ready. With much deliberation and a coldhearted selection process, on May 21, 1924, they accosted fourteen-year-old Bobby Franks walking home after classes from Harvard School on the South Side. Loeb knew Franks and was a distant relation.

Taking Bobby into their car, Loeb struck him on the head with a chisel as Leopold drove away. Bobby bled to death in the car's back seat floor from his injuries.

But the perfect crime began to unravel. The body was poorly hidden in a culvert on the Far South Side and was discovered just as the ransom note was arriving at the Franks' home. The discarded typewriter used for the ransom demand was recovered and traced to Loeb. Eyeglasses dropped at the culvert were traced by their prescription to Leopold.

The two were brought in for questioning by the police. Intense pressure on both cracked Loeb first, and Leopold's confession followed. Loeb was disowned by his family, but Leopold's father stood firm and hired the only lawyer he felt could possibly help, Clarence Darrow.

In a thirty-three-day bench trial before Judge John R. Caverly, Darrow took on State's Attorney Robert E. Crowe in what everyone presumed would be a solid case against Loeb and Leopold with well-deserved death sentences. Stories circulated of a savage mutilation.

After an ingenious and eloquent plea against the death penalty by Darrow, Judge Caverly imposed sentences on each defendant of life imprisonment for murder, plus ninety-nine years for kidnapping. Caverly's stated rationale in not imposing death was the age of the youths. The State of Illinois had never executed anyone so young. Judge Caverly made a proviso in the sentencing that neither killer was to ever be eligible for parole, and they should be kept apart the rest of their lives.

Despite public opinion running strongly for executions, Darrow had succeeded in saving his clients' lives. Many thought that justice had not been done, and it was family money and connections that had made the difference for Loeb and Leopold.

Their high-priced legal talent saved their lives, and bribes would provide them relative luxury at Stateville Penitentiary. They were not separated and had the run of the prison. Spe-

Bobby Franks' Crypt

cial meals, private dining in the officers' lounge, and personal phone privileges set them apart from ordinary criminals, as did their open access to liquor and narcotics.

Ironically, Darrow, who was reputedly hired at the fee of $1 million, received only a miserly portion of $30,000 from Leopold's father, who even begrudged that amount; yet, it was reported that the father had begged Darrow on his knees to take the case.

In January of 1936, Richard Loeb, while attempting to coerce inmate James Day into sex in a shower, was seriously slashed in a fight with a razor. Shortly after the fight, Loeb died. Leopold was at his side.

Against the specific wording of the sanctions by Judge Caverly decades before, Nathan Leopold was eventually paroled in 1958 after thirty-three years behind bars. He settled in Puerto Rico, took a job as a lab technician, and married a widow in 1961. Heart failure claimed his life in 1971.

It was a spring day in 1988, and I was driving through Rosehill Cemetery with a caretaker acting as my guide. "Bobby Franks is buried here, you know," he stated. He proceeded to point out a small weathered-stone crypt with the name of Franks carved over the doorway.

Stopping my car to get a better look, I walked up to the door and purely out of inquisitiveness, gave the handle a turn. To my amazement, it opened. The caretaker was shocked to see that the door was unlocked, and said to me in a not entirely humorous tone, "Maybe the ghost of Bobby wanted you to go in." I entered the crypt and said a silent prayer for the child.

The caretaker explained to me how years ago cemetery workers claimed that a young boy was seen from a distance, but would vanish when approached. It was thought to be the ghost of Bobby wandering nearby the crypt haunting the spot where his body was buried.

And what has happened with the ghost of Bobby Franks? Only after the deaths of his killers did the boy find rest, it seems. According to Rosehill Cemetery tradition, the boy's ghost has not been encountered since Leopold's death.

May Bobby Franks rest in peace.

19 FRANKS MAUSOLEUM ROSEHILL CEMETERY (SECTION †)

Location: 5800 North Ravenswood Avenue, Chicago.
Type of Occurrence: Alleged apparition of child.
Characteristics: Fully formed, solid and substantial vision of child seen playing near crypt where body was interred.
Status: Probably extinct.

GHOST SOLVES HER OWN MURDER

Teresita, The Possession Case

As Teresita Basa looked out of the window of her high rise building, her view was a typical cold and wintry February day in Chicago with gloom pervasive. It was 1977. Teresita, forty-seven and a native of the Philippines, had come to Chicago hoping to pursue her dream of teaching music, but for now she was working as a respiration therapist at Edgewater Hospital.

The doorbell rang. Teresita Basa hurried to the door and glanced out the aperture. She recognized the face outside, slipped off the safety chain, and unlocked the door, allowing the caller to enter her apartment. She closed the door and slid the chain back in place. Out of the corner of her eye, she caught the quick blurring movement of an arm grabbing her from behind. Before she could react, the strong arm encircled her neck with a crushing grip. As the arm jerked back, her body raised up, intensifying the effect of the chokehold, and instantly her body fell limply into unconsciousness.

The intruder dragged Teresita's body to the bedroom and stripped off her clothing, then went to the kitchen, quickly searched through the drawers, pulled out a large butcher knife, and hurried back to the bedroom. Leaning over Teresita's unconscious body, the intruder plunged the knife deeply into her chest. The killer rummaged through her purse, finding only thirty dollars. Angry, he ransacked the bedroom looking for valuables. As he poured out the contents of a jewelry box, he grabbed a necklace and a pendant. He pulled the mattress from the bed and threw it over Teresita's lifeless body, then some clothing and lit them on fire.

The Chicago Fire Department arrived at the scene and extinguished the fire, but when they found Teresita, they called the Chicago Police Department. The brutality of the case and the fire set to destroy evidence and throw off the investigation gave the police extra motivation to track down the murderer. Assigned to the case were Detectives Joe Stachula, a ten-year police veteran and an ex-Marine, and his partner Lee Epplen.

The detectives aggressively pursued the case. As the police team questioned dozens of Teresita's associates, they always arrived at a dead end. Months passed by and winter turned to spring and then summer. It seemed that as more time passed, chances increased that Teresita Basa's killer would never be found.

Remedios "Remy" Chua worked as an inhalation therapist on the midnight shift at the hospital. She knew Teresita, but seldom saw her, since they worked different shifts. They usually did not socialize, but Remy had attended a party given by Teresita. On July 11, while on a break in the locker room, Mrs. Chua, feeling unusually exhausted, positioned herself on two chairs. As she began to close her eyes, she saw someone standing in front of her. It was Teresita Basa. Driven by panic, she jumped up and ran from the room down the hall. She breathlessly asked her coworker if he had seen Teresita, also. He scoffed and assured her he had not. She was embarrassed by the incident.

One evening, the usually reserved Remy broke into a tirade in front of her coworkers. She complained about her job, her fellow employees, working conditions, and more. When

Edgewater Medical
Center

confronted by a coworker saying, "Mrs. Chua, you are sounding more like Teresita Basa every-day," she was puzzled by her outbursts of emotion.

Mrs. Chua was exhausted and asked to take a few days off. On July 16, Mrs. Chua came to Edgewater Hospital on her day off accompanied by her husband, Dr. Chua, to get her paycheck. She was confronted with the news that her supervisor had decided to discharge her from her job. Although feeling hurt, Remy felt sure she would be able to find new employment quickly with so many opportunities in the health field for hard workers.

One evening after dinner, the Chuas were relaxing in their living room. A strange look came over Remy Chua's face as she rose from her chair and walked into her bedroom. Dr. Chua followed her to check if everything was all right. He found her lying on the bed, staring blank-eyed at the ceiling.

After asking her repeatedly what was wrong, Remy's lips began to move. The voice, however, was not his wife's nor in his wife's dialect. It was a Spanish accent.

"I am Teresita Basa," was the reply.

The stranger in his wife's body then pleaded with Dr. Chua to call the police and tell them who killed her. But before giving up the murderer's name the entity slipped away, and Remy Chua awakened to find her husband looking over her with grave concern. He asked her if she was aware of what had happened. She recalled nothing.

The possession of Remy Chua by Teresita Basa's spirit happened twice more. On the third incident, Remy's voice also described how Allan Showery, an orderly at Edgewater, had stolen jewelry from the apartment and had murdered Teresita. Her voice pleaded for help to go the police with the information.

The Chuas now were faced with the problem of finding someone in authority who would believe them or act upon the information they obtained through such an unorthodox source. After contacting the Philippine Consulate and the Evanston Police, they were interviewed by Detective Joe Stachula who took their statements and with trepidation acted on the tip.

Upon being questioned, Showery denied ever having been at Teresita's home. He soon contradicted that denial and other statements he gave. When the missing jewelry was found in his common law wife's possession, the psychic noose was tightening. Allan Showery confessed.

Frank Barbaro, a distinguished judge with thirty-two years of experience as a lawyer, sixteen of those serving on the bench, had heard almost every conceivable story in his courtroom, but this case was his most unusual. It was the first case in Illinois annals where a psychic experience was accepted as evidence.

Showery's public defender attempted to save his client by arguing that the "claimed supernatural contact" negated the confession, since Showery was arrested without sufficient evidence, making his confession inadmissible. Showery might have gone free, but strangely, against the advice of his attorneys, he pleaded guilty. On February 23, 1979, Allan Showery was sentenced to fourteen years in prison for the murder of Teresita Basa.

Edgewater Hospital is a nine-story building serving the medical needs of a multi-ethnic neighborhood on the City's far North Side. Where death is commonplace and the emotions of the sick and dying, as well as their loved ones, runs high, it is natural to suspect that hospitals might be good places for ghost stories. But of all the supernatural tales involving Chicagoland hospitals, none is as bizarre or well documented as those surrounding the 1977 murder case of Teresita Basa. After the murder of Teresita Basa, three other Filipinos who worked at Edgewater Hospital claimed they too had been visited by the apparition of the victim, begging them to help, but all were too frightened to respond.

Two in-depth studies of this case have been published. *A Voice From The Grave, A Documented True Life Happening* by Carol Mercado tells the story from the point of view of the Chuas. An "Unsolved Mysteries" segment and an NBC made-for-TV movie have been produced based on Carol Mercado's work. *Teresita: The Voice From The Grave*, by crime reporters John O'Brien and Edward Baumann, recounts the case from the police perspective.

Things seems to be quiet at Edgewater Hospital now that justice has been served. But the corridors, halls, and the cafeteria here still bring back vivid memories to some who remember the life, times, and afterlife of Teresita.

20 EDGEWATER MEDICAL CENTER

Location:	5700 North Ashland Avenue, Chicago.
Type of occurrence:	Documented possession of hospital employee by spirit of a murdered coworker.
Characteristics:	Spirit of victim invaded personality of another and speaks and acts in ways that only the dead person could.
Status:	Incidents stopped when police solved case and restless spirit found closure.

EMPTY GRAVE FOR A GHOST

GRAVE OF THE CHRISTMAS TREE SHIP'S CAPTAIN

Many Chicagoans prided themselves in buying their Christmas trees each holiday season from one source in the early 1900s, Captain Herman Schuenemann. He seemed to have the freshest, fullest, and the brightest trees for sale each year. Brought down from the great northwoods of Michigan just before Christmas each year, they were sold directly from his ship, the *Rouse Simmons*, at his dock at Clark Street.

Herman Schuenemann was simply known as the "Christmas Tree Captain." The sign on his ship read, "The Christmas Tree Ship. My prices are the lowest."

Safe and snug in the warm comfort of their homes, many Chicagoans enjoyed the fine holiday tree they had just purchased, but few gave any thought to the long and potentially dangerous winter trip necessary to bring such trees down Lake Michigan to Chicago. The Christmas tree voyage, a 300-mile trip from Manistique, Michigan to Chicago, took place each year in late November, a time on the Great Lakes when serious storms could cause havoc with the frail wooden ships plying the cold waters.

It was near Thanksgiving 1912, when the three-masted schooner, *Rouse Simmons*, was fully loaded with freshly cut trees. There were trees everywhere, in the holds, tied down on the deck and even to its masts. The scent of the fresh cut pine filled the air like perfume. It was time to set sail.

Winter, it seemed certain, would be early and harsh that year. One storm had already hit northern Lake Michigan, and as the *Rouse Simmons* was setting sail, a bigger storm was brewing. Captain Schuenemann had a mission, however, he felt obligated not to disappoint those waiting for his Christmas cargo in Chicago.

As they left Manistique, ice was already beginning to form on the rigging when the new storm began to blow. The gale was fierce as the *Rouse Simmons* continued fighting her way down the Wisconsin coast toward home port. Everyone knew that ship by her cargo, with thousands of trees for the season. Sightings of the *Rouse Simmons* battling along were made by the tugboat *Burger* and the brig *Dutch Boy*.

The ship was by now in great peril. The storm, a nor'easter, was full blown, and the temperature was below freezing. A Coast Guard lookout at Sturgeon Bay, Wisconsin spotted the ship flying distress signals, but the storm was too fierce to allow an approach. Snow killed visibility and swallowed up the ship.

There was to be one last sighting of the ship by a lifeboat crew farther down the shoreline. Ice had coated the hull and cargo and her sails were in tatters. The weight of the ice was forcing the ship to ride lower in the water. Approach was impossible, and the ship disappeared from sight, swallowed up by the treacherous storm.

Captain Herman Schuenemann and his crew were lost in Lake Michigan waters during that very harsh November of 1912; all went down with the ship.

Monument for the captain of the "Christmas Tree Ship"

A last message from the captain would be discovered after the storm blew out. Near Sheyboygan, a bottle washed up on shore containing a note. It read: "Friday. Everybody goodbye. I guess we are all through. Sea washed over our deck load Thursday. During the night the small boat was washed over. Ingvald and Steve fell overboard Thursday. God Help us. Herman Schuenemann."

Other reminders of the last voyage of the "Christmas Tree Ship" would be discovered the next spring. Local fisherman found their nets tangled with numerous Christmas trees, the lost cargo of the doomed ship.

A red granite stone stands among rows of similar stones bearing the family name Schuenemann at Acacia Park Cemetery. Acacia Park Cemetery is not famous for elaborate tombs and crypts like Graceland or Rosehill cemeteries. Most of those buried here were of the hard-working middle class who upon death were laid to rest with just a simple stone containing a name, dates of birth and death, and perhaps a cross or fraternal emblem. But among these ordinary-looking plots is a unique grave representing one of Chicago's most colorful mariners, Captain Herman Schuenemann of the fabled "Christmas Tree Ship," the *Rouse Simmons.* The Schuenemann stone is unique in that it bears a carved pine tree to honor the Christmas Tree Ship's captain.

Barbara Schuenemann carried her love for Herman to the grave. She outlived him for two decades and when buried had his name engraved upon her tombstone along with hers: Captain Herman and Barbara. His name may be placed on the stone but his wife, Barbara, lies alone.

On a spring day in 1996, as I once again visited the Schuenemann grave, I began thinking about the brave captain who sailed into the face of a storm rather than disappoint those waiting for his Christmas trees. Suddenly, I realized my nose was picking up the scent of fresh cut Christmas trees. The psychic scent lasted for less than a minute with the scent coming and going a few times. There were no trees or fresh cut timber nearby to explain the experience.

Since that initial encounter, I have experienced the scent of Christmas trees at Acacia Cemetery a number of times. Although it never happens to all in the group, usually some of those with me claim the same experience. It serves as a reminder of Captain Herman Schuenemann's gallant efforts to uphold the spirit of Christmas.

21 ACACIA PARK CEMETERY

Location: 7800 West Irving Park Road, Chicago.
Type of Occurrence: Psychic scent.
Characteristics: Scent of freshly cut spruce and balsam with no natural explana-
                       tion.
Status: Ongoing.

THE HAUNTED INDIAN BURIAL GROUND

ROBINSON WOODS

Indian burial grounds traditionally are thought to be abundant sources for ghostly happenings. Robinson Woods Indian Burial Ground is the only marked Native American burial ground within the city limits of Chicago. It is situated on East River Road just north of Lawrence Avenue. It was named after Alexander Robinson. He was a chief of the local tribes around Fort Dearborn back in the days when the fort was being built, prior to the War of 1812. Robinson's father was Scottish and a British soldier. His mother was a Chippewa Indian. Chee-Chee-Pin-Quay was Robinson's Native American name.

During the War of 1812, very violent, often bloody, frontier warfare took place, as sections of the Midwest were fought over by pro-British Indian tribes in opposition to the American frontiersmen and militia and their Native American allies.

Robinson was a hero of the Fort Dearborn Massacre staged when the Sauk and Fox Indians from Wisconsin, acting on orders from the British, came to the south end of Lake Michigan to destroy Fort Dearborn and obliterate the American military presence.

Some Native Americans living around the Fort Dearborn area were more friendly to the American cause, than to the British. Those who were, hid-out and helped various members of the garrison and their families who were holed up at the fort, including local notables like John Kinzie and Captain Nathan Heald and his wife.

Alexander Robinson was credited with saving many American lives and after the war, a grateful United States government gave the Robinson family a tract of land that currently sits along East River Road, now part of the Cook County Forest Preserve.

Robinson and his family chose to stay on their land near the Des Plaines River during the Federal Government's notorious Indian relocations, rather than moving west to reservations.

It was in 1958, with the construction of O'Hare Airport, that this land was annexed by Chicago to become part of the connecting link between the bulb of land where O'Hare sits and the rest of the city. That neck of land was necessary under Illinois law to connect the airport to Chicago and make it part of the city proper. At that time, the last of the Robinson descendants were moved from the land but were promised they could be buried in Robinson Woods. By 1972, the last Robinson descendant died. Before his death, he was granted permission to be buried at his ancestral plot wanting to join his family. But after death, his wishes were denied by the City of Chicago.

Perhaps, this broken promise could account for some of the psychic unrest that takes place here, for ghost stories abound at this spot.

I first learned about the Robinson Family Burial Ground in the early 1970s when Bob Zmuda and Joe Troiani, hosting a local TV program called "News of the Psychic World," brought it to my attention. They recounted the myriad of ghost stories circulating about this spot. One recurring tale was of a mysterious streak or ball of light that seemingly bounced and darted around the woods at night.

Alexander Robinson Memorial at Robinson Woods Indian Burial Grounds

This small ghost light has not only been observed, but also photographed; a streaking effect appears on the film. Besides that, strange sounds are often heard at night.

The most common psychic sound is thumping, as if someone were in the woods beating on an Indian tom-tom. Those sounds were recorded back in the early 1970s by Joe Troiani on one of his nighttime vigils while conducting research on these phenomena.

From time to time another sound occurs, a constant hacking—chop, chop, chop—as though someone were out in the woods chopping firewood. The sound is heard on a regular basis, and when anyone goes to check, there is no earthly evidence to account for the strange sounds, nor are wood chips ever found.

Maybe a key to understanding why these sounds are heard dates back to the 1940s and early 1950's when the last members of the Robinson family were still living on the property.

According to accounts I have collected, the remaining Robinson descendants lived an isolated life in the woods and earned extra money doing odd jobs for neighbors. They cleaned garages, washed windows, and most often chopped firewood to sell. Reportedly they were often out in the woods chopping in an intoxicated condition. There is the strong possibility, if this is true, that some of them did die under the influence of alcohol.

I did not have any experience personally for many years, but when I eventually did, it was luckily with a bus full of people on my Supernatural Tour who were co-witnesses to what occurred. It was on November 2, 1980, two days after Halloween, All Souls Day, a very good day for the dead to interlope among the living in order to take care of unfinished business.

The group joined me as I walked back to the boulder standing in the middle of the clearing inscribed to the memory of the old Chief, and we gathered around the spot.

Suddenly, someone remarked that there was a very strong scent. It did appear to be a very sweet smell of violets. The group began to search the area to try to find a rational explanation to this perplexing fragrance. They found no flowers blooming, (after all, it was November) nor were there any freshly cut flowers laid about.

Some of the group sought to find a place where perhaps perfume could have been spilled. They found nothing. They became agitated, and in a bizarre act, began to accuse one young woman of wearing strong perfume. "It's you," they said. "You! You're the cause of all of this." Mortified by the accusations of the others, she fled to the bus to wait by herself.

I went back to the bus to apologize to her for the rudeness of the others in the group and assure her that nothing said should be taken personally. As I talked to her, I realized she seemed to be wearing a fragrance with a very slight scent of rose, but nothing that could account for the sweet essence that emanated from around the boulder.

When I returned to the site to tell the rest of the group it was time to board the bus and leave, the scent was still there and lingered as we left that day. I had just had my first encounter with a psychic scent at the Indian burial ground. It was the first time an olfactory paranormal event was noted here.

Since that time, I have encountered the psychic scent a number of times at Robinson Woods. It is not always as pungent as lilacs; sometimes, it has more of a subdued fragrance of roses.

In January of 1990, I was hosting a Japanese film crew. We stopped at Robinson Woods to shoot a location film for a TV program in the Far East. It was nighttime. One man left the group and wandered down a trail farther back into the woods. He hurried back and excitedly told the story of encountering an intriguingly strong scent of flowers.

I investigated. It was true. Even though there was still ice upon the ground and no flowers anywhere to be seen, the scent was quite strong, reminding one of entering a floral shop. My Japanese guests had been given more than they bargained for that night at the Indian burial ground. They got a psychic rush.

Often debris in the form of beer cans and assorted liquor bottles are found by our groups when we visit the site. Local teenagers gather here to party and imbibe on a regular basis. I noticed they have a curious custom that they partake in when they visit. Many times, they spill some of their freshly opened drink on the ground. I've questioned some of them about the reason, and the reply is, "We've always done it this way. Just an old custom."

By pouring the drink, however, they are unconsciously bestowing an offering to the spirits. This old Indian custom is something that I have seen practiced in parts of the Southwest. When one is out having a drink, first, he or she should always spill some of it on the ground for those who have gone before.

Think about this: Beneath the feet of those standing at the Robinson Woods grave sites are many who might have had "a taste for liquor," and for these ghosts who find something to their liking and do not want to move on to the Happy Hunting Ground, perhaps, it is better to be here in limbo.

With the advent of spiritualism in the 1840s and 1850s, the belief that Indian burial grounds were haunted, or that Indian sites had some strange connection with another dimension, had become widespread. The Indian spirit guide and the haunted Indian burial ground became part of our popular culture.

Certainly, many reasons exist why this site should be haunted. The descendants of the Robinson family were not warmly treated by the local governments that grew up since Alexander Robinson first settled in the area.

The broken promise to Robinson's descendant may be another factor.

If there was a family pattern of overindulgence of alcohol, the traditional spilling of the drinks on the graves may account for some of their ghostly resurfacing. But all in all, the site just seems to follow a general pattern of hauntings which cannot be pinpointed down to one or even a few ghosts.

During the 1980s, yet another type of psychic activity was reported. Visitors to the site had taken photos and thought they had caught something usual. Photographs, particularly Polaroid film, seemed to "capture" shadowy faces, appearing to be Native American, in the background of the monument bearing the Robinson name. This phenomena is typical simulacra. Although the imagery is subject to one's imagination, in the shadows, there appears to be faces with Native American features. Blowing up the photographs causes great loss of detail, and so far, nothing can verified.

In all likelihood, the Robinson Woods site will remain haunted for many decades to come. This Indian burial ground will not disappoint anyone with an interest in the supernatural. However, be wary of going there at night.

22 ROBINSON WOODS INDIAN BURIAL GROUND.

Location:	East River Road, just north of Lawrence Avenue (part of Forest Preserves), Chicago.
Type of Occurrence:	Activity runs the gamut of visual to olfactory along with photographic anomalies. Small, unexplained balls of light sometimes seen at night. Psychic floral scents are encountered often in winter season. Sounds similar to Indian tom-toms drumming or chopping sounds are heard on certain nights.
Characteristics:	Most reports fit Native American and early pioneer profile.
Status:	Active throughout year.

HAUNTED HOTEL

ROOM FOR ONE MORE

The O'Hare Hilton is the only hotel located on the grounds of O'Hare, "the world's busiest airport." This ten-story hotel with 858 rooms, houses three restaurants, including the last Gaslight Club, an 1890s counterpart of the Playboy Club. The hotel has easy access to O'Hare's several terminals and is the most convenient refuge for those needing an overnight stay before continuing their journey.

The soundproof hotel was constructed with sound-resistant windows so once inside there is complete silence from the roar of the jets overhead. But for many years, in at least one room, weary travelers toss and turn and find no rest. They have unknowingly checked into the haunted room.

I have been a member of the Chicago Convention and Tourism Bureau for over twenty years. The monthly business exchanges are a great way to meet people in the hospitality industry. Representatives of restaurants, transportation companies, hotels, and tour companies all mingle and make contacts. I first heard about the O'Hare Hilton's special room while attending these gatherings in the mid-1980s.

O'Hare Hilton employees told me that there was one specific room that seemed strange to visitors, though there was nothing outwardly different looking. It had the same look as countless other rooms on similar floors. It's just that people had an adverse reaction to this one room. It wasn't every night, but it did happen often. Guests in this room sheepishly made complaints to the registration desk. There was never anything precise that the guest could complain about, but just that the room "wasn't right" and that the guest "couldn't sleep" and "was it possible that they could be switched to another room?"

The obliging clerk took care of the situation by moving the guest to another room, and all was well. As incident after incident of this sort began collecting, the "haunted room" became a topic of conversation with the hotel employees.

Why would this one room act up? The only possibly incriminating history discovered about the room was that years before a man had committed suicide by hanging. As I discussed this puzzling activity with O'Hare Hilton staff, I offered my help in investigating the room. I suggested that on an off night, so that other activity in the hotel would be quieter, I would check into the room and give the unknown a run for his money.

It was a summer night when I arrived at the hotel. Assisting that night was my team, a psychologist and his wife and three other researchers. But, it was not a night to relax. We had the physical layout to investigate.

The haunted room was near to the elevator. And, there was a section of lobby with an ice machine and vending machine for soft drinks between the room and the actual elevator shaft. My first suspicions were that noisy machines might be at the bottom of things. Could a thin wall and constantly humming vibrations be the answer?

My team then traveled by elevator to floors above and floors below. On each floor, there was an identical floor plan: room/machines/elevator. If each floor were the same, wouldn't each room on each floor have similar problems? Why just one floor?

O'Hare Hilton

In the very early evening, there were few guests present to disturb us as we began round two of the investigation. From floor to floor we went, listening to the ice and vending machines to try to detect any difference in sound. As we checked each floor, we knocked on the outside walls. We wanted to ascertain if any walls sounded different, perhaps thinner. We also did extensive knocking and searching of the haunted room.

After hours of such activity, there was nothing left to do but to wait in the room to see if anything would happen. As sunrise began, we had to admit that our searching produced nothing and no unusual effects, and this troubled us. Our vigil proved fruitless. We did prove, however, there were no physical reasons that would explain why that room was considered haunted.

The first rule of ghost hunting is that when you stake out a "known" haunted site, there is no guarantee of contact. Ghosts do not always show up for command performances.

The only convincing evidences that something was amiss here, were the unsolicited testimonies of many guests suggesting there was just something "off" in the room. So, it just became something that the O'Hare Hilton learned to live with.

By the late 1990s, my tour business was drawing more and more visitors from out-of-town and out-of-state. I was regularly asked if I could recommend a good hotel, and particularly if there were any that were haunted. I once again contacted O'Hare Hilton staff and learned that conditions had changed.

The haunted room has been quiet in recent years. The unexplainable something that haunted here has been absent. The building has been completely renovated. Physical change at a sight can sometimes stir up a ghost if one is present, or conversely extinguish an active ghost.

Has the psychic residue of that tragedy long ago dissipated with time? Is it gone for good or biding its time to return? Or yet, will another room turn haunted?

23 O'HARE HILTON

Location:	Chicago International Airport Terminal 2.
Type of occurrence:	Originally, one room at hotel proved to be impossible to sleep in. Guests demanded that front desk switch then to another room.
Characteristics:	Although nothing overtly supernatural took place, a panic attack, or feeling of fear caused customers to leave. This only took place in one room and lasted for years.
Status:	No recent activity. Seems extinct or at least dormant at moment.

CHICAGO SOUTH

CHICAGO SOUTH

A CHURCH FULL OF GHOSTS

PHANTOM ALTAR BOYS AND OTHERS

Holy Family Church was built between 1857 and 1859. Additions were added in 1862 and 1886. This Gothic splendor was one of the few public buildings to survive the Chicago Fire. For generations, Holy Family Church was the point of entry for ethnic groups coming to Chicago—the Irish, the Germans, the Italians, the African-Americans and Hispanics.

The parish's founder was a Jesuit missionary, Father Arnold Damen. Damen Avenue in Chicago was later named after him. According to Father David McCarthy, S. J., the site of Holy Family Church itself was selected with great care.

I first met Father McCarthy in 1973 when I was putting together my first Chicago Ghost Tour for De Paul University. He was then the assistant pastor of Holy Family and had a great love for the history and lore of this magnificent building. He gave me tours of the church, pointing out its unusual architecture while filling me in on its fascinating historical background.

Father McCarthy was particularly knowledgeable in the sacred symbolism and religious themes that made this church unique. He said the church was built over running water, a very ancient practice in Europe. The church's main altar was positioned directly above a blind stream traditionally thought to have been where an Indian battle was fought long before, where the waters ran red from the blood of the slain warriors. Because of the loss of life, the site was believed to be sacred by the Native Americans.

When the magnificent cathedral-sized church was erected, the main pillars of the church were built off plumb. The pillars are some eighteen inches off plumb, so when you walk toward the main altar, the columns appear to be leaning away from you. This design creates an optical illusion, a bit hypnotic in a subtle but effective way. As Father McCarthy described it, "The pillars look as though they are trees being felled in the forest."

Some architectural writers have suggested the real reason for the optical illusion is that the heavy slate roof displaced them, but others who have studied this church's history think it is mysteriously deliberate.

Above the high altar is an enormous painting of the Holy Family, a splendid reproduction by a Flemish Jesuit placed in the middle of a fifty-two-foot intricately hand-carved walnut alcove, or reredos. Several elaborately carved statues stand atop each other, sheltered in alcoves, on each side of the altar. In front of the high altar is a wood-carved reproduction of "The Last Supper" by DaVinci.

A larger-than-life wooden statue of Our Lady of Perpetual Help is in the east transept of the altar. Created by a local man prior to the Chicago Fire, the statue is the protective guardian of the church. The statue is ill-proportioned: the head is too large and torso and limbs don't quite match, but this locally produced, naive art has quite a supernatural tale behind it.

Statue of Blessed Mother where mystery "faces" were discovered in 1973. Indian girl is to the left of the crack, demon head to the right and partially obscured by ornate top of pillar.

A crack was discovered one day making its way down the wall of the church from roof to floor. A structural flaw such as this might mean the entire church was threatened. If the crack enlarged further, a wall or walls could collapse. Father Damen placed the church under the protection of Our Lady of Perpetual Help at that time, and her statue was put in position directly next to the crack. According to Father McCarthy, the crack had not changed or worsened in more than a century. Despite years of plaster damage from the seepage of rain water dripping from the crack, the church continued to survive this structural threat, and Marian intervention is credited by many for this modern and ongoing miracle.

Another miraculous tale connected with the church involves its near escape from the Great Fire of 1871. Tradition places the starting point of the fire at Mrs. O'Leary's home at DeKoven and Jefferson Streets, just a few blocks away from the church. Father Damen was in New York at the time leading one of his famous missions. A telegram reached him that Chicago was in flames and that his church and parish were in danger.

All that the concerned Father Damen could do, halfway across the country, was to pray and trust in God. He vowed that if the church were spared, he would acknowledge this as divine intervention. Strangely, the fire did zigzag out of the area, burning a path further north into the downtown business district and beyond. The parish was indeed saved, and a miracle was proclaimed.

When Father Damen returned home, he ordered seven candles to be kept burning at a side altar to commemorate this event. After some years, the candles were replaced by gas jets, and then light bulbs. Since 1871, Holy Family parishioners have remembered the providence that caused the fire to veer away from their homes and church.

The most famous ghost story of Holy Family Church, the tale of phantom acolytes or altar boys, dates back to the period just after the Chicago Fire. I first heard a version of this story from Father Charles Carmody at Visitation Church when I was an altar boy there in the 1960s. I was later able to find historical references to the incident in parish histories of Holy Family.

Late one stormy night in the days of Father Damen, as the story goes, a furious ringing of the bell at the rectory aroused the porter. Two young boys were at the front door anxiously asking for a priest for an urgent sick call. They insisted that a priest was needed immediately and that the sick patient, a woman, was not expected to make it through the night.

Father Damen overheard the conversation and told the boys that he would leave with them immediately. As the priest followed the boys into the night, they walked for blocks into a remote part of the parish. Finally, they came to a rundown home, and the boys said that the woman was in the garret.

In haste, the priest started up the rickety old stairs and realized that the two boys were gone. He came to a small room where an old woman was lying on a bed in the corner. She looked at the priest with astonishment and thanked him for coming. He heard her confession and gave her the last rites of the church.

The old woman said, "Father may I ask who called you to me? I have been very ill and I have wanted a priest, but I had no one to send." Father Damen told the woman about the two boys who had come for him. He suggested that they must be neighbors.

"No, Father," the woman said," there is no one, and nobody knows of my illness."

"Have you no boys of your own?" the priest asked.

"None living," the woman replied. "I had two boys who were acolytes of the Holy Family Church, but they are dead."

Father Damen told the woman that he believed that her two sons had come for spiritual help for her in her hour of need. She died before morning, trusting that she would soon be reunited with them.

The incident so moved Father Damen that he commissioned two statues carved from fine wood to be made of two young boys, acolytes, holding candles and placed high above the main altar of the church. The life-like figures have gazed down upon the altar of the parish for many of years. The statues' eyes seem to follow you wherever you stand at the altar.

Father David McCarthy told me that he found an historical record of two Holy Family altar boys, brothers, who had drowned while on a parish picnic during the Civil War. Perhaps they returned years later to bring comfort to their mother.

Preaching in New Orleans in 1877, Father Damen converted former Confederate General James Longstreet. One of Holy Family's priests baptized Stephen A. Douglas into the Catholic Church while the "Little Giant" was on his deathbed.

In October of 1973, Cindy Graham, a placement counselor at De Paul University, was photographing the interior of Holy Family Church, including the statue of Mary. Later, when she developed her black and white photographs, she noticed some unusual images in the water-damaged plasterwork behind the statue. Two images appeared quite plain in the photo. One was the head of an American Indian girl with high cheekbones and a headband. The other image was a grotesque devil head. Although the images seemed obvious on the photo, going back to view the wall proved different. These "simulacra" images can only be observed from a

Seven lights burn at this side of altar to praise God for saving the church at the time of the Great Fire.

set distance. When you are either too close or too far away, the illusive forms just fade into the background and dissipate.

Modern hauntings of the church were personally witnessed by Father McCarthy. On many mornings while saying mass on the main altar, he turned to face the congregation and noticed a lone figure in the choir loft. There was no way that someone could be there since the loft had been found to be unsafe years before and was always kept off limits to the public. After mass was over, McCarthy investigated and found the door to the loft still locked. He continued to check the spot where the shadowy figure was seen, but he always found that no dust had been disturbed. There is an old Catholic belief that those who miss Sunday mass in their lifetime may have to attend services after death to make up.

Another incident reported by Father McCarthy was that he saw an African-American youth on the church grounds. The priest was shocked. He had learned earlier that day the boy had been electrocuted in a train accident. This story was reported on WBBM Radio.

Tales of the church, its founder, and its priests are larger than life, and Holy Family Church recently survived a threat far greater than the Chicago Fire and structural cracks—a money crunch, by perhaps yet another miracle. During the 1980s, the Jesuits considered destroying the landmark for financial reasons and selling the empty lot. However, donations from parishioners and friends of the landmark were raised in time. In 1991, the much needed restoration began to turn the church back to its glory.

24 HOLY FAMILY CHURCH

Location:	Roosevelt Road (1200 South) and May, Chicago.
Type of occurrences:	A traditional tale of phantom altar boys and a ghost in the choir loft. Additional tales abound of miracles and divine intervention.
Characteristics:	Ghost stories reflect the age of the church with Victorian tales of great drama and impact leading to 20th Century tales with less flash.
Status:	Traditional stories still believed and told. Current happenings rare but seemingly still active.

THE HAUNTINGS AT HULL HOUSE

THE DEVIL'S BABY

In 1889, Jane Addams came to Chicago to work with the urban poor on the old West Side. This was the port of entry for Italians, Jews, Greeks, Russians, Poles, Gypsies, and many other ethnic groups finding a new life in America. She set up her school of social work in the former home of the Hull Family, built originally in 1856, and her pioneering settlement house would become known worldwide as Hull House.

Upon moving in, Addams learned that Hull House was considered the neighborhood haunted house. She mentioned this local belief in her autobiographical book, *Twenty Years at Hull House*. A pail of water had been kept at the top of the stairs on the second floor leading into the attic to keep the ghost from coming downstairs.

"I am sure it was a survival of the belief that a ghost could not cross running water," Addams wrote.

Other traditions included Hull House being haunted by a phantom monk and by a pesky poltergeist that was responsible for small fires. The ghostly monk tale probably stems from the time when the Little Sisters of the Poor, a Catholic religious order, had used this location for a while as a home for the aged.

Outwardly, the college educated, science-minded Jane Addams feigned non-belief in the supernatural, but privately it fascinated her, and she relished the local tales around Hull House. In her writings, she often made references to those around Hull House who were true believers. She was a friend and correspondent of Irish folklorist and poet William Butler Yeats with whom she shared her stories.

The most famous supernatural tale on the old West Side of Chicago is undoubtedly the "Devil Baby at Hull House." Jane Addams' routine was shattered in 1913 as thousands of curiosity seekers came to the settlement house in search of a baby born in the area with horns, hoofs, and a tail. The popular belief was that the demon child and its mother were hidden at Hull House by Addams. All her denials merely reinforced the suspicions of neighborhood folk.

Jane Addams wrote about the devil baby in her book, *The Second Twenty Years at Hull House*. She described how for six weeks during the spring and summer of 1913, Hull House was virtually under siege as people from all over Chicago and beyond came in search of the demonic baby.

There were a number of stories to explain the existence of this child. The Italian version, popular in the Taylor Street area, described how a religious woman had foolishly married an atheist. One day her husband found a holy picture hanging on his bedroom wall, and in a fit of anger, ripped it down. He told his pregnant wife that he would rather have a devil in the house than the religious icon. When his wife gave birth, it was to a misshapen imp that ran about the house shaking a finger at the blasphemous husband. The fearful father caught the child and brought him to Hull House.

Nothing seemed to be able to exorcise the evil from the child. When the child was brought to church for christening, the baby leaped from the shawl he was wrapped in and bounded over the pews, fleeing from the holy water in a panic.

South of the Italian Taylor Street district is Maxwell Street and home for 135 years to the outdoor markets of "Jewtown." The Jewish belief here in the devil baby was widespread. In the Jewish version, a father of six girls proclaimed before the birth of his seventh child that he would rather have a devil born into the family than have another daughter. Of course, the devil obliged this invitation.

In a version quoted by devout Catholics, the father of the devil baby had committed a hideous crime that he never confessed. When he married years later with this sin still on his soul, he deceived both the priest and his bride and invalidated the wedding vows. The sin then incarnated into a child born with the physical attributes of a devil.

The people who came to Hull House were sent away unhappy, told by Addams and her staff that no such baby was there. The curious offered to pay a quarter, a half-dollar, two dollars, or more just to see the demonic infant. Many were old and infirm, some near death. Perhaps many were in need of a look at such a supernatural wonder to give their faith a boost.

Despite Jane Addams' personal and condescending disbelief in a devil baby born in the neighborhood, another Chicago writer seems to have taken it seriously enough. Ben Hecht, colorful newsman, Hollywood scriptwriter, and co-author of the play "The Front Page," was a young reporter at the time. In his memoirs *Gaily, Gaily* (published in 1963), Hecht relates how he investigated the case.

Hecht, known as a reporter with a flair for the bizarre, was given the assignment of running down the devil baby story for his paper. With the help of an Italian-speaking boxer named Joe Govani, Hecht spent days chasing down leads. Although he found many who were believers, Hecht lamented that, "After three days of darting from authority to authority, I was still without the name or address of the satanic infant."

Hecht's investigation did dig up some interesting "facts" about the devil baby: the child was born with a full head of hair, had a complete set of thirty two teeth in its mouth, and sported a small tail. It was born with the ability to speak, cursing like a sailor in the midwife's arms.

When all his leads turned up dead ends, Hecht was pulled off the story by his editor. But he still kept on the story on his own time, visiting Italian midwives, trying to find out who assisted at the birth of the imp child. Everyone on the West Side seemed to be a believer, and the neighborhood churches were full of penitents with renewed faith, saying the rosary on their knees and lighting vigil candles in profusion.

Hecht finally gave up on the story, but for decades the legend of the devil baby was a vibrant part of local folklore. It is still a popular topic in Italian American neighborhoods. When the supernatural suspense novel *Rosemary's Baby* topped the bestsellers charts in 1966, those familiar with the Chicago account easily recognized author Ira Levin's literary inspiration. Although the location of the novel is set in New York City, Chicagoans know the real story is a local one.

By a twist of fate, the actor who played the demonic father of the devil baby in the movie version of *Rosemary's Baby* had Chicago ties. Anton LaVey, founder of the Church of Satan, was born in Chicago in 1930. LaVey was hired in 1967 to act as an advisor to the film by director Roman Polanski. For his character, LaVey was outfitted in a traditional devil costume of fur and scales. He played a small but essential role in the movie.

Hull House, sightings have been reported in the second floor windows.

The supernatural element aside, there just may have been a deformed baby born in the Taylor Street neighborhood in the spring of 1913. Jane Addams in her role as social worker would naturally have been sought out for help by a grief stricken mother. But after all these years, we may never know with certainty the real story.

Today, Hull House is a museum and library dedicated to the memory of Jane Addams. It is listed in the National Register of Historical Places and was honored by a commemorative postal card by the US Postal Service in 1989. Even the TV game show "Jeopardy" has used Hull House as a question.

The campus of the University of Illinois at Chicago (UIC) was created in the 1960s with Hull House as its hub. The campus was literally built around this haunted house. And with the influx of thousands of students, the ghostly tales continued with a new vibrancy. Hull House is one of the longest, continuously haunted buildings in the Chicago area with over a century's worth of ghost stories tied to it.

Campus police are well aware of Hull House's connection with ghost reports. It is very common for motion sensor alarms to go off at night at Hull House. When the police arrive on the scene there is never any sign of break-in or disturbance, and the building is, of course, empty of anyone—anyone alive, that is.

One member of the campus police force with personal experience is Eric Von Kondrat, who started with the cadet program at UIC in 1994. "No building on campus has as many phony calls as Hull House," Von Kondrat reports. "Due to the frequency of calls, as long as there is no sign of entry, we just call it in." In about three years, Von Kondrat claims he has personally responded to ten to twelve false alarms there. Other campus police make similar claims.

Besides the alarms being triggered quite often, students and faculty have called the police to report somebody inside the building after hours. Once again, the police find nothing awry when they arrive.

The street lights on Halsted directly in front of Hull House malfunction from time to time. When they go out, all of the other street lights nearby function properly, only the stretch of lights near Hull House is affected. Cars also mysteriously stall or die out in front of Hull House. Derelict cars are often found here.

I began to use Hull House as a location on my evening bus tours around 1980. It wasn't very long before strange happenings were noticed while stopping at this landmark building. Often the decorative wooden shutters inside the second floor windows were moving back and forth. No one is in the building late at night when this happens. The shutters are inside the windows, not on the outside, so they cannot be moved by wind. They are not over any air conditioning or heating ducts, and the back and forth motion is so extreme that it is obviously not just a trick of eyesight and shadows.

One spring night in 1985, I set up a stakeout with video equipment in the median strip of Halsted directly in front of Hull House. It was April 30, the halfway point to Halloween. Two video cameras on tripods were trained on the top floor windows where the shutter activity is often noted. Taping continued for two hours in hopes of catching any movement. After midnight we packed up the gear and prepared to leave. Then, with the cameras safely stowed away, two of our group saw the shutters start to swing back and forth.

Throughout the 1980s and the 1990s, the after-hours shutter movement happened sporadically but regularly. Then in 1995 a new claim was made.

About 9:30 p.m. on a Friday the 13th in January of '95, my tour bus pulled up in front of Hull House. Suddenly a number of screams rang out as some of my passengers claimed that they saw a child's head looking out of a second floor window. Since the witnesses reacted in unison, it could not have been imagination or hysteria. Once again no one was in the building that night, adult or child.

The head in the window, sometimes described as a pale silhouette, is now commonly being reported. The question always arises, "Is it Rosemary's baby, back again?"

25 HULL HOUSE

Location:	800 South Halsted, Chicago.
Type of occurrence:	Traditional ghost stories, a devil connection, and modern reports of sightings and poltergeist-type activity.
Characteristics:	A large home from the 1850s, now a museum, continues to produce reports of apparitions of a head or body in the window at night, electrical problems with alarms, movement of window shutters, and more.
Status:	Definitely ongoing.

THE GREAT CHICAGO FIRE

Its Psychic Side

The late summer months in Chicago of 1871 were brutally hot. There was a drought in the city and everything was dangerously dry: the air, the ground, the wells, and the trees. But what presented the most serious situation were the dried-out wood-framed structures that made up most of Chicago's building stock. Starting in September of that year, there was a succession of smaller, but rampant fires that ran for blocks, destroying several blocks of buildings and foreshadowing what was to come.

On October 8, 1871, fire almost destroyed Chicago. The fire was thought to have started about a half mile west of the South Branch of the Chicago River and spread as far as the city's northern limits, which at the time was Fullerton Avenue. Approximately thirty hours later, the flames were finally squelched by rain. The legend that predominates is that the fire started in Mrs. O'Leary's barn. The barn was located at the rear of the house on 558 West DeKoven Street. One story is that her husband, Mr. O'Leary, in a drunken state, knocked over a lantern in the barn. Another story blames their cow for overturning the lantern.

How the fire got started is not known, but there are clear reasons why it became an inferno. The city was parched, which made it a perfect breeding ground for a fire. The wind, for which the Windy City gets it name, carried the flames at twenty-five miles an hour throughout the city. The wooden buildings stood defenseless against the fire as it leaped from one house to the next. The City's fire department was poorly trained and undersupplied to fight a fire of this magnitude. No one was prepared for such a disaster. Although figures vary, approximately 300 people were killed, and over 100,000 people were left homeless. The fire took one-third of Chicago.

The fire opened, rather than closed, opportunities in Chicago. Industrialization in America had begun. The City had a remarkable potential for growth because of its accessibility to resources, both raw material and human, and also because of its location on the inland waterways. There may have been brief moments of doubt about the City's future by some, and added to that a negative economic blip, but within days after the blaze, businesses started springing up among the ruins, basic services were reestablished, and traffic started moving: the revitalization of Chicago was launched.

The fire did not destroy the spirit of people of Chicago, nor its "spirits." The Chicago Fire has left its mark psychically on many area locations.

The haunted Hooters, the Excalibur Club, the Water Tower, and many other sites still bear the scars of paranormal unrest because of the 1871 conflagration. This disaster inspired numerous folktales and legends.

A vivid dream that predicted the horrors may be the most unique Chicago Fire tale. From 1868 to 1872, our nation's president was Civil War hero Ulysses S. Grant. Although he was born in southern Ohio, Grant, like Lincoln, was claimed by Illinois. He had lived in Galena, a scenic town set by the Mississippi River, for a number of years and was very popular in Chicago, which was a Republican city in that era.

The City of Chicago invited the President to visit our city in the fall of 1871. There were

Chicago Fire Academy
Great Fire Memorial

to be parades and dinner parties and all manners of festivities to welcome the Commander-in-Chief to Illinois and its largest city. Plans were well underway when the unexpected intervened.

Julia Dent Grant, the First Lady, excitedly told her husband that he must call off the trip to Chicago. She had just had a dream in which she claimed she saw Chicago in flames. A fire was destroying the metropolis on Lake Michigan in her vision and hovering above the scene was a giant bird, a phoenix, the symbol of destruction by flames.

Although fully aware of the political ramifications that canceling the trip could have, the President informed the city officials that he must respectfully decline.

The visit would have coincided with the October 8 to 10, 1871 Great Chicago Fire. Heeding his wife's pleas probably saved the President and the First Lady's lives.

This was not the first time that Mrs. Grant exhibited psychic abilities. Six years before she was the reason the Grants were not at Ford's Theater on Good Friday, 1865, the night of President Lincoln's assassination. It was published in the newspapers that the Grants were to be special guests of the President and Mrs. Abraham Lincoln. John Wilkes Booth planned to kill both Lincoln and Grant, but because of Mrs. Grant's uneasy feelings, she and her husband stayed away—and lived.

In recent years, we have had other First Ladies dabble with the supernatural: Nancy Reagan with astrologers and Hillary Clinton with mediums. More than a century ago, we had a first lady who actually was psychic herself, and proved it, Julia Dent Grant.

Today in Chicago, the legendary site of the start of the Great Fire, Mrs. O'Leary's home and barn, is remembered in a very fitting manner. In 1961, during his second term in office, Mayor Richard J. Daley dedicated the Chicago Fire Department Training Academy, now the Robert J. Quinn Fire Academy, at DeKoven and Jefferson. The building of glazed brick, fire red in color, was built at the site of Mrs. O'Leary's home and barn, the anecdotal starting place of the 1871 blaze. In front of the building is the bronze memorial, "The Pillar of Fire," that marks the location. Noting the significance of the location, Mayor Daley saw to it that the Great Fire would inspire generations of Chicago Firemen to duty and trust.

The fire that was put out on October 10, 1871, is still very much alive today in Chicago traditions, legends, folklore, and ghost stories.

26 ROBERT J. QUINN FIRE ACADEMY

Location: 558 West DeKoven Street, a block-long street between South Clinton and South Jefferson Streets, Chicago.

Type of occurrences: Many different manifestations from traditional tales to ongoing hauntings.

Characteristics: Large-scale disaster leaves psychic unrest and motivates many legends.

Status: Traditions and real hauntings very much ongoing

THE 2,700 YEAR-OLD SCREAM

THE HAUNTED EGYPTIAN MUMMY "HARWA"

Glistening on a sunny day, the imposing white-marble Field Museum resembles a Greek temple scenically sitting on the shore of Lake Michigan. Although the Field Museum was founded in 1893 with objects remaining from the popular World's Columbian Exposition, this neoclassical building, housing the world-renown collections, was built in 1921. Its benefactor was Marshall Field, and its designer was architect Daniel H. Burnham.

When you enter the Main Hall of the museum, you are greeted by two battling African elephants locked in mortal combat, and folkloric carved and brightly painted totem poles from the Pacific Northwest. In May of 2000, Sue, the largest, most complete, and best-preserved Sixty-seven-million-year-old Tyrannosaurus rex skeleton fossil to be found was put on display.

The Museum has twenty-million objects warehoused in its collection, but only one percent is on display in its vast exhibition halls. There is everything from meteorites to fossils, from gems to wildlife, from insects to ferns, with items from ancient to recent times. The Museum's cultural exhibits display artifacts on life from every corner of the earth.

For the lover of the odd and curious, there are the Tibetan skull bowls, made from actual skulls. Buddhist monks had created these sacred objects from human bones, a probable reminder to themselves of how fragile life is. There is also in the "Life Over Time" exhibit that holds what may be the earliest recorded murder. The victim has a bone knife wedged in her rib cage. Found in what now is France, scientists determined the skeleton is a seventeen-year-old Cro-Magnon girl who lived 15,000–16,000 years ago. Could it be foul play?

Another popular exhibit in the Museum is "The Man-Eating Lions of Tsavo" from Kenya. In 1898, this deadly duo terrorized the Tsavo railroad workers, slinking stealthily into their tents and dragging them off into the night, hungrily devouring them. More than 100 people were killed by these lions before they were shot.

But it is the "Inside Ancient Egypt" exhibit that many may want to head to at first, in order to see Harwa, "the screaming mummy."

The Egyptian collection at the Field contains a large number of superbly preserved mummies ranging from animal mummies, birds and small mammals, to the classic human mummies, children and adults. Of all of these mummies, Harwa is the most famous.

Evidently, Harwa was not royalty but a successful businessman, the overseer of storehouses at a large estate during the Twenty-fifth Dynasty, of the late period from about the 712 to 525 BC. His place in society guaranteed him a first-rate mummification upon his death, but his long wait for resurrection would be interrupted. Although "wrapped for eternity" he would eventually find his body partially unwrapped and transported thousands of miles from his homeland to a land undreamed of in his time.

Harwa certainly stands out, perhaps because his bare head has an uncanny resemblance to Boris Karloff's seen in his classic portrayal of the 1932 movie, "The Mummy."

Harwa, "the screaming mummy," a popular attraction at the Field Museum.

Because museums often have ghost stories and supernatural tales associated with them, it is no surprise, that the Field, with its immense collection of unusual articles drawn from all corners of the world, could have a few. Harwa, "the screaming mummy," is the Field Museum's most famous.

The screaming mummy story was first reported by Henry Field, a curator in physical anthropology at the Field Museum from 1926 to 1941. In his 1953 book, *The Track of Man*, he gives a straightforward account of a remarkable incident.

One winter night, long after the museum closed, and the last of the visitors were home in bed, a nightshift guard was making his rounds through the basement near the Egyptian Hall. Suddenly, the quiet night was pierced by a bloodcurdling scream coming from the mummies on exhibit.

Switching on all the lights, the frightened guard blew his whistle for help, and soon other guards were at his side. A search of the basement was made, but no trespassers were found. As the guards searched the area closely, they checked the 125-feet-long case containing numerous mummies arranged chronologically.

One of the guards shouted, "Look here, this mummy is off its base!" Harwa had fallen from his base and was lying face down inside the case.

Henry Field was on hand the next morning to investigate. He could find no natural explanation as to why the mummy moved. It stood on a solid base that extended at least four inches in circumference around the mummy's wrapped feet, so it could not have slipped off due to mere vibrations. Besides, since the museum was built upon an island of concrete on a lakefront landfill, no vibrations were possible.

The most amazing aspect of the jumping mummy mystery is that it happened in a sealed glass case. The case was kept airtight and filled with noxious poison so that moths or other pests could not attack the exhibits. The case had only one access door at the back, and it was found properly locked.

Egyptian mummies have not fared very well over the centuries. Ancient grave robbers who plundered the tombs of the wealthy often desecrated the mummies they found. From the Fifteenth Century, mummies were often pulverized into medicinal powders. And during the Nineteenth Century, mummy bodies were used to create the pigment called "mummy brown," while the linen wrappings of mummies were used by paper manufacturers to create expensive bond.

Harwa's body did not meet such a tragic destruction in his long wait for eternity, but he is perhaps not very happy about his current fate: usurped from his beloved homeland and brought thousands of miles away, then forced to stand hours in the glass encasement to be viewed by visitors daily. Of course, there is the matter of the scream. Is Harwa overdue for another psychic outburst?

27 THE FIELD MUSEUM

Location:	1400 South Lake Shore Drive, Chicago.
Type of occurrence:	Ancient artifact (mummy) exhibits special powers.
Characteristics:	Presumed psychic auditory scream and movement.
Status:	Only one initial incident documented.

BLOCK FULL OF GHOSTS
In Chinatown

C hicago's Chinatown may not be as large as those of San Francisco, Los Angeles, or New York, but it is a vibrant community. The main Chinatown in Chicago is on the south side and dates to 1910. Prior to that, there was a small Chinese community around Van Buren and Clark, but rising rents began to squeeze residents out. The On Leong Businessmen's Association contracted a number of ten-year leases on buildings around Cermak Road and Wentworth in a previously Italian and Croatian neighborhood, and a large Chinatown began to grow. Eventually Chinatown would extend solidly down Wentworth Avenue from Cermak Road to 26th Street, half a mile long, and is still expanding north of Cermak.

The architecture here dates to the early days of the City of Chicago. Many homes are below current street level, since they were built years before the current sewers and streets were constructed. As you walk down the street, you are about four feet above ground, walking atop "vaulted sidewalks." You get the feeling that you are traveling back in time in this area.

For centuries, the Chinese have observed that some surroundings are better than others. "Feng Shui" literally means wind and water. This mystic science of geography and placement is practiced to ensure well being. It is important for both business and private life.

In ancient Chinese astrology, five elements—water, wood, fire, earth, and metal—interact and shape and stimulate one's daily life. This natural order leads to harmony, prosperity, and happiness. If there is an imbalance to this natural order, or destructive sequence, it could cause bad events and calamities, or hauntings.

A small round mirror, a "bagua" or "pakua," can often be seen above shop entrances or in front of windows of homes to bring good luck and drive away the bad. Since "8" is considered a lucky number, most businesses in the area try to have at least one "8" in their phone number. The colors red, green, and gold predominate because of their special symbolism of health, longevity, and prosperity.

With such a philosophy on life, it is no surprise that the belief in ghosts and spirits exists among many in the community. Memories live long about which buildings have been the scenes of tragedy or death, since that might lead to Feng Shui imbalance. Psychic history may repeat itself, unless precautions are taken to put the elements back in order.

Curiously, it was later discovered that the area of Chinatown was originally an Indian burial ground in the Eighteenth Century and earlier. Arlene Wong, a Chinatown resident for many years and keen local historian, discovered this fact while researching the community's past. "An Indian burial ground covered the area all the way to the Chicago River," Mrs. Wong said.

There is one block in Chinatown that is acknowledged by the entire neighborhood to be haunted. The 200 block of West 22nd Place is primarily residential but also contains two restaurants and the Chinatown Community Center. This is the very oldest part of Chinatown. Down this short block, just off the main shopping corridor of Wentworth Avenue, can be found more locations thought to be haunted than any other block in Chicago.

Chinatown's haunted block

"On 22nd Place many homes are haunted because the souls are not at rest," Mrs. Wong believes. "People hanged themselves, and a couple of houses burned down for no reason. It was believed that a ghost was responsible. One building was rebuilt and caught fire again."

Other problems constantly plague this block. Electric company crews are often found here working on the lines. Strange power surges are common and have been ongoing for years.

An apartment building at 211 West 22nd Place was converted in recent years into a restaurant. Now named the Triple Crown, this local favorite is considered haunted because of a suicide that happened here years before. Traditional colors, a shrine to the Chinese god Kuan Ti, and even a lucky turtle in the aquarium with the catch of the day combine to produce good Feng Shui, but the ghost stories remain.

An old story involves a friendly ghost who lends a hand when the restaurant is really crowded. The overworked staff facing a mounting pile of dirty dishes and crockery finds the situation miraculously resolved when they look around and find the dirty dishes all washed and put away.

Traditional Chinese good luck signs in red and gold were hung upside down to "dehaunt" the place by confusing the spirit. Or was the ghost originally responsible for turning them upside down to attract attention to itself?

The suicide supposedly took place in the area now occupied by the washrooms. Late at night some patrons have claimed to have seen a figure in that area, a figure that is semitransparent and obviously a spirit.

A building just a few doors west of the restaurant acquired the reputation of being the local "haunted house" during the 1970s and later. The basement apartment of this private home was infested by a poltergeist responsible for moving things about in the kitchen area and causing the curtains to move when anyone was bold enough to try to look inside.

Former resident Kelly Wong, who lived in Chinatown for nineteen years during the 1960s and 1970s remembered, "We heard that someone had hung himself or herself there. I think that 22nd Place is the most haunted street in Chinatown."

"We'd cross the street so we shouldn't have to walk in front of that building," recalled Dr. Karen Eng. Now living in the northwest suburbs, Dr. Eng still avoids walking directly in front of that spot when revisiting her old neighborhood.

The Chinese Community Center sits at the end of 22nd Place, guarded by two white marble "foo dogs" and a large bronze statue of the ancient sage Confucius. Opened in 1963, it is still old enough to be considered haunted by some, or perhaps the ghost was there on the location from earlier times. A story attached to this building involves the women's washroom on the second floor. A little old lady is seen in and around the facility but disappears in an instant. Who she is and why she haunts here has yet to be determined.

Helen Moy, a volunteer at the community center, has made an interesting discovery. She said, "Most of the ghost stories are from the people who have newly immigrated here." Perhaps these recent arrivals are more attuned to the psychic possibilities present in Chinatown.

Other telltale signs that the locals actively believe in restless spirits can be seen by just walking down the street. Bagua mirrors can be seen protecting a dozen homes along this short block.

28 Chinatown

Location:	The 200 block of West 22nd Place, Chicago.
Type of occurrences:	Various poltergeist acts, some apparitions.
Characteristics:	Mostly traditional beliefs. Sites believed to be haunted are all believed to be scenes of earlier tragedy or suicide. Area believed to be haunted before homes were even built.
Status:	Belief is currently strong, but actual status of sites may be dormant.

TITO'S ON THE EDGE

FORMER FUNERAL HOME BECOMES A HAUNTED BAR

For many years, 26th Street at Wentworth was the "edge," the southern boundary of Chinatown and an older Italian neighborhood. The local funeral home catering to Italians was Coletta's founded in 1908 at 2600 South Wentworth, a corner building with the first floor occupied by the undertakers and apartments above.

As many Italian families began moving out of their original neighborhood in the 1960s and 1970s, Coletta's moved as well. They relocated further south and their original building was sold.

The corner location was the perfect setting for a bar, and the current owners of this popular spot, the Tito brothers, opened for business in the summer of 1995. The bar's name, "Tito's On The Edge," refers to its geographic location on the edge of two old Chicago neighborhoods. The clientele is mostly local, predominately Italian and Chinese, but there is one thing they all agree upon—the place is haunted.

From the beginning, owner Bobby Tito found that some of his friends were a bit reluctant at first to drink here at a former funeral parlor. "They said that they felt uneasy drinking at a place where their relatives had been laid out," he told me.

Since this was the major funeral home in the area for Italian families, almost everyone in the neighborhood had a personal tie to the place.

Because the Chinese view funeral homes as places of potential psychic unrest, they are also wary of the spot. Bartender Karen Moy steadfastly refuses to go into the back room of the building, the original embalming room, or to go downstairs to the cold storage area.

"That's where the bodies were!" is her reply to questioning.

All the bartenders here, as well as the patrons, are accustomed to the TV sets changing channels by themselves. It is not just one temperamental set; both sets act up.

The first reported apparition sighting here was in the summer of 1995. Owner Russ Tito often slept over at the bar after working a double shift. During the night he awoke and realized he was not alone.

"I saw someone with a trench coat walking from the bar area toward the side door," Russ recalled. "It was an older man and solid, but it didn't seem real. It disappeared in the stage area."

The figure had vanished in the area where the bodies had formerly been placed on display for the mourners.

Russ Tito kept this incident to himself for about a year; then he received independent confirmation of the haunting from his bartender Roseann Vercillo.

"It was late at night and I had just closed the bar," Roseann remembered. "I was sitting here with another girl reading a magazine with all the lights on when a big cloud, thick and white, crossed the room from the end of the bar."

Frightened by her encounter, the bartender told Russ Tito about the experience, and only then did he tell Roseann about his.

Although Roseann's ghostly figure was cloudlike and nebulous, its path across the room and the place where it vanished were exactly the same as the actions of Russ' image.

"Tito's on the Edge"

The obvious presumption is that the ghost haunting the stage area has something to do with the old funeral home, but the exact reasons or motivations for the haunting remain unknown.

On a regular basis, strange shadows are reported in the hallway, and one night it appeared that there was an extra member of the band on stage for a few seconds. Most reports are subtle and all are of a nonthreatening nature.

A belief that the building is haunted does not keep away bar patrons. Weekends are particularly busy. It has effected the rental of apartments upstairs, however. Of eight apartments only two are rented, six are usually vacant.

Roseann Vercillo perhaps sums up the situation here best: "I have seen them. They are here."

29 Tito's On The Edge

Location: 2600 South Wentworth, Chicago.

Type of occurrences: Apparitions of man in trench coat and a blob of mist.

Characteristics: Hauntings cluster around section of room where caskets were formerly displayed.

Status: Sporadic, but widely talked about due to local superstitions.

LINCOLN'S GHOSTLY FUNERAL TRAIN

PHANTOM FUNERAL PROCESSION OF ABRAHAM LINCOLN

It was in Chicago that our sixteenth President, Abraham Lincoln, was nominated by the Republicans on May 18, 1860. Opposed by Northern Democrat, Stephen A. Douglas and Southern Democrat, John C. Breckinridge, Lincoln was elected the first Republican President on November 6, 1860. He had received 180 of 303 possible electoral votes and almost forty-percent of the popular vote.

President Lincoln led the North during the Civil War, and he is credited for determinedly preserving the Union.

The southern states had slavery, and the vast majority of the northern states were against slavery. Those in the southern states believed abolition of slavery would eliminate manpower and create disaster since their economic base was mostly agriculture.

Just after Lincoln's election to the presidency, on December 20, 1860, South Carolina seceded from the Union. Within two months, other southern states followed: Mississippi, Florida, Alabama, Georgia, Louisiana, and Texas. These secessions created an impetus that led to the Civil War and split the United States in half. The Civil War lasted from 1861 through 1865. Three million fought and 600,000 died.

Lincoln was not only a wartime president, but also our first president to die by an assassin's hand. He was shot and mortally wounded on April 14, 1865, by John Wilkes Booth. Booth and his associates plotted to kill others in Lincoln's cabinet but did not succeed. They had hoped to preserve the South.

Abraham Lincoln may have been born in Kentucky, but was an Illinoisan by adoption. The first thought of many was that Lincoln would be buried in Washington, D.C.; even New York City vied for the honor. The final decision rested with his widow and surviving sons. The burial would be in Springfield, Illinois. Lincoln, in death, would return to his roots.

Because new advances in embalming had just been developed at the time of his death, Lincoln's body would be transformed into a celebrity corpse. Chemical embalming allowed the funeral of Lincoln to become a moveable feat, a fourteen-day journey back across America from his presidential heights in Washington, D.C. to his political beginnings in Springfield.

After a wake at the White House, the presidential casket was moved in procession to the Capitol. Thousands mourned and visited the casket in Washington. Then the long journey home was about to begin.

At the Baltimore & Ohio depot, the funeral train waited. A pilot engine led, followed by a black-draped engine pulling eight cars. From Washington, the procession slowly traveled through Baltimore, then into Pennsylvania, New Jersey, and New York. Heading west, the route went through Ohio, Indiana, and then finally Illinois.

The procession was accompanied by church bells pealing, cannons blasting, and local bands playing funeral marches. Burning tar barrels lit the way after dark. America had never seen anything like it before or since. Even in rural areas as cities or towns were visited, the crowds were uncontrollable.

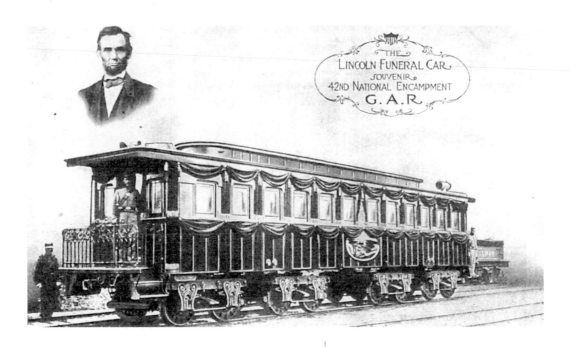

THE
LINCOLN FUNERAL CAR
SOUVENIR
42ND NATIONAL ENCAMPMENT
G. A. R

Ghostly stories circulate about Lincoln's funeral train car

The images of that lonely last ride would be etched into the memories of tens-of-thousands. Within a few years however, it became obvious that the Lincoln funeral procession was more than just a moment in time.

The Victorian era, in America as well as Europe, saw the rise of an incredible interest in ghost stories. Spiritualism was in vogue, and in literary circles, anthologies of ghostly tales, both fictional and "true," were popular reading. Ghost stories of the rich and famous are always more interesting than those of commoners, and in the United States, our presidents are our royalty. With this background, it is not surprising that ghost stories of Abraham Lincoln took hold, and the most intriguing involve his ghostly funeral procession.

Chicago was one of the North's most important cities during the Civil War. Chicago's industry and commerce were crucial to the Union cause. Its links with the war were many. Camp Douglas was located here where thousands of troops enlisted and where thousands of Confederate prisoners of war were confined.

As the veterans of the Grand Army of the Republic aged and war memories became cracker barrel yarns, tales were often told of the Lincoln train reappearing during the springtime of the year, its ghostly return along lonely stretches of rail, once again taking that sad trip back to Springfield.

An exceptionally graphic account of the ghost train was carried in the Albany, New York, *Evening Times* of April 28, 1896, thirty-one years after Lincoln's burial:

> Regularly in the month of April, about midnight, the air on the tracks becomes very keen and cutting. On either side of the tracks it is warm and still. Every watchman, when he feels the air, slips off the track and sits down to watch. Soon the pilot engine of Lincoln's funeral train passes with long, black streamers and with a band of black instruments playing dirges, grinning skeletons sitting all about.

> It passes noiselessly. If it is moonlight, clouds come over the moon as the phantom train goes by. After the pilot engine passes, the funeral train itself with flags and streamers rushes past. The track seems covered with black carpet, and the coffin is seen in the center of the car, while all about it in the air and on the train behind are vast numbers of blue-coated men, some with coffins on their backs, others leaning upon them.
>
> If a real train were passing its noise would be hushed as if the phantom train rode over it. Clocks and watches always stop as the phantom train goes by and when looked at are five to eight minutes behind.
>
> Everywhere on the road about April 27 watches and clocks are suddenly found to be behind.

Although this particular account was colored with vivid and gruesome Victorian imagery, the incredible possibility remains. An actual ghostly recreation of the Lincoln funeral train procession along its route decades later must be considered as a possibility.

The British rail historian, Richard Peyton, estimated that the Lincoln ghost train was seen by "literally thousands of people." In the United Kingdom, where "train spotting" is a popular pastime, stories of haunted stations and ghost trains are widely believed.

The Lincoln ghost train legend became an inspiration to a well-known TV and motion picture scriptwriter. Rod Serling's interpretation on this tale would form the plot of his ghost story, "The Ghost Train," and became an episode of his classic TV series, "The Twilight Zone." The popular definition of a ghost is usually that of paranormal contact with an individual, a person, not an inanimate object. Could an entire funeral procession of two railroad engines and a number of cars of mourners haunt hundreds of miles of railroad track across America?

When President Lincoln was assassinated, it was a time of national crisis and intense psychological trauma. War, death, and uncertainty threatened both personally and communally. As the long and bitter civil unrest had drawn to a close, suddenly the leader died.

The long funeral of Lincoln, crossing the country from East to Midwest, gave the northern states a distraction to focus upon. The grief and anguish of the people centered upon the funeral procession and reached fevered pitch in Illinois. The crowds at each stop were growing larger and larger as the train approached Illinois. In Chicago, one million met the train, the largest gathering of the entire procession. Then it completed its doleful journey downstate to Springfield. It was a quasi-religious experience, honoring the savior of a nation slain on a Good Friday.

No one has claimed to have encountered the ghost train in living memory. But ghosts are often cyclical, able to go dormant for years before returning again. Perhaps another national crisis will be necessary to cause the ghost train to return again.

When this visualization does return, the odds are it will be along the Illinois Central Line from the Indiana border into downtown Chicago. Here the numbers of the mourners were the highest, and the emotions the most profound.

So on a dark spring night, when you are driving down Lake Shore Drive southbound from McCormick Place, keep looking over your right shoulder toward the century and a half old rails of the Illinois Central Line. If the night becomes uncannily quiet, suddenly devoid of insect and the bird sounds, it may herald a new beginning for an old story.

A psychic postscript: Thirty years after Lincoln was buried, and after many attempts, his body was stolen from his tomb. Following the recovery, Lincoln was reburied in a block of concrete.

Although the flesh may now be secure, Lincoln's spirit gives no evidence of being restrained having been sighted on numerous occasions and in various locations across the country.

30 ILLINOIS CENTRAL RAILROAD

Location:	Illinois Central Railroad tracks south from the former 12th Street depot, 135 East 11th Place, Chicago.
Type of occurrence:	Vision of funeral train.
Characteristics:	Graphic re-enactment of funeral procession visually but with total silence that blankets out all other sound. Vision is accompanied with clocks or watches stopping or running slowly
Status:	Traditional tale. Nothing past late 19th Century, but may merely be dormant.

CLARENCE DARROW'S RETURN

CLARENCE DARROW MEMORIAL BRIDGE

Clarence Darrow was recognized as the "attorney for the damned" because he would take on legal cases no one else would touch. The Ohio-born lawyer eventually moved to Chicago's south side, the Hyde Park neighborhood near the Museum of Science and Industry. The museum is the most notable building in Jackson Park, constructed for the World's Columbian Exposition of 1893. The park has acres of lawn, formal gardens, and mature trees, making it a peaceful refuge for wildlife and many species of birds. There is a pleasant yacht harbor and even a Japanese tea garden. Darrow loved walking through Jackson Park, and in particular, stopping at the bridge spanning the picturesque winding lagoon. He called this spot "the prettiest view on Earth."

Known as a civil libertarian, Darrow was strongly against the death penalty. One of his best known cases was the 1924 murder "trial of the century" of Nathan Leopold and Richard Loeb, two scions of wealthy families who murdered a neighbor, little Bobby Franks. That a fourteen-year-old's life was brutally taken in a sick "thrill kill" did not phase Darrow in his defense of the indefensible. In a case where guilt was obvious, Darrow proceeded to get the killers off with life in prison instead of the execution the public was sure they deserved.

The 1925 "Monkey Trial" pitted Darrow against William Jennings Bryan, populist and former presidential candidate. Darrow defended teacher John Scopes in Dayton, Tennessee for illegally teaching evolution in a state school. This trial was the first to be broadcast live on radio. WGN radio in Chicago gave Darrow and Bryan national coverage.

It was during the Scopes trial that Darrow's agnosticism, or some would say atheism, became widely known. Darrow's defense for Scopes was based upon an attack on organized religion and the Bible as literal word of God. Such a defense did not fly well in Bible-belt Tennessee, but Darrow got the national attention he sought.

Yet, Darrow was a man of contradictions. Despite his views on traditional religion, Darrow had some sort of personal belief in an afterlife. He told his son that after he died he wanted his body cremated and the ashes scattered over the waters of the Jackson Park lagoon. In the area he loved so much in life, he wanted to spend eternity after his death. He promised that if there were a way, he would return after death and give a sign from beyond at this very site.

This sort of promise to give a sign from beyond is similar to Houdini's famous pledge to return that he made before his death on Halloween of 1926. Despite numerous annual séances at the penthouse of the Roosevelt Hotel in Hollywood, Harry Houdini has never made it back.

A few days after his death on March 13, 1938, Darrow's final wishes were carried out. Family and friends gathered on a bridge within sight of the rear entrance of the museum, a bridge now known as the Clarence Darrow Memorial Bridge. With a brief service, the urn was tipped over the side of the bridge, and the cremains of Clarence Darrow settled over the dark green waters below.

*Clarence Darrow
Memorial Bridge*

The following year, at 10:00 a.m. on March 13, 1939, the one-year anniversary of his death, Darrow's family and friends returned to the bridge. In a commemoration, they recited speeches and poems in Darrow's memory and scanned the area for a promised sign. Nothing was noted that year, nor the next or the one after that.

The March 13 vigil on the bridge became an annual event, and as the original Darrow followers died out, they were replaced with new blood. Despite a day often quite blustery and sometimes snowy, dozens gather each year for this traditional ceremony.

In March of 1991, I took part in my first commemoration at the Darrow Bridge. As I stood on the bridge with some fifty others, I heard speeches and witnessed the tossing of the wreath into the waters below. No, Darrow did not show up. It was obvious to me that those taking part that day were motivated far more by the ideals of Darrow than by the thought that Darrow might actually intervene psychically.

As I left the park that day, however, I thought to myself that this was just too good of a story to save for once a year. This seemed like a natural story to incorporate into my Halloween bus tour package, so I prepared to use it in my 1991 tour material.

When October finally rolled around, I began to stop at the Darrow Bridge on nighttime tours around 10:00 p. m. On one of the first stops there, as my group stood on the bridge and faced the massive rear entrance of the Museum, we noticed someone standing on the stairs. Across the water in plain sight stood a nicely dressed, elderly man in a long camelhair type coat, a rather stereotypical choice of lawyers and politicians.

There was no event ongoing in the Museum that evening that we could tell, and the man certainly seemed strangely out of place. During better and warmer weather, fishermen with gear in hand often frequent the area late into the night, but from the way the man looked, he was no fisherman.

Some of the group thought it humorous and began to yell across the lagoon to the figure, "Hey, Clarence! Look over here!" Comments of that sort were shouted, but the figure stood unmoving and silent. It seemed obvious that he must have heard us, but he just ignored us. The thought occurred to me that his attire could actually place him in some danger, since being alone in any Chicago park long after dark could invite crime, and one should not throw caution to the wind like this. I told the group it was time to board the bus and go on to our next location. I had no reason at that time, however, to suspect anything unnatural.

During the next week, I totally forgot about the well-dressed stranger on the museum stairs. The following Friday night, I was back again with a new group of tourists. Prepped with the Darrow stories I was telling on the bus, we approached the bridge. Then it happened again, at least to some of us.

Some of the group asked, "Who is that on the stairs across the lagoon?" As I looked to the stairs, I saw nothing. I squinted some more and still saw no one there. The area was partially lit by the museum floodlights and in plain sight.

"There's no one over there," I said, but some of the crowd loudly disagreed.

"Over on the left, by the railing," they said, "wearing a long tan coat." They were describing the same spot and the same man I saw there one week before, but I could not see him. I took a show of hands and about one half of the group, around thirty, saw the man.

I came back again with another group a week later. It happened once more. But again, I could not see the dapper older man this time either, although about half of the people on the bus did. He still appeared silent and unmoving in the same location, to those who could see him, that is. If I wasn't convinced the previous week, I was now.

The form that I saw, and the others saw without me, was fully formed and substantial. There was absolutely no reason to think that it wasn't just a fashionably dressed man in the wrong spot after dark, except for the unnerving fact that some could see him and others could not. Had that disparity not been noted, there would be no reason to suspect anything out of the ordinary. A ghost like that, if indeed this were a ghost, could haunt a location for decades and never be identified as more than a mere mortal, his disguise being his normalcy.

Was it really Clarence Darrow, returning as he said he would? Well, this is the spot that Darrow loved and where he vowed he would return, and the figure was dressed in the fashion of Darrow. There is no other ghost tradition at this location except the Darrow legend.

He finally materialized.

I have been back to the Darrow Bridge many times in recent years, by day and by night, but Darrow's ghost has proved to be elusive. On a 1992 October tour, some of my group claimed to see a shadowy figure on the top of the museum stairs to the right of the entrance doors. Once again, I did not.

The most dramatic sighting of what is believed to be Clarence Darrow's ghost took place on Halloween night in 1995. After a hiatus of some three years, Darrow came back in style.

The annual tour on Halloween night is a much-anticipated event. It usually sells out more than a month before and even though October 31, 1995, was a Tuesday, all seats were sold well before the event.

The bus for that night's tour was an articulated seventy-capacity Prevost highway coach. There were sixty-eight passengers, plus the driver and myself.

When we arrived at Jackson Park shortly after 10:00 p.m., we had the entire area to ourselves. No one else was in the parking lot, and the crisp weather meant no fishermen were about. The museum interior was dark, no private party taking place inside. As the bus unloaded, I led the group from the edge of the parking lot some 100 yards to the small bridge. I described the 1938 ceremony and the spilling of the cremains over the side of the bridge. We all eagerly scanned the edges of the lagoon and watched the rear entrance of the museum directly in front of us, hoping for an encounter with the famous spirit.

After some ten minutes of futility, we began to head back towards the coach. Then, about halfway back, someone shouted, "There he is!" We saw the figure of an elderly man walking with steady, even steps down the sidewalk on the museum side of the lagoon. He was heading from west to east, parallel to us, on the opposite side of the water. When he got in front of the entrance, he stopped, did a half turn towards us, and seemed to look down into the dark water.

Yelling and waving our arms did no good. We could not attract his attention this time either. En masse, we all ran to the edge of the lagoon to take an even closer look. Two passengers with video cameras began to tape the event. Due to the poor light available, the image of the man appeared grainy and fuzzy, but he was captured on film.

Then two young men asked me if they could chase the figure. "Do it!" was my reply. They took off around the edge of the lagoon. The route to the strange figure was around the water of the lagoon and past the Omnimax Theater and the U-505 submarine. As they gained ground on the figure, we shouted encouragement from our side of the lagoon.

When the pursuers got within about fifty feet of the figure, they both froze in their tracks simultaneously. The rest of the bus party went berserk at this point, urging the two to "knock him down!" and "tackle him!" Nothing we screamed could get them back into action.

After some thirty seconds or more of this stalemate, the old man did a half turn and began to retrace his steps back the way he came. He was soon around the side of the building and out of our line of sight. The two "ghost chasers" sheepishly walked back to the rest of the group.

When we questioned the two about why they stopped short, they could only explain that, "Something was not right!" and "It was too scary!" And, what never could be explained was why both of them they stopped exactly at the same time, as though they had hit an invisible wall.

All the rest of the tour that night was focused on our dramatic sighting, although, we could not fathom how an old man stylishly dressed could be that frightening to his two pursuers.

It still stands out as the most exciting evening I have had in leading bus tours for a quarter of a century. It affected my bus driver to the extent that he quit the company a short while later to drive a truck instead.

Regardless of one's personal take on Clarence Darrow, either as a champion of civil liberties or mere lawyer for hire, his promised return to Jackson Park seems to be an accomplished fact and lends substance to this Chicago legend.

31 Jackson Park Lagoon

Location:	Jackson Park on south end of Museum of Science and Industry, 57th St. and Lake Shore Drive
Type of occurrence:	Promised supernatural return after death and probable apparition
Characteristics:	Apparition reported as fully formed and solid in certain cases and as hazy and shadowy in others
Status:	Occasional with Halloween season seemingly favored.

LUCIFER'S LAST WALTZ

KAISER HALL

Bridgeport, now a neighborhood on Chicago's South Side, was a town founded during the days of the Illinois and Michigan Canal before the Civil War. It was annexed by Chicago and, some say, took over Chicago, becoming the nerve center of local politics for many years. Over a third of Chicago's 20th century was ruled by mayors from Bridgeport, and the heritage continues into the 21st century.

There are things different about Bridgeport that distinguish it from other parts of Chicago. It has street names that are unique: Mary, Stark, Bonfield, and Gratten. The street pattern follows a geography of its own, like the spokes in a wheel. Then there is the folklore.

Old world immigrants, first and second generation Irish, Germans, Poles, and other nationalities settled Bridgeport. Their cultural and religious perceptions still remain in the surviving folktales and ghost stories of the neighborhood. A center for these traditions is an old building in the heart of the community called Kaiser Hall.

Time has not been kind to many of the old buildings in Bridgeport. Kaiser Hall, a massive three-story building at Archer and McDermott, now houses Loung's Corporation, a Chinese-American firm. In its early years, however, this grand building housed a butcher shop on the first floor, apartments on the second, and a magnificent ballroom on the top floor. It was a hub of community activity.

Despite the outward appearance of successful commerce and gaiety, the building housed dark secrets. According to Lily Joy, whose family built and owned the property until the 1970s, there was a curse on the Hall placed by the family of the original owner's wife.

The Kaisers came from a small town in Wisconsin to Bridgeport as newlyweds. It seems their hopes for financial success and the good life would destroyed by family discontent.

"My mother's family built Kaiser Hall," recalled Lily. "My great-grandmother's sister and her husband came from Wisconsin, and her family was upset that he took her away," she said. "They didn't believe in cursing a person, but they would curse what a person owned. They cursed his wealth."

At first things seemed to go fine. Business was good for the butcher shop, restaurant, and dancehall, and the apartments were all rented. Prosperity then withered. Illness followed; then both Kaisers died young.

"It was just one problem after another. The building was left to my mother's mother," recalled Lily Joy, "and immediately upon taking possession of the building, my mother's family fell into ruin. My grandparents were well off up to that point. My mother still won't talk about it."

Lily's grandfather, a successful carpenter, fell from a roof and was unable to work again. His wife suddenly took ill and died at the age of thirty-nine of a brain tumor.

More bad luck would follow: City inspectors declared the ballroom unsafe, and it had to be closed in the 1940s. The magnificent windows were bricked up, and all furniture had to be removed from the top floor for safety reasons. A grand piano was broken up with an ax.

"The whole atmosphere of the building changed. There were a lot of rats up there," Lily said. "It was a spooky place."

Kaiser Hall, where the devil was said to dance.

Lily's grandfather stayed on as the last tenant. His apartment had cold water only and one toilet at the end of the hall. Every Saturday night as a child, Lily and her family would visit and watch television on an old black and white set. It was during those visits around 1959 or 1960 that a strange new haunting began.

"The orchestra pit was right above my grandfather's apartment," Lily vividly recalled, "and we would hear a drum beating above us. We went upstairs several times and it would stop. All the chairs and tables were gone, and the only thing left up there was an empty drum case on the floor.

"Every time we went up, the drum case was open and my grandfather was the only one with a key. He'd lock the drum case up, and we'd go back downstairs. The next week the drum would start beating again. "

After many fruitless attempts to catch someone playing a prank, the family realized that the supernatural must be involved.

"Finally my dad and my grandfather couldn't take it anymore and they called St. Bridget's Church down the street," Lily remembered. " The pastor came down and took the drum case away and the drumming didn't happen anymore."

Besides the episode of the phantom drummer, there was a psychic cold spot in the hall under the center staircase. Lily often noticed this occurrence. "It was under or alongside the center staircase, and was always cold despite the temperature outside."

The history of the cursed hall would take another turn in 1972. Lily's grandfather died at the age of seventy-one, and a new generation was given the opportunity of ownership.

Lily said, "When my grandfather died, the Hall was left to his three children, but they didn't want anything to do with the building. I was the only grandchild over eighteen. My mother told me that if I took the building, paid the back taxes, and signed the papers, that the family would disown me."

Since Lily was only a senior in high school, and quite aware of the curse and its potential, she prudently decided not to take the tainted property. "It was bought for back taxes by District National Bank, who then suffered a mysterious rash of robberies. It eventually was sold to a Chinese construction company," said Lily. The family curse on the property may have finally run its course.

The curse was not widely known outside of immediate family circles, but other neighborhood tales about the building still flourish in the Bridgeport community. The most familiar tale is about "the night the Devil came down to Bridgeport."

There are a number of versions of the story about Satan's appearance at Kaiser Hall, but they all contain common threads about disobedience to your parents or higher authorities and being wary of strangers, especially after dark. Most storytellers place this tale in the pre-World War I days of the last century.

A popular version of the story I originally heard has deep religious connotations. One Saturday night in Lent, a dance was being held at Kaiser Hall. Because it was unseemly for a good Catholic to attend such an activity during this religious time of year, a young girl was forbidden by her parents to attend.

Disregarding her parents' wishes, the girl went to the dance anyway and soon was out on the hardwood floor dancing with a mysterious dark stranger. As she was being whisked around the floor, the others at the dance were aghast to discover that this outsider dancing with a local girl had hooves instead of human feet — cloven hooves, the sign of a devil!

At this point the two dancers were whirling about, faster and faster in frenzy. Some say that the music being played by the orchestra mysteriously became church hymns. Then with an explosion, a cloud of smoke and an evil stench of sulfur, the dancers crashed through a tall window and disappeared.

The crowd rushed to the window and expected to see two bodies on the sidewalk three flights down, but there was no one there. Both completely vanished.

Only two burnt hoof prints remained in the hardwood floor in front of the smashed window as visual proof of the satanic abduction.

The owners of Kaiser Hall were well aware of the Devil tale connected with their building. With everything else that had happened there, why wouldn't they believe?

Lily Joy's version of the story, based on family tradition, is somewhat different. It has less of a religious overtone. "A young girl from the neighborhood came here for a Halloween costume ball. For some reason, she was forbidden by her parents to come but ignored them. She was dancing with a masquerader dressed as a devil. He waltzed her right through a side window facing McDermott Street. As the crowd rushed to the window and looked down, they saw both bodies lying on the ground. But when they ran down the flights of stairs and outside, the girl's body was still there, but the Devil was gone. She was dead."

Other versions of this classic story undoubtedly exist, but the lessons remain the same: your life and even your immortal soul may be the price of breaking religious or parental taboos.

Folklorists can point to such tales in many other places, but the reality of the Kaiser Hall incident is not doubted in old Bridgeport.

32 FORMERLY KAISER HALL

Location: 2988 South Archer Avenue (Archer and McDermott), Chicago

Type of occurrence: Family business cursed: plagued with bad luck, a phantom drummer, and even an appearance by the Devil himself.

Characteristics: Multi-generation psychic problems manifesting in various ways involving family as well as outsiders.

Status: Curse may or may not have run its course. The Devil has not returned recently.

BLOOD CURSE OF THE STOCK YARDS

STOCKYARD CURSE

"Hog butcher for the world," begins Carl Sandburg's poetic ode to Chicago, but cattle, sheep, goats and other meat-providing creatures were also slaughtered with assembly-line efficiency in the Chicago's Union Stock Yards from 1865 to 1971. Their flesh nourished the country. Chicago became the meat capital of the world. Fortunes were made in the meat packing industry by families like Armour and Swift.

From Upton Sinclair's grim indictment of the stockyard's despicable conditions in his novel, *The Jungle* (1906), to the vaudeville-style ballad "Back of the Yards," the Union Stock Yards left its mark on Chicago's culture.

The giant meatpacking complex was the brainchild of John B. Sherman, a Chicago businessman. At the time on the outer limits of the city, Union Stock Yards consolidated a half-dozen meat packers and nine railroads into a square mile area. It became one of the city's largest employers and continued as such for well over a century.

The stock yards were ready in December of 1865. However, for some strange reason, Christmas Day was selected as the first day of operation, and the rivers of blood began to pour forth.

The parishioners of a Catholic Church nearby named their church Nativity, which was a touching symbolic gesture to Christmas and the Christ child born in a manger; even though, the Christ child was born amist the animals, and not in a slaughterhouse.

The Union Stock Yards was the number-one air polluter in Illinois for many decades. The smell of the stockyards filled the air for miles around. I can remember waking up with tears in my eyes from the stockyard's stench. Our family home was just a mile away. On certain nights, when the wind was right, you could go to sleep listening to the lonesome lowing of cattle awaiting slaughter in their crowded pens.

Millions of animals were killed by the sledgehammer blow to the skull and the sharp slit across the neck. Hopefully, the fortunate ones didn't feel pain for long.

Locations of mass deaths, human or animal, are often considered to be unlucky. There may be psychic connections surrounding the Stock Yards.

Over its long history, Union Stock Yards has faced inexplicable misfortune in the shape of disastrous fires. The city has not faced anything like them since the Great Fire of 1871.

Just before Christmas, 1910, a killer fire broke out in Warehouse No. 7 of the Nelson Morris and Company plant in the complex. The fire alarm was given at 4:09 a.m. on December 22. The fire burned for over twenty-four hours until it was struck out at 6:37 a.m. on December 23, and twenty-one firemen were killed when a wall collapsed.

In was a sad Christmas for Chicago that year as the Fire Marshall, his Second Assistant, three Captains, four Lieutenants, eleven pipemen and truckmen, and one driver were laid to rest. The property loss was only $400,000, but the lose of life was the worst in the Chicago Fire Department's entire history.

Stock Yard Gate

Two dozen years later, another horrific blaze broke out in the Union Stock Yards. On the evening of May 18, 1934, the Swift and Company stock pens burst into flames at 45th and Morgan. With winds fanning the fire, it rapidly spread toward the north and the east, jumping Halsted Street and burning out residential housing and businesses. The summer had been unseasonably warm and the old buildings, often wood, were perfect kindling. Were it not for the bravery of the Chicago Fire Department, a disaster on the scale of 1871 might have been repeated. Landmarks like the Stock Yards Inn, Saddle and Sirloin Club, and the Dexter Park Amphitheater were destroyed. It took 1,500 firemen from 138 companies citywide to quench the flames. The two-day fire ended on May 20 with 1,100 people injured and financial losses of $10 million. Miraculously not one human life was lost although thousands of cattle died trapped in their pens.

While researching, I found an interesting coincidence relating to the area. What is the strange chance that Chicago's two most financially disastrous fires would be connected to cattle? Mrs. O'Leary's fabled cow in 1871, and the cattle pens of the Union Stock Yards in 1934?

The red brick International Amphitheatre was built at 4300 South Halsted Street as part of the Stock Yards complex on the site of the old Dexter Park Amphitheater that was destroyed in the wake of the 1934 fire.

The life span of the Chicago's Union Stock Yards was just over 105 years. After its peak years in the mid 1920s, a long decline set in, and the yards went out of business at midnight on July 30, 1971.

There is, I believe, an interesting link to the Stock Yards era and other bloodshed. Stock Yards construction began at the time of war; just two months after Lee's surrender at Appomattox Courthouse in 1865, the finish of the Civil War, our nation's greatest human bloodletting. The Stock Yards closed at the time of war, during our nation's long, bloody involvement in Vietnam. These two civil wars, one fought on home soil and the other fought on foreign soil, threatened to tear America apart amid great divisiveness and social upheaval.

What seems thought provoking to me is the significant center-stage role the Chicago Stock Yards played in both the political scene and social movements in our country.

Between 1832 and 2000, there have been eighty-seven national presidential nominating conventions of major U. S. political parties. Of those eighty-seven conventions, twenty-seven have been held in Chicago. About one-third of all decisions as to what person would be selected to run for the highest office in the land were made here in Chicago.

During the tumultuous Cold War era election years of 1952, 1956, 1960, 1964, and 1968, of ten national conventions of the Democratic and Republican parties, five, or one-half, were held in Chicago. And all five were held at the International Amphitheatre.

An argument could be made that the decisions made here on the South Side of Chicago shaped much of America's foreign and domestic policies for the last half of the 20th Century. The national leadership, selected here, conducted the Cold War against the Soviet Union and Red China, and the undeclared bloody, hot wars against North Korea and North Vietnam.

In 1968, the Democratic Convention was held at the International Amphitheatre. The convention was marked by violent confrontations between the opponents and proponents of the Vietnam War. As Chicago was rocked by rioting in Grant Park, downtown, the Amphitheatre was under heavy guard by the Chicago Police and the Illinois National Guard. There might have been constant talk of "pigs" at that time, but it was not about the unlucky porkers about to be slaughtered behind the Amphitheatre. This epithet was the hurled at the police by angry protesters who were outraged because of the United States' involvement in the war.

That year, President Lyndon Johnson withdrew from the election process, and Hubert Humphrey, nominated as the Democratic candidate, ran against Republican candidate Richard Nixon. Nixon was elected President, and policies enacted during his administration eventually led to the United States withdrawal and end of the Vietnamese Conflict in 1975. The protests made an impact on our collective social and political consciences for years to come.

As the 1990s drew to a close, the International Amphitheatre was sentenced to destruction. Its last days were far from its glory years of hosting national party conventions. Its last venues included Mexican rodeos and a Halloween season "world's largest haunted house." Bulldozers quickly leveled decades of history and political aspirations. What the now-vacant lot at 4300 South Halsted will next become is anyone's guess. For those who know the "bloody" traditions of this piece of land, it will certainly be something to watch.

Today, the area is an industrial park.

33 STOCK YARDS INDUSTRIAL PARK

Location:	Pershing (39th) to 47th Streets, Halsted to Ashland (one square mile), Chicago.
Type of occurrences:	Bad luck and disaster, especially from fire.
Characteristics:	Locations of mass death, human or animal, are often considered to be unlucky. Those locations of mass slaughter even more so.
Status:	Stock Yards are now closed, but blood-soaked land remains. Future uncertain.

A Debt Beyond The Grave

Visitation Church

During the Baby Boom years, Monsignor Richard Wolfe often claimed that Visitation Parish had the largest grammar school in the U.S. For an urban parish, Visitation probably had the largest number of parishioners, as well.

For those of us growing up around Visitation Parish during the fifties and early sixties, we had the feeling of being more in a self-contained village than just a neighborhood of Chicago. We certainly had our own folklore.

One of the more popular tales told, especially among the altar boys and parishioners who resided on the surrounding blocks near the huge gray Gothic stone church building, was the eerie tale of the midnight Mass.

In the innocent years, before the Vietnam War and widespread drug use, it was commonplace for church buildings to be open twenty-four-hours-a-day. At any hour, the faithful could go into their local church, kneel, and pray. Then churches and the devout were safe from harm.

On certain nights, however, those approaching or passing by Visitation Church might have noticed something strangely astray. Sounds emanating from the church were obviously the recitation of the Latin Mass. But what kind of Mass would be taking place at the ungodly hour of midnight or at one o'clock in the morning?

Curious but apprehensive, some brave soul would carefully open one of the massive wooden church's double doors a crack, or another might strain a peek in a partially opened stained glass window to take a look inside. There they saw standing on the altar, oblivious to an empty church, a priest in his religious garb performing the sacrament. But he was no priest known at the parish; he was a stranger.

A day or so later, the puzzled parishioner might visit the rectory or happen to meet one of the parish priests in the neighborhood and ask about the incident. "Who was the strange priest and why was he saying Mass to an empty church in the middle of the night?"

The parish priests could not provide any answers, since the description fit no priest at the church and there were no visiting priests at the rectory at that time.

But a mystery like this needs an explanation, even if only a theory. It did not take long before the parishioners thought they had a probable answer.

One of the most sacred duties that a priest can perform is to say a Mass for those who request a special intention. Very often the Mass is said for the soul of a departed loved one. A donation made to the priest seals the obligation.

But what if the priest never gets around to saying the Mass through forgetfulness or too busy a schedule, and his death intervenes? The debt is still owed from beyond the grave. Therefore, the priest might still feel compelled to perform his duty, even if that means a ghost Mass at midnight.

As an altar boy at Visitation Church, this was a lesson I never would forget. If serious obligations are not taken care of in this life they will follow you into the next.

Visitation Church

34 VISITATION CHURCH

Location:	843 West Garfield Boulevard (Corner Garfield Boulevard and Peoria Street), Chicago.
Type of occurrence:	Apparition of priest on altar or just sounds of religious service.
Characteristics:	Ghostly priest says Mass at midnight in an empty church.
Status:	Traditional. No recent reports.

GHOST GUILT

THE DOLL IN THE WINDOW

Baby Boomers in the early 1960s will remember when the craze of the life-sized "Patty Playpal" doll began. Her appearance, if taken at a glance, would be enough to make you think you were looking at a real person. You had a choice, a blonde with powder blue eyes or a brunette. The doll could be dressed in regular clothes, perhaps even children's clothes and become "your child."

At the same time these dolls were becoming popular, a story began circulating in a certain South Side neighborhood about a little girl who was savagely struck down in the street outside her home by a hit-and-run driver. The cold-hearted killer charged off and was never identified. The grief-stricken family buried the little girl and returned to a house full of memories. All around them were the reminders of their loss.

The dead girl's clothes, schoolbooks and playthings, mementos that all seemed to call out her name, and what about her life-sized "playmate," Patty? Her doll with the sweet, cheery round face, cute nose and blonde hair was a continual reminder of their daughter.

Her parents chose to cope with their loss in a curious way. They dressed their child's favorite doll to look exactly like her, in the clothes she was wearing at the time of her death. They placed this replica of their lost little girl in a picture window overlooking the scene of the tragedy and watched, believing the driver would likely return again down the same street and the same site where their daughter died. They hoped that the doll would shock the killer into a fit of remorse. If he saw the doll dressed in the clothes the girl was wearing at the time of death, then he might take the doll for a flashback image of the dead child or even her ghost. Therefore, justice could be accomplished when the lawbreaker would turn himself in to authorities.

I first heard this sad tale in the mid 1960s. I was told about a corner apartment complex at Garfield Boulevard and Racine Avenue on the edge of Sherman Park. I went to investigate. Standing vigil in a second story window was a large doll that could be seen from either Garfield or Racine. It appeared almost real, but odd, motionless and staring endlessly. I heard about the supposed purpose of the doll and accident from friends who lived close to the immediate neighborhood.

Doll in window

Asking around, however, I found that no car-incident death had occurred there. So, the reason for the doll in the window puzzled me.

In the 1970s, the tale had migrated south to the Beverly neighborhood. On scenic Longwood Drive just south of 103rd Street, a similar account was popular. It involved a doll facing Longwood from an apartment complex. A local precinct captain was my initial source and was positive of his "facts." My inquiries to the police showed that no accident had taken place there. By this time, I was sure a new urban myth was blooming.

Like all great folktales, this one would eventually go cross-cultural. In the 1980s, "the sentry doll in the window tale" popped up in an Hispanic neighborhood near McKinley Park, again on Chicago's south side. This time the grieving parents were Mexican-born Americans.

In all of the stories, the same the elements of the myth were in place: the death of a little girl killed in an unconscionable hit-and-run act; the doll dressed in the deceased child's clothing and placed in a window overlooking the tragedy; and the hope that the driver of the vehicle would return to the exact location, be shocked at seeing the "child," then become so remorseful, he would confess to this deadly deed.

The rationale for the doll in the window could be the shared desire for justice to be served. For whatever reason, I have heard this tale only on the south side of Chicago. It seems to favor busy streets and apartment buildings. Maybe the transient nature of apartment dwellers helps the myth survive. As an urban myth, the tale of the life-sized doll could always surface again.

Perhaps, there are deeper lessons to be learned. If we don't know our neighbors, we cannot know their joys, sorrows, or losses, let alone any past that may haunt them.

35 DOLL IN THE WINDOW

Locations:	5501 South Racine Avenue; Longwood Drive just south of 103rd Street; and a street just off McKinley Park.
Type of occurrence:	A life-sized doll is dressed in a dead girl's clothes and placed at scene of her death to represent her ghost or image.
Characteristics:	Folkloric explanation for a doll in a window involving a desire for justice to be done.
Status:	No accounts in recent years, but probably will turn up again.

ALL SOULS' DAY APPARITIONS

THE PHANTOM MONKS

Growing up Catholic on the South Side of Chicago during the Kennedy years was exciting. In 1960, America's first Catholic president was elected, Castro was painting Cuba red, and the pope was supposed to reveal the terrifying third secret of Fatima. Because of the 1958 Our Lady of Angels School fire, we had numerous surprise fire drills, and they were supplemented with air raid drills: we hid under our desks in preparation for a nuclear bomb attack.

Suddenly the grammar school grapevine was abuzz with yet another concern. Normal class curriculum could wait; there were sightings of ghostly figures at nearby St. Rita's Church.

October 31 through November 2 is a special period in the Catholic Church calendar. Halloween (October 31) is the eve of a holy day of obligation, All Saints Day (November 1), a day to honor all the saints of the church. November 2, All Souls Day, is a day to remember all the dead who have gone before. It was widely believed to be a day when the dead could communicate with the living and make their needs known.

Not long after November 2, while in seventh grade at Visitation grammar school, I heard about the psychic activity at St. Rita's, a neighboring parish about two miles away.

The version we heard was that while people were attending St. Rita's to say their devotions for their departed loved ones that All Souls' Day, a commotion broke out. The organ, located in a loft over the main church doors, began screeching with random notes. When those in the church looked around in annoyance, they were shocked to discover mysterious figures, "monks" for lack of a better word, standing there.

There were six figures in all: three dressed in white and three in black, standing on each side of the organ as it continued to give off wild sounds.

Panic set in, and those in the church tried to flee via the large doors on the east and west sides of the building. The doors were held shut by an unknown force. Struggling to get out was to no avail.

The figures were next to the main floor of the church, semitransparent, and gliding through the pews. A strange voice was heard in a hoarse whisper crying, "Pray for me!" A mysterious wind inside the church swirled, and the doors blew open. Those who were trapped moments before, fled outside in fear, eager to put distance between themselves and the spirits.

As this account, or similar ones, made the rounds, we speculated on the meaning. As good Catholics, most of us were sure that some lost soul or souls had visited the living that special day set-aside for such contact. They came to holy ground and begged for prayers to be set free from the torments of purgatory. If our interpretation was correct, they got what they needed. Many prayers were offered by those of us who heard the St. Rita's tale.

The St. Rita's All Souls' Day account has been the center of controversy over the years. Officially, this never happened. The parish either denies that anything ever took place, or

St. Rita's Church

attempts to write it all off as an out-of-control teenage prank. The Archdiocese of Chicago's archives reportedly hold no records of this incident. Perhaps officialdom would prefer that the St. Rita's case would go away, but there are still the witnesses.

Mary Kelly lived through the incident. She knows that it was real. She also vividly remembers how seriously the clergy reacted and investigated.

Mary was a sixth grader at St. Rita's Catholic School in November 1961. A sacristy girl, it was her duty to clean the altar area, keep flowers fresh, and attend to the candles. All Souls Day meant compulsory attendance at Mass for all students. But early that morning, things began turning strange.

"At 7:00 a.m. Mass that morning," Mary remembered, "there were some shrill notes coming from the organ. The priest turned from the altar to look, but no one was there." Those at Mass paid scant attention to maverick organ notes until later that day when things escalated.

"There were five of us on sacristy duty, and the church became very eerie. Then there was a whistling sound in the church. There was a stillness, a chilling effect," Mary related.

Mary was originally in a side room behind the altar. She came out to investigate when she heard the strange noise and commotion. Then she spotted the figures.

"In the organ loft there were three black and three white figures. The figures were transparent wrapped in gauze like veiling, a wispy kind of fabric. There were no faces or hands visible.

"The figures were first in the organ loft, then on the main floor. They asked that we would pray for them. It was one voice.

"The kids were trying to leave the church and were very panicky.

"One of the girls was trying to leave the church but couldn't. There was a weird vacuum effect that held her back."

By the time Mary had crossed the altar area and entered the main floor, things were winding down. She headed towards a side door, which by this time was functioning, and left the church building. Decades later, she still finds it difficult to discuss the event.

There was official interest, Mary remembered: "Some of the kids were interviewed by a priest from the archdiocese. They did not talk to me because I was behind the altar and wasn't in the main fray. I came out after the initial commotion."

Mary also remembers an attempt to cover up the story. "I was never asked not to talk about it," she recalled, "but some of the others were."

There was no doubt in Mary's mind that something unusual had taken place. She totally rejects the possibility that it was a teenage hoax. She also heard from others that supernatural events such as statues moving by themselves were reported at various nearby churches.

St. Rita's Church has remained quiet ever since. There have been no repeat performances of the All Souls' Day apparitions of forty years ago, and most of those personally involved have moved away. Mary Kelly moved to a southwest suburb, married, and became the mother of three.

And as for the apparitions, the three black figures and the three white figures seen, the dichotomy is equated with goodness and evil, lightness and darkness, and all the connotations that go with it. Hopefully they will have received the prayers they needed and have resolved any spiritual debts they may once have owed.

But every year when All Souls' Day rolls around, parishioners at morning Mass are known often to look over their shoulder's towards the organ loft, just in case.

36 St. Rita's Church

Location:	6243 South Fairfield (63rd and Fairfield).
Type of occurrence:	Multiple apparitions of shrouded or veiled figures and a verbal message, all accompanied by strange winds, whistling sounds, jammed doors, and screeching organ music..
Characteristics:	The church setting of this contact from the dead incident gives it a quasi-religious quality. The color symbolism and plea for prayers give it an almost medieval feel.
Status:	Incident one of a kind, but the folklore grows stronger year by year.

GHOST NUN

THEME UNFINISHED

Lourdes High School, a Catholic girls' school, was founded in the heart of the Depression in 1936. There is a main three-story building, and years later Stritch Hall, a theater and assembly room was added on. Next door is the convent building. The school is run by the Sisters of St. Joseph, Third Order of St. Francis, who staff the school supplemented with lay teachers. The school is located in a conservative middle-class neighborhood in Chicago's heavily Polish American South Side.

In recent years, the enrollment is around 400 students, but at the peak of the baby boom, it reached as many as 1,300. But no matter what the class or staff size, there was always a ghost to add to census rolls.

Sometimes you can find a ghost by just going to school or the workplace. I taught English and journalism at Lourdes High School for the 1972-73 academic year. While running the school yearbook and newspaper and teaching classes, I was able to observe close-up how students fostered a belief in an in-house ghost. Rather than being something scary, the ghost was accepted as just one more addition to campus life.

The journalism room was on the third floor of the school next to an antiquated Otis elevator. On many a late-nighter, making newspaper or yearbook deadlines, that elevator took on a life of its own. When everyone else was gone for the day except for the journalism students and me, cutting and pasting copy, the elevator loudly came to life. The old elevator, notoriously slow, would make the torturous journey from the first floor to the third. We expected one of the sisters from the convent to be coming up to check on us, but when the elevator doors opened, there was no one there.

The ghost in the elevator became a joke that all of us involved in journalism enjoyed. But there was more.

The third-floor hallway was dark and ominous at night. It was down this stretch of vintage linoleum that phantom footsteps were heard plodding away when everything else was still. The shuffling of uncomfortable shoes was in sharp contrast to the light steps of the students. No doubt about it, the girls said, it must be the ghost nun. Besides the sounds of someone walking, a shadowy image was claimed to be seen on rare occasions.

One of the first things that a freshman learned when attending Lourdes was the haunted third-floor legend. Marianne Sudd, a student in the early 1970s, remembered well: "There was always a story about a ghostly nun on the top floor."

Maureen Harney, a 1977 graduate, recalled: "The upperclassmen would scare us by saying that there was a ghost on the third floor and dare us to take the elevator there."

The longevity of the ghost story is attested to by a ninety-year-old sister, now retired, that I talked with. Although she did not personally believe in the ghost, she confirmed that the belief by the students went back decades.

There is also another part of the school with strong ghostly traditions, Stritch Hall. If this is the same ghost or yet another, it is impossible to tell. Both areas have firm claims on paranormal activity.

Lourdes High School

Stritch Hall is a beautiful auditorium annex built in the 1950s. Besides assemblies and theater productions, the foyer is used as a polling place on election days. Like many a theater, this one claims a ghost (or more) that manifests itself primarily as poltergeist activity during rehearsals or play productions.

Lights malfunctioning and other electronic mishaps are attributed to ghostly interference. The phantom footsteps have been heard in this area as well.

A widely held theory is that this area is haunted because of an old tradition of the Sisters of St. Joseph. Decades ago, when the sisters died, they would be waked on campus. Today nuns are waked in funeral homes, but the memory of these rituals are strong and fuel the belief in spirit possibilities.

One ghost nun? Two? Maybe even more? The students of Lourdes High School, class after class, have kept the belief in their local hauntings alive. They have no doubt someone is up there on the third floor.

37 LOURDES HIGH SCHOOL

Location:	4034 West 56th Street, Chicago.
Type of occurrence:	Ghost nun haunts top floor of Catholic girls' school and school hall.
Characteristics:	Phantom footsteps are common, a shadowy image has been reported. Elevator moving by itself also thought to be a part of haunting.
Status:	Student belief in ghost is still current. Sporadic reports continue.

THE PRIEST WHO NEVER RETIRED

ST. TURIBIUS CHURCH

Roman Catholic St. Turibius Church is located on the southwest side of Chicago, one mile east of Midway Airport. A large percentage of the parishioners are Polish and Polish-American with many foreign-born. The neighborhood also has a good representation of Hispanic, Irish, and Italian families. Middle class and mostly single-family homes, it is considered a quiet, conservative part of the city.

One man deserves much of the credit for the neighborhood's high reputation, a former pastor, Father Joe Lechert. Guiding his flock of Baby Boomers during the Cold War years, Father Lechert ran the parish with a firm but guiding hand. The school, church, hall building, and physical plant were always under his watchful eye. In those days, the local pastor was almost autonomous. Decisions of how to spend parish monies and what jobs had priorities were all his to make. There were no cumbersome church bureaucrats or parish committees to deal with. The pastor was respected and powerful. It was the way things had been since pioneer days in America.

Change came to the archdiocese of Chicago when John Cardinal Cody arrived on the scene. A centrist with no use for the old ways of strong pastors and semiautonomous parishes, he soon began to change the financial face of the Catholic Church locally. The purse strings were now controlled by downtown bean counters, and pastors were ordered to toe the new line. For pastors who had operated for decades independent of outside control, who had nursed their congregations through financial hard times and national emergencies, this was a bitter pill to swallow. For them, this new corporate behemoth was the antithesis of their faith.

Holdout pastors soon found themselves forced into a form of early retirement. Those resisting change found themselves named "pastor emeritus" and were essentially stripped of all real power. This sad treatment was meted out to Father Lechert and a number of other area priests.

The psychological blow to Lechert proved too much for him to bear. Shortly after his removal from power, he died of a heart attack. Friends of the priest described it as a broken heart.

But Father Lechert, who had for some two decades guided and guarded St. Turibius Parish, was not about to let go. His presence remains, vibrant and active, as a ghost still dutifully acting as pastor.

My family moved into this parish in the late 1960s. Living just around the corner from our new parish church, I began to hear tales that Father Lechert haunted the building. I had no solid confirmation of these stories until a few years later.

In June 1974, a new priest was assigned to the staff of St. Turibius. Father Marc Pasciak was a seminarian with me at Quigley South in the early 1960s. It was good to have an old friend stationed at my family's parish. He stayed at this assignment until 1979.

In many of our conversations, the topic of the supernatural was brought up. Father Pasciak confirmed that Father Lechert did indeed haunt St. Turibius. Although, Father Marc

St. Turibius Church

had never personally seen the ghost, he had heard from a number of witnesses who had. Reports were often from altar boys in the church.

"Some of the servers spoke to me," Father Marc remembered, "about a figure they had seen when the lights were turned off. They said that a priest was walking down the aisle with a strange hat on and that he walked funny."

The hat they described was a biretta, a square hat with a tassel, out of style for years, once popular with monsignors of the Catholic Church. Lechert was known to wear a biretta. The unusual walk also indicated Lechert, as he had suffered a stroke a number of years before his death that affected his walk and his posture.

"The boys wouldn't know about a biretta or know anything about Lechert's ailments," Father Marc concluded. "It's enough to convince me."

In the sacristy of the church, an unusual scent of cigarette smoke is sometimes encountered. No one would ever think to smoke inside the church, but years ago, Father Lechert, a heavy smoker, sometimes did. Many take this seemingly psychic scent as another sign from the dead pastor.

Besides haunting the church's interior, Lechert's ghost has been seen walking around parish buildings. He is always looking down, preoccupied, it seems, inspecting the foundations of the buildings to make sure that things are all right.

The Roman Catholic Church in America is currently suffering from a severe shortage of priests. This is especially true in the Chicago diocese. At St. Turibius Church on Chicago's South Side, however, there will always be one priest that can be counted upon, ever loyal and vigilant, the ghost of Father Joe Lechert.

38 St. Turibius Church

Location:	5646 South Karlov Avenue, Chicago.
Type of occurrences:	Former pastor haunts church and grounds as an apparition and sometimes indicates presence by scent of cigarette smoke.
Characteristics:	Someone so actively involved with their job feels obligated to continue even after death.
Status:	Sporadic but active.

A HAUNTED CASTLE

Beverly's Irish Castle

The Beverly area on the south side of Chicago is well known as a neighborhood of beautiful homes and mansions. Historical plaques are found in front of many homes, especially along Longwood Drive. The Irish Castle is architecturally the most interesting home in Beverly. For over a century, this stone fortress has stood on the high ground of the "Ridge" and has come to symbolize the neighborhood. The local community organization, BAPA (the Beverly Area Planning Association) depicted this building on its logo.

The builder of the Irish Castle was an Irish American named Robert C. Givins, who had made a fortune in real estate around Chicago during the 1880s. The flamboyant Givins was a promoter who used all sorts of gimmicks to attract attention to his business. He once gave a free house lot away by releasing a number of helium balloons at a promotion. One balloon had a deed attached and the finder was to be given the free lot. Years later, a farmer near Summit found the deed in a tin container while plowing on his farm.

But Givins, the master promoter, also had another side. He was the author of a widely read book, *A Rich Man's Fool.*

Givens made a grand tour of Europe. He had a love of Irish history, and while in Ireland, he made sketches of a long-abandoned castle that would later serve as the inspiration for the dream home he built in Chicago. The finest materials were used inside and out for his castle. Limestone blocks were quarried from the Lemont area, a canary yellow stone sometimes called "Athens Marble." The three-story structure is topped by four serrated turrets. Inside were 15 rooms, with a massive living room thirty-six feet long and twenty-four feet wide. The first-floor ceiling stood twenty-four feet high. Tapestries collected by Givins decorated the walls and a medieval look was accomplished overall, except for one design change. Instead of arrow slits, modern windows were a concession to the current age. Givins completed his castle in 1886.

Givins and his wife and son moved into the home upon its completion, but happiness would seem to elude Givens. The ideal retirement haven that Givins hoped for was not to be, and in 1908, the home was sold to John B. Burdett.

In 1920, Dr. Miroslaw Siemens of the Chicago Ukrainian Society bought the castle. The castle was also for a time the home of the Chicago Female College and a boarding school for young girls. For the past fifty years, the castle has been home to the Beverly Unitarian Church.

The majority of ghost stories told about the Irish Castle date to the time after it became a church. With so many more people coming and going for church activities, more attention was given to the site and more neighborhood people claimed personal incidents.

For years in the wee hours of the morning, Beverly neighbors have noticed strange lights, like flickering candle flames in the windows. No church services were being conducted at those odd hours, and electrical lights certainly would be used by anyone up and about in the church, not old-fashioned candles, unless these candles of another time were being carried by people of long ago.

The best-known tale about the castle dates from the early 1960s. A night watchman was on duty on a cold wintry evening. As he made his rounds through the building he was shocked

*Beverly Unitarian Church,
the "Irish Castle"*

to see a young blond girl in a white dress come out of nowhere. She spoke to him for a minute with an Irish lilt and then seemed to disappear. The watchman went to the outer door to open it and look outside. A layer of freshly fallen snow covered the ground and there were no footprints. She had not left but was not still inside, so where was she? What was she?

The story goes that the watchman spoke to the minister the next day and then promptly quit his job.

Reverend Roger Brewin served as the minister here from 1980 to 1991. This was during the centennial celebrations of the building and during its restoration work. He is a believer in many of the tales. "I think it is haunted in the sense that it inspires stories, highly credible, about the supernatural," he says. "I heard accounts directly from the people who experienced them." Reverend Brewin thinks that the little girl ghost is highly believable. He has heard various reports of her sighting in the building. In an account that he heard from a former tenant who lived in a third-floor apartment, the little girl ghost seems to have come back on yet another wintry night.

The woman was entertaining a friend in her apartment when the two ladies were startled by sudden loud banging at the front door. Her friend offered to go downstairs and check. As she opened the door, she found a little girl, cold and wet, as a snowstorm raged all around. Letting the child into the building, she heard the girl mumbling something about "being home."

The woman then ran upstairs to report on the strange visitor. Her friend asked, "Was she wearing a white dress?" She continued, quite aware of what the visitor was, "Did she speak with an Irish brogue?"

Reverend Brewin concluded the story by stating that, "Both women then hurried downstairs only to find a puddle of water from the melted snow on the floor."

The pretty little child is seemingly fond of parties. According to Reverend Brewin, she has been seen at a number of events; however, he noted, "Later, upon checking, he learned that there was no real little girl present." Reverend Brewin may never have seen this famous little girl ghost of the Castle, but he did have a first hand encounter with a strange auditory phenomenon in the early 1980s.

During the Christmas season each year, the church sells Christmas trees as a fundraiser in their parking lot behind the castle. After closing up the tree sales late one night, about 10:30 p.m., Reverend Brewin walked up the back stairs to the rear door of the church. As he entered the building, he recalled that he heard sounds, primarily music, but also voices and laughter. "These sounds of a party were coming from the church sanctuary on the first floor adjacent to where I was. I pulled open the two wooden doors and stepped into the room. It was empty and the sounds completely died away. When I went back into the entry room area, the party noises started again, and it was clear that they were coming from the sanctuary."

His curiosity aroused, Reverend Brewin went back in a second time, turned all the lights on, and walked around the room. The sounds again stopped when he entered the big room. "When I was standing in the entry room, that was the old kitchen," Reverend Brewin said." The sanctuary, where the sounds were coming from, was originally the dining room, where the parties would have taken place. It was the same room where the little girl was reportedly seen on several occasions."

Reverend Brewin tried to find a natural explanation for the party noises. He thought at first that maybe the cold night air and the old windows might have somehow been responsible for the situation. But there was no easy answer. "What puzzled me was that when I stepped into the room, I couldn't hear the sounds at all. It was audible only from one specific spot."

Another woman who had lived in an upstairs apartment of the castle told Reverend Brewin of related incidents. She told him she heard the same kind of sounds coming up the stairs, but when she came downstairs, no one was there, and the sounds stopped. This went on for a period of time until she found that yelling at the ghostly sounds would silence them. When she yelled down the stairs, "I'm trying to sleep!" the party sounds would cease.

The current pastor of the congregation is the Reverend Leonetta Bugliosi. She has had two very vivid experiences with apparitions at the castle, the first during her installation service.

"It was February 27, 1994, at my installation," she recalls. "I was on the second floor talking with some well-wishers when I noticed two very slim arms, those of a young woman, reach around from behind my husband's back and around his waist."

At first she thought it was someone saying good-by; then, she realized there was no one there. "My husband felt nothing," she added.

Four years later in February of 1998, Reverend Bugliosi had another sighting. "I saw a black cloak scurrying down the stairs to the second floor," she said. "There was a woman working upstairs, and I thought it was her walking down, so I called to her."

The woman upstairs was still there when Reverend Bugliosi checked. Although she didn't see more than just the flash of material as it went down the stairs and not the full figure, she believes this could only have been the ghost. "I heard that sometimes the ghost was on the third floor," Bugliosi said.

A number of the older homes in the Beverly area have legends and ghostlore associated with them, but all agree that the most haunted house in Beverly is the Irish Castle.

39 The Beverly Unitarian Church

Location: 10244 South Longwood Drive, Chicago.
Type of occurrence: Traditional apparition, strange lights and sounds.
Characteristics: Haunted house type occurrences that seem to remain from the heyday of this building before the dawn of the 20th century.
Status: Sporadic but ongoing over the years.

THE HUNGRY FENCE

MOUNT OLIVET CEMETERY

The southwest side neighborhood of Mount Greenwood was originally founded by Dutch farmers. Times changed, and the once pastoral community was eventually annexed by the City of Chicago. Its new claim to fame is being the home of more City Hall employees, police, and firefighters than any other section of Chicago.

Humorist John Powers wrote about the Mount Greenwood neighborhood in his autobiographical books, *The Last Catholic in America* and *Do Black Patent Leather Shoes Really Reflect Up?* Powers nicknamed the area "Seven Holy Tombs" because of the number of cemeteries located here. One tale that Powers never wrote about, however, is the legend of "the hungry fence" at Mount Olivet Cemetery.

More than a century old, Catholic Mount Olivet Cemetery has a large population of Irish graves. It also boasts of being the original gravesite of Al Capone. But in the 1970s, its historical importance was overshadowed as a tale of a supernatural menace, "the hungry fence," began to unfold.

Young people in the area know the route down 111th Street very well. It leads to a number of popular pubs from Western to Pulaski Avenues.

In the later 1970s, a series of strange traffic accidents began to occur here. Anyone could fall victim.

You drive down the street approaching the low rise between Western and Kedzie Avenues, and the next thing you know, you are crashing into the fence of Mount Olivet Cemetery. For some, it is a blackout, then a crash; for others; a strange compulsion or possession seems to take hold. Since many of those who crash are completely sober, the local Irish bars are definitely not to blame.

The colorful term, "the hungry fence," was coined by longtime Mount Greenwoodian, Terry McEldowney, around 1978. Terry, a financial investor by day, is better known by his part-time work as an Irish folksinger. He is a co-author of the anthem of the area, "The South Side Irish," that has sold a 100,000 copies.

Since 1976, Terry has been a popular performer at local Irish bars, especially Reilly's Daughter Pub at 111th and Pulaski, just a few minutes drive west of Mount Olivet. As part of his closing at the end of performances, he began to sign off with a warning to his audience to "be careful, and beware of the hungry fence."

As Terry recalls, "About 1978, while going home at night, I noticed that all manner of cars seemed to be "magnetized" into the Mount Olivet fence, so I started calling it the 'hungry fence.' I lived on Maplewood," Terry continued," and I had to drive right by the fence on my way to Reilly's. So I had to watch that I didn't get drawn into it."

Chicago Fireman Joe Jamen has the unique distinction of having been involved in two accidents at the notorious fence. "I hit it the first time in 1979, and then about six months later in 1980," Joe recalls. "The first time I was heading east from the Fr. Perez Knights of Columbus Hall just about ten o'clock at night. It was just like I was magnetized. I drove right into the fence."

"Hungry Fence"

When Joe discussed this accident later at the firehouse, he learned about others, including other firemen, who had hit the fence. After he was involved in his second accident at the fence, he began to avoid that stretch of roadway whenever possible.

It was not the fence at all that was the problem, but the rows upon rows of shiny tombstones just inside. At night, the reflections of headlights from passing traffic and the tall street lamps flash hundreds of times. Since motorists were concentrating on the road directly ahead, these flickering lights played havoc with them.

But is there a natural explanation for the strange powers this fence seemed to wield over passing motorists? It seems the answer is the psychological effect known as the "flicker phenomena."

For instance, you are driving down a straight road at 30 or 40 miles an hour, and the flashing lights on your left in your peripheral vision distract you slightly, so that a slight turn on the steering wheel toward that diversion can within seconds have you drifting across the road, crossing over the median, jumping the curb and feeding the "hungry fence."

The effect is similar to "white line fever," watching the lines on the highway become white dots as you speed up and disassociate.

Oddly, just across the street from the hungry fence is Mount Greenwood Cemetery. It was seldom the scene of an accident, undoubtedly because the geography here was totally different from its sister cemetery across the street. At Mount Greenwood Cemetery, the gravestones are flush with the ground or set much further away from the road. There were no stones positioned to reflect the lights.

On certain weekends during its heyday, there could be as many as three or four accidents along that stretch of road. From the late 1970s into the early '90s, the accidents continued in steady numbers, then they dropped off dramatically. In 1993, traffic accidents mangled so much of the old fence that most of the decades-old wrought iron bars were replaced by modern chain-link fencing. With these vertical bars gone, the "Doppler effect" lessened. The groundsmen also planted thick shrubbery along much of the fence line, shielding many stones from view.

Although the answer to the enigmatic "hungry fence" seems to be just a strange optical illusion, the legend lives on. There is hardly a Mount Greenwoodian around who doesn't offer a quick nod to their St. Christopher medal as their car climbs the high ground while passing by Mount Olivet's legendary barrier.

40 Mount Olivet Cemetery

Location: 2755 West 111th Street, Chicago.
Type of occurrence: Series of unexplained car crashes blamed on possible supernatural influences.
Characteristics: Motorists black out and crash into cemetery fence or have uncontrollable urge to ram it.
Status: Formerly quite common, now rare.

THE GRINNING PHANTOM

NOCTURNAL JAYWALKER OF ST. CASIMIR CEMETERY

The Mount Greenwood neighborhood on Chicago's southwest side was nicknamed "Seven Holy Tombs" by local humorist John Powers because of the seven cemeteries found here. The furthest cemetery west, jutting into the suburbs of Oak Lawn and Alsip, is St. Casimir Cemetery. Originally called St. Casimir Lithuanian Cemetery, this Catholic cemetery was initially founded for immigrants from Lithuania and their descendants.

Driving along 111th or 115th Streets heading west from Pulaski Road, you realize the well-lit and bright Chicago streets quickly are transformed into ill-lit, darker suburban roadways. Automatically, you become a more cautious motorist, watching the road and wary of the shadows on either side.

A number of those who have driven this area have had the unnerving experience of encountering a dark-garbed figure. The image suddenly appears in the path of your car. You take evasive action, swerving to avoid hitting the image. You are frustrated and almost angry. You glance up at your rear view mirror only to discover the mystery figure has disappeared.

The figure is usually described as a tall, thin man in dark, tight-fitting clothes. His pale face is unforgettably etched in one's mind. His lips are curled back in a grotesque configuration spelling fear or horror. Because of the toothy grin, this image has been called the "St. Casimir vampire," as well as the more common "cemetery phantom." But he is no true vampire. There are no accounts of blood sucking from this area. Then why the exaggerated teeth?

The first report I uncovered about this apparition was from September 27, 1979. I happened to cross paths with a former neighbor of mine, Mary Agnes Hogan, at a Western Avenue restaurant. "I was just going to call you", Mary said. "I think I saw a ghost last night."

Still somewhat shaken by her experience, Mary gave me a very detailed account of her curious encounter. "I was driving down 115th Street between Central and Cicero where the railroad tracks cross the road," Mary said. " Directly in front of my car, it's a '79 Caprice Classic, this person appeared. He had a grinning, frightened, hysterical type of look. His lips were wide; his mouth was open; his teeth were bared. His hands were up, crossed in front of his face, like he was gesturing me to stop."

Mary Agnes reacted instinctively: "I just hit the brakes and swerved into the next lane and then veered back into my lane." Mary continued. "I stopped the car and looked back and didn't see anybody. I turned around and came back, and I looked on both sides of the road but I didn't see anything."

Mary then drove home to her apartment and found a neighbor. The two both went back to the location to check. However, Mary still wasn't totally convinced that she had not hit a real person.

"We got out of the car and looked on both sides of the road," Mary said. "We walked up and down the road. There was nothing."

Mary Agnes, a City Colleges employee, had a fine eye for detail. She could describe exactly what the figure looked like and what he wore.

St. Casimir's Cemetery

"He wore dark pants, dark blue or black, and a silk-looking shirt. His shirt was dark blue and had a swirl or circle design. He was very pale, and he had a full-head of sandy-blond, longish hair," Mary remembers.

After their search of the roadway, Mary's neighbor suggested that she might have seen the "Alsip vampire." Her cousin, Jack Ryan, also had heard about this ghost and he volunteered the same possibility.

Hearing such a detailed account from Mary Agnes, I began to make inquiries of my own in the area. It wasn't long before I found other similar reports. The locations varied somewhat, but the figure was seen along 111th Street, 115th Street, or Pulaski Road, always around or fairly near the St. Casimir Cemetery.

After gathering a collection these accounts, I began to use this story on some of my bus tours.

One evening in 1981 while leading a private tour for the Lake N Park Inn, a local country and western club, I had a breakthrough.

As I told the story of the St. Casimir's haunt, a voice from the back of the bus shouted out, "Its Ernie!" A woman soon came up to my seat behind the driver and anxiously told me about a former neighbor of hers.

Ernie, she said, was a disabled man who often walked this area in life. He was constantly walking the roads in the area around St. Casimir's Cemetery after dark, usually wearing dark clothing. But the dark clothing eventually cost him his life. He was struck and killed by a motorist who apparently didn't spot him in time. It was hit and run. Ernie's body was found sometime later. The frozen expression embedded onto his face when he died was the wide grimace of fear and pain, an expression that "Ernie the ghost" has borne ever since.

Someone on a later tour once suggested that Ernie's ghost may walk the area until "the killer returns to the scene of the crime."

That old adage about the killer returning is based on common sense. Ernie's killer was probably somebody in the general neighborhood, maybe even someone who finds himself or herself on a bus trip some evening. I always recommend, "If the guilty party is on board, you should confess and give up to the law rather than some night finding yourself confronting the eerie, restless spirit of Ernie."

Perhaps the motivation that fueled this haunting has cooled. Maybe Ernie no longer needs to walk because justice has been done by the death of the perpetrator.

To my knowledge, there have been no sightings of this ghost in recent years.

41 St. Casimir Cemetery

Location:	4401 West 111th Street, Chicago (and nearby roads.)
Type of occurrence:	Phantom figure seen prowling area by night.
Characteristics:	Figure seen dressed in dark clothing but has distinct pale skin and exaggerated grin on face. Appears in line of traffic, then disappears.
Status:	Many reports from late '70s and '80s. May now be dormant.

SUBURBAN CHICAGO
NORTH AND NORTHWEST

SUBURBAN CHICAGO NORTH AND NORTHWEST

SEAWEED CHARLIE

Drowning Victim Ghost of Evanston

Calvary Cemetery, an old Catholic cemetery from antebellum days, sits on an "S" curve on Sheridan Road where Chicago ends and Evanston begins.

Markers with crosses, crucifixes, and angels are abundant throughout the cemetery, and there are also many mausoleums. It has unique markers also that denote the departed person's occupation.

Many famous Irish figures from Chicago's past lie buried here including, Colonel James Mulligan, a Civil War hero, and Doctor Patrick H. Cronin. Cronin was a leading member, but also, murder victim in 1889 of the Clan-na-Gael, the American branch of an Irish nationalist organization. A more radical faction of this quasi-secret group disagreed with the direction Cronin wanted to take the organization and assassinated him.

This cemetery is halfway between and minutes away from two large universities, Loyola in Chicago and Northwestern in Evanston. Students from these schools have often found themselves driving late at night along the stretch of roadway next to Calvary.

Many people have heard about the Calvary Cemetery ghost for years. The most accepted story is that sometimes around midnight as a motorist approaches the "S" curve that snakes between the cemetery on one side and Juneway Park and the beach on the other, an image is caught in the glare of the driver's headlights. This soggy, dripping configuration of a man emerges from the breakwater, crawling or slouching across the road, heading towards the cemetery.

The more graphic retellings of the story literally describe the man trailing seaweed as he crosses the road, hence, his unofficial name, "Seaweed Charlie."

Tradition claims that the man is a drowning victim who drowned in Lake Michigan and whose body was eventually washed ashore at this site. Some versions of the story state that this man's body was never found and therefore was never given a proper burial. Perhaps, his being is cursed and remains restless, forever on a mission to find the blessed and consecrated ground of a Catholic cemetery, otherwise, he must haunt this spot until his earthly remains are found and disposed of properly.

There is some speculation of a connection to an historical plane crash that occurred on May 4, 1951. An instructor from the Glenview Naval Air station, flying an FH-1 Fathom, had a double flame out and landed on the lake just 200 yards east of Northwestern University. The pilot was seen alive on the wing waving his arms, but drowned before help could arrive. Two days later his body was found on the rocks adjacent to Calvary Cemetery.

The tales of Charlie the Ghost have been circulated widely along the North Shore since at least the 1960s and are still popular folklore.

On a pleasant summer night in 1993, shortly before midnight, two Columbia College students were driving southbound along Sheridan Road headed toward Chicago. Jenny Trisko was driving and chatting with her cousin, Lisa Becker, when they noticed traffic in front of them was swerving wildly.

They were in the middle of the "S" curve when they saw the reason for the commotion. A strange man in a long trench coat had come from the breakwater and was blindly crossing

*Breakwater in front of
Calvary Cemetery*

the road, heading toward the cemetery, paying no attention to the cars maneuvering to avoid hitting him.

Lisa Becker remembers the incident well. "It was too nice to be wearing a coat," Lisa stated. Although it was a clear, pleasant night, this enigmatic figure was unseasonably dressed in a heavy trench coat. To Lisa, his heavy garb only fueled the mystery.

"He was very thin and tall," Jenny Trisko recalls. "He did appear to be glowing."

"We saw a human form with almost an aura of light around him," Lisa affirms. "It was obvious it wasn't a person, but some form of light or being."

Neither Jenny nor Lisa had remembered hearing ghost stories about this location, but as they told their family and friends about their haunting experience, they soon learned more. "I was telling my boyfriend about my experience," Jenny said, then she added incredulously, "and his mother had seen the same guy, same location, ten years before."

From that night on, Jenny Trisko and Lisa Becker preferred not to take that route home after dark.

Evidently "Seaweed Charlie" cannot find rest. The stories about him remain remarkably similar. He seems to be drawn electromagnetically to the gleaming headlights of passing cars, and although appearing ambivalent, he may be asking for help.

Many eyewitness accounts from the area do seem to validate the belief that a ghost really does haunt the spot. At least, this one urban myth may be based on a kernel of truth.

42 Calvary Cemetery

Location:	301 Chicago Avenue, Sheridan Road side of Calvary Cemetery, Evanston.
Type of Occurrence:	Tradition of ghost seeking out consecrated ground may be motivation for this haunting of man entering or leaving cemetery near possible site of his death.
Characteristics:	Strange figure, sometimes crawling and dripping wet, sometimes walking.
Status:	Sporadic but continuing.

ONLY TENANT FOR 46 YEARS: A GHOST

A HAUNTED LAKESIDE ESTATE

L ake Forest is known for magnificent homes on large lots surrounded by majestic trees. It was here in 1913 that newlyweds Charles H. Schweppe and Laura Shedd were presented with an imposing brick and stone Tudor revival mansion as a wedding gift from the bride's father. The Schweppe Mansion, as it became known, was the largest private residence in a five-state area. Designed by architect Frederick Wainwright Perkins, the house was a massive 33,000 square feet sitting on twenty acres of prime North Shore real estate. It had twenty bedrooms and eighteen bathrooms and was perched on a ninety-foot bluff with a spectacular view of Lake Michigan. There were fabulous gardens surrounding the house and an outdoor swimming pool.

Fitting with their social standing, Charles and Laura Schweppe held lavish parties that attracted not only the movers and shakers of business and politics throughout the country, but also foreign royalty. Sweden's Crown Prince Gustavus Adolphus and Princess Louise stayed here for a time as guests, as did the Duke and Duchess of Windsor, Edward VIII and Wallis Simpson. The guest list was a Who's Who of power and prestige in post-World War I America.

The Schweppe family fortune began to unravel with the stock market crash of 1929. Charles, a financier, lost vast amounts of money during the Depression. His wife died in 1937 at the age of fifty-eight. Although she had inherited millions from her father and had a personal estate worth some $6 million, Laura left less than $200,000 to her husband in her will. The bulk of her wealth went to their two children.

If his financial future looked bleak, his health condition was even grimmer. Schweppe suffered from chronic insomnia. He was also being treated for a nervous condition. Eventually his monetary woes drove him to despair.

One night in 1941, a single gunshot rang through the mansion. Charles Schweppe had taken his own life with a bullet through his forehead. A small .32 caliber pistol was beside him in the bed. A note, unsigned, was on a dresser next to his bed reading, "I've been awake all night. It is terrible."

For whatever reasons, the heirs to the Schweppe estate decided not to live there or do anything else with the property. The house stood vacant for forty-six years. The home and grounds were maintained by a caretaker as the house remained frozen in time, just as it was in 1941 at the time of Schweppe's suicide.

Neighborhood stories spread about how Schweppe had planned one day to return. A dinner table was said to be set, prepared for his eventual homecoming. The temperature at the house was always kept cool at a constant 55 degrees. Schweppe believed in reincarnation, so the local legends relate, and his homecoming might be in either human or animal guise.

In 1987, progress finally caught up with the Schweppe Mansion. Donna Denton, the restorer and renovator of four other historic properties, acquired the estate for $5.5 million. Donna's family planned to live there and tackle the challenge of undoing decades of emptiness and neglect.

Mayflower Place

A grand party was planned to show off the legendary home to neighbors and friends shortly after the new owners bought the estate. It was to be a night of fine food and drink and, of course, ghost stories. A mutual friend told Donna about me and my ghost research around greater Chicagoland, and I was invited to play a part in the big gala.

On Friday night, April 7, 1987, over 100 guests were on hand, anxious to tour the legendary mansion. For most it was the chance of a lifetime, an opportunity to see a home that was shuttered in the era of their parents or grandparents. This was the house that three generations of north suburbanites considered haunted. All the old ghost stories were re-hashed as we prowled the home from basement to attic in search of anything paranormal.

A legend was recalled that, years before, a pregnant maid was found dead in the eleva-tor. Since that time, the elevator had a mind of its own and would move between floors by itself with sound effects, clanking and banging. Schweppe's bedroom was pointed out and said to be a place of dread and despair.

The wildest tale recounted was that of the devil's footprint discovered in the concrete floor of an upstairs room. In the center of the floor, a clear but misshapen footprint was imprinted into the concrete. It was somewhat human in general shape, but twisted as if a foot had been broken and not properly set to heal.

How such an imprint came to be in the center of a concrete floor with all the cement around it perfectly smooth, caused much discussion that night.

Charles Schweppe himself starred in the most popular ghost tale of the evening. The story of "Schweppe's window" is not only a good yarn, but also one with physical evidence to back it up. Beautiful leaded glass windows were created for the mansion; however, only one window offers a clear view of the path leading up to the front door. From this second floor perch, Schweppe's ghost was believed to watch for those who entered his property. One section of cut glass in this old window, and one section alone, was always kept clean. Over the years the windows became dirt and grime encrusted from neglect, except for this one pane. The ghost was said to rub the piece of glass clean to see outside.

During the restoration work that Donna Denton undertook on the mansion, the old leaded glass windows were temporarily removed to be releaded. When no longer in place, the pane that had faced the driveway became dirty like the other panes in the window. There was no need for the ghost to rub that section clean once it was removed.

The Schweppe Mansion now goes by the name of Mayflower Place. The cobwebs, dust, and neglect are gone, and the long vacant haunted house of the North Shore is once again an architectural gem. It sports a well-deserved listing in the National Register of Historic Places.

Mayflower Place now houses Donna Denton's magnificent collections of art and antiques that rival anything to be found in the days of the original owners. There have been no ghostly manifestations since the restoration work has been completed. Perhaps that is because Charles Schweppe is pleased with the results.

Visitors to Mayflower Place are overwhelmed by its many facets. The sheer size of the home is as breathtaking as its contents. The view of Lake Michigan to the east is stunning. There is a sense that the past is still present. But there is also an otherworldly feeling.

Shelly Chapman of P.P.S. Promotions, who since 1990 has assisted Donna Denton in managing the property, said, "The house has an attitude. The whole feel of the house is paranormal."

Mayflower Place is available for private parties on a limited basis. Maybe on a stormy night when a full moon hangs in the sky, the magic will be just right for the long awaited return of Charles Schweppe. The guests at that party will certainly be in for an evening they will never forget.

43 MAYFLOWER PLACE, FORMERLY, SCHWEPPE MANSION

Location:	405 North Mayflower Road, Lake Forest.
Type of occurrence:	Traditional haunted house.
Characteristics:	Folkloric tales but some physical manifestations.
Status:	No activity noted since recent renovations.

GOT THE SCHOOL SPIRIT

Chapel Ghosts at a Co-ed College

Barat College occupies a picturesque campus, with thirty acres of lawn, woods, and gentle rolling ravines located in Lake Forest, an old, affluent suburb north of Chicago set along the shore of Lake Michigan. Barat began as an academy for young women in Chicago in 1858. It was named for Saint Madeleine Sofie Barat, a religious, who founded the Society of the Sacred Heart in France in 1800. Her commitment was to give young women a strong educational foundation. In 1904, the school moved to Lake Forest. The college became co-educational in 1982.

The Old Main Building, a Georgian Revival structure, is the college center that houses faculty and administrative offices, most of the classrooms, and the chapel.

I had the pleasure of being invited to Barat College to present a program of storytelling for students and guests one night near Halloween in 1984. As the people sat comfortably around a dimly lit room near a glowing fireplace in the student lounge, outside the fall air had turned crisp and the branches of stately trees swayed, softly nudging their leaves to the ground. The setting and mood were perfect as I regaled the listeners recounting local area ghost stories.

After finishing my stories and answering questions from the audience, a young woman hesitantly mentioned that Barat College was considered haunted. More specifically, there were stories of unusual occurrences that focused around the chapel. My curiosity was piqued. Within minutes, all of us enthusiastically headed down the long corridors towards the chapel, the supposed area of psychic unrest, on our own ghost hunt.

The chapel itself has changed very little since its construction. It is an old-fashioned Catholic chapel with a carved altar, antique wooden pews, and some pews arranged along the wall in choir stall fashion. It was a custom for the religious to face one another during the liturgical services. There are traditional fixtures of saints and religious figures carved into the wall and a magnificent refurbished pipe organ. The candelabras hang from the vaulted ceiling, and the stained glass windows are two stories high. The chapel is where spiritual and cultural ceremonies and celebrations are conducted year after year.

As we reached the chapel, we noticed a strong scent of flowers, which came and went. It seemed to be strongest along the corridor just outside the chapel. At first, I thought that the scent must be due to flowers in the immediate area, but my search of the area revealed there were none. There was nothing "natural" about this.

Soon, I was leading a number of students around the chapel and out into the corridor searching for the "flower patches." There were a number of places by the stairwell, a few feet across from the chapel, where we would suddenly walk into a "wall of flowers," an olfactory barrier. Once we passed through the aura, everything was normal again.

As we retraced our steps, we found that there was a range of space, or "spot," where the scent could be picked up, but if we moved a couple of feet in any direction, the scent was gone. The scent did not trail off when we moved slightly. It was either very strong or not there at all.

Barat College

Catherine McCole, one of the students in the group, had a slightly different experience. She said that she smelled both roses and candles, and the scents were very obvious to her. However, she remembered, "It was just on the stairs. Once we would hit the landing, we couldn't smell it."

Catherine was so intrigued by the phenomenon that she later did research on the chapel's history and uncovered a possible explanation. "We talked with a nun who had been with the school for many years," she said.

This nun told Catherine that Barat College has had several decades of ceremonies that included the presence of flowers. One of the college's earliest and best-loved traditions was a Daisy Chain ceremony, which she thought, began in the thirties. A long chain of real daisies interwoven with fern was used in the ceremony. After a chapel ceremony, the students proceeded through the front doors of the main building and to the Scared Heart Statue, positioned duly prominent on the front grounds. The juniors and seniors each formed a circle around the statue and the senior class handed the daisy chain to the junior class. This very formal affair symbolized the forging of bonds and hope for the future.

In the last twenty years, the college has presented an annual Rose and Candle ceremony. It is both a spiritual and social occasion. During the convocation in the chapel, the seniors pass the candles to the junior students "to preserve the light of knowledge," and the juniors pass the roses to the seniors "to signify the growth and beauty that will be unfolding in their future."

The students carried the long-stem roses and the lighted taper candles down the stairs from the chapel in the exact area where the phantom scents occurred to Catherine and her friends. During her time at Barat College, Catherine experienced the mystery scent four times, always in the same area immediately on the stairway.

Finding a haunting is one thing. Learning the reason for it is sometimes more difficult. Is this floral scent caused by one particular incident in the school's past, perhaps tied to one early day student? Or could the psychic scent be something caused by years of collective activity, the repetitive ceremonies that were held with the daisies, then the roses and candles?

Here is a psychic tradition to replay alongside the living traditions of a famous college.

44 Barat College

Location:	700 East Westleigh Road, Lake Forest.
Type of occurrence:	Psychic scent.
Characteristics:	A strong floral scent, probably roses, encountered in well-defined "spots" around the chapel.
Status:	Sporadic but seemingly ongoing.

The soil cries murderer

Lot of the John Wayne Gacy Murder House

A common manifestation in European folklore involves nature itself, exposing an evil deed. Murder, in particular, it was said, cannot be hidden. The spot where a corpse is buried will be exposed due to barren ground, a sterile patch of soil that draws attention and leads to the discovery of the dastardly deed.

Such an occurrence seems to have happened in suburban Chicago in the case of the greatest mass murderer in the annals of American criminal justice, John Wayne Gacy.

Gacy owned a small construction and maintenance company for his livelihood, but was also a Democratic Party precinct captain and active member of the Jaycees. He was famous for throwing lavish parties where he often entertained the children of his neighbors and business associates as "Pogo the Clown." He once had his photo taken with the then-First Lady, Rosalynn Carter. Despite this public posturing, Gacy was a man with a dark side. An overachiever in private life and business, he would become an overachiever in murder as well.

He lured young men to his home near O'Hare Airport. Reportedly, he would drug and forcefully subdue them and perform sexual acts, then torture and kill them to keep them from talking and to keep his reputation as "normal" intact.

Finding himself with incriminating dead bodies on his hands, Gacy began to hide corpses in the crawl space beneath his home, under a shed in his back yard and even beneath his barbecue pit. Finally, he just ran out of room. The last of his victims, just before he was caught, were dumped into the nearby Des Plaines River.

Local police investigations finally zeroed in on Gacy after so many of the young men who had disappeared were found to have had ties to him and his construction company. Search warrants, surveillances, and the questioning of associates gave the police their break-through. In late December 1978, a body was found buried in the crawl space of Gacy's home, then another, and another.

Eventually he would be convicted in criminal court of thirty-three murders, but the number of deaths may have been even higher. He was put to death for these heinous crimes May 9, 1994. Opponents of the death penalty were against this decision; some believing his life should be spared in order that he could be clinically studied.

There were a number of psychic connections to the Gacy case that attracted my interest from the beginning. Some of the victims' families had hired psychics to aid them in their search when the police seemed unable to assist. One ominous incident occurred by chance.

It was a pre-Christmas party on a cold Saturday night, December 2, 1978. Florece, nee Florence Branson, a well-known local psychic, was hired to give each guest a psychic reading with her euchre deck. The party was being held in the home of a contractor associate of Gacy.

The night was almost over when it came time for Gacy to have his fortune told. Florece became physically ill when she saw his hand and interpreted the cards. The psychic could not discern details but did pick up that Gacy was a deviate who was a multiple murderer. She bluffed her way through the reading, much too frightened to divulge her findings to Gacy.

Former lot of Gacy house, soil barren where bodies were buried.

Florece wrapped up the evening's readings, but before leaving, she divulged to her hostess what she saw in the chunky contractor's cards. "I'm afraid of him," she confided. "He's perverted and violent."

The hostess refused to hear such things about "John," a friend of the family for years. Florece didn't argue, but trusted her cards. She left the party that night and went home to a sick bed. Within weeks the story broke and the psychic was proven right.

I later asked Florece how she could be so positive about Gacy's killer status. Florece replied, "I have entertained at Italian restaurants for years, and I had read cards for hit men a number of times. I have an ability to pick up on those things."

By late January of 1979, the former Gacy residence at 8213 West Summerdale was just a muddy, vacant lot. All vestiges of the house, driveway, even the barbecue pit were dismantled and hauled away in the hunt for bodies. The lot, conspicuous as the only vacant site on the block, was a local tourist attraction of sorts, visited by curiosity seekers who drove through the previously quiet residential area.

I visited and photographed the lot at least three times between 1979 and 1981. By the spring of 1981, there was no doubt in my mind that something unusual was taking place at the still empty lot. Although close to eighteen months had passed since the house was demolished, the empty lot was still strangely barren in the area where the building had previously stood. Two overlapping, roughly oval sections of soil were still without any vegetation at all. There was some weed growth in the front of the lot near the sidewalk, but the back section of the lot, where the house had stood and where the bodies were hidden, was devoid of any plant life.

There was absolutely no logical reason for that soil to be bare.

The strange sterile patch of ground at the Gacy lot was confirmed by Pat Jones, a former Cook County Sheriff's Police Officer who worked the case gathering crime scene evidence when the murders were first uncovered. Jones was with Cook County from 1968 to 1989 and still remembers the Gacy case as his most harrowing.

Jones was on the team of police responsible for the recovery of the bodies from the site. He said that to preserve evidence, the bodies had to be removed with almost archaeological precision. The shallow graves were unearthed with tools that looked like large soupspoons and all soil had to be sifted for evidence. Eventually, floors had to be removed and then the entire house, by then just a shell, was demolished.

"We brought in a backhoe to go down eight to ten feet to make sure nothing was missed," Jones remembered. For a little over a month, the site was dug up by evidence technicians, then put back. By the end of the investigation, twenty-nine bodies had been retrieved from the lot.

Jones realized that there was something unusual taking place at the lot the spring after the bodies were removed. Jones recalled, "One of our guys went up there after everything was torn down and took a photograph, and there wasn't anything growing there. It was just totally barren."

Trying to find a natural explanation, Jones and other police at first suspected that the lime that Gacy had used to dust the corpses might be the answer. They had to drop that theory after some further research.

"There was some lime sprinkled over the bodies, but after a period of time lime mixes with the rest of the soil. And the lime was only in the crawl space which was under about two-thirds of the house and did not extend under the family room in the back. There was, of course, no lime under the garage or in the backyard. So, there wasn't a whole lot of lime down there," Jones said.

With his curiosity up, Jones kept an eye on the location: "Periodically during that summer, we just drove by the place every once and a while. It continued to look barren, except for a couple of weeds here and there, but no real vegetation."

Jones finally stopped driving by the site. He concluded, "I needed to put that part of my life behind me."

The riddle of the sterile soil lasted for a few years, then the house lot was sold and a new home built on the infamous site. The new owners even went to the trouble of having the address changed to remove the stigma. Fortunately, their efforts worked. There is a rebirth. The grass grows normally. Psychic unrest is no longer at this location.

The authorities have closed the books on this case, but it might not be closed psychically. Rumors have cropped up about other locations.

John Wayne Gacy was convicted of thirty-three murders, but is that number complete? His construction company did business throughout the Chicago area. Could there be another body buried beneath a southwest side roller skating rink's concrete floor? Or a victim plastered inside the wall of a north side church?

Psychic clues could surface and lead to further discoveries.

45 Death House

Location:	Formerly 8213 West Summerdale Avenue, Norwood Park.
Type of occurrence:	Supernatural sign.
Characteristics:	The soil in most of the lot where the Gacy house once stood was totally sterile for a period of years.
Status:	Location no longer has psychic unrest, but rumors have surfaced about other sites.

jet Crash Hauntings

Crash Site Flight 191

O n the Friday afternoon of Memorial Day weekend 1979, May 25, the greatest air disaster on American soil, and in our country's aviation history, happened when American Airlines Flight 191 crashed after takeoff from Chicago's O'Hare Airport. All on board were killed, as well as two on the ground, when the DC-10 lost an engine upon takeoff and plowed straight into the ground. The death toll was 173.

The flight, meant to be nonstop Chicago to Los Angeles was full of fuel for the cross-country trip. When the jet crashed the fuel exploded in a fireball, sending a small mushroom cloud into the air. The dark smoke was visible for many miles in the distance.

Every great tragedy seems to leave a legacy of psychic and ghostly tales. Even before the crash was a reality, a Cincinnati man dreamed of the event nine times in great detail. He saw an airliner crash just as 191 would. He plainly saw the American Airlines markings on the jet. Night after night he awoke in a cold sweat plagued by this nightmare. He alerted the FAA about his visions, but nothing could be done. What airport? What particular flight? All American flights could not be grounded based upon a dream. Only after the crash was the prediction proven true. The worst part of a psychic vision is not being able to change the inevitable.

People I have met over the years tell of another sort of psychic intervention prior to the crash. I have heard from those who tried to book that particular flight, only to give up when the American Airlines telephone line was constantly busy. They then gave up and booked other airlines—and lived. A friend decided to cancel his trip that day due to a bad cold and sore throat—a fateful choice.

Many on the flight that afternoon were writers and publishers. The annual convention of the American Booksellers Association was being held in Los Angeles over Memorial Day weekend, and the Chicago area was strongly represented. I lost a number of friends that day.

The crash site was not far from O'Hare. It was a strip of land between the Des Plaines Mobile Home Park and the Chicago K-9 training area. It was vacant ground for the most part, although fire damaged a number of mobile homes on the edge of the trailer park. Had the plane crashed just a short distance anywhere else nearby, the loss of life could have been staggering. It narrowly missed fuel storage tanks on Elmhurst Road and the nearby heavily traveled I-90 Expressway.

Ghost stories soon sprang up about the site of the crash. Within months of the disaster, motorists claimed that they could see tiny lights in the field where the jet crashed. A potential explanation, some thought, was some ghoul with a flashlight looking for diamonds believed to be lost when a jewel merchant was killed that day. But it is highly unlikely that anyone would be foolhardy enough to trespass near a K-9 dog training area. For many, ghost lights are a better answer.

I was originally told about these reports by a Des Plaines police officer. His department was the first to respond when calls came in regarding these strange lights. Officers who went to the scene never found anyone or anything.

In Europe, at the sites of ancient massacres or old battlefields, tiny flickering lights at night have been reported. These ghostly manifestations are known as "corpse candles," a

Des Plaines Mobile Home Park

Chicago Police Canine Training Facility

belief found from the Scottish Highlands to the Ural Mountains. Perhaps the O'Hare crash site lights are a modern version of this old belief.

But far more intriguing are the ghost accounts from residents of the Des Plaines Mobile Home Park adjacent to the crash area.

Residents have reported various psychic encounters. A very common auditory event is they hear footsteps approaching their trailer, a clanging noise coming up the metal stairs, and then someone rapping on their door. When they answer the door, no one is there.

A variation of this encounter is when they open their door they find a frazzled figure saying something like, "I have to get my luggage" or "I have to make a connection," the figure then turns and runs away. Although a prankster was suspected at first, no one has ever been apprehended during these bizarre episodes.

The tragedy caused a large number of residents to move. The turnover meant new people came in, many unaware of the tragic history next door. It wasn't long, however, before they too had psychic contact.

Ron Schroeder, now living in Minnesota, lived in mobile home #284 from 1988 until 1992. A musician in the popular rock bands, "Stancy" and "Bullet Proof Babies," with a CD to his credit, Ron had a number of encounters here after moving into his dad's trailer.

Although Ron's father had claimed certain experiences, Ron didn't become a believer until he had his own personal contact.

"My dad had bought the place in 1986," Ron recalled. "He would tell me that he'd feel someone get into bed with him and crawl over him."

When Ron's father moved, Ron and his girlfriend moved into the trailer. Ron said, "My girlfriend didn't know about the ghost stories, but she told me about two experiences. Something sat down next to her in bed. The only thing visible was the impression made on the mattress next to her."

Ron had his own ghostly encounters. "I noticed the doorknob shaking. My father still had a key and I thought that it was him. I opened the door and I looked out—there was no one there."

Ron quickly searched through the trailer but discovered he was alone. Ron was very shaken by the incident. He said, "I just decided to run. I left and went to a friend's house."

Hearing phantom footsteps is a commonplace phenomenon. Ron remembered, "I would hear footsteps. You would hear them bang on the stairs. I would hear footsteps inside the trailer, so I had to sleep with the radio on."

One night, Ron and his friend saw an actual apparition. "My friend was on an exercise bike and I was lying on the floor watching TV. It was about 10:30 p.m. My friend saw a man standing in the doorway and thought it was my dad. 'What's up?' he asked, but the stranger didn't answer." Puzzled, Ron's friend gave him a kick to get his attention. Ron recalled, "It was an old guy standing there wearing army boots and the old style green uniform. "I jumped up and said, 'I think you are in the wrong trailer,' and the old guy left. He didn't make any sounds when he stepped down the metal stairs. I ran to a side window, but there wasn't anyone there."

Ron experienced an odd glowing light outside his trailer for three nights in a row. "I could see a glow coming through the curtains. At first, I thought it was moonlight, but the light was moving straight up and down," Ron reported. By this time he was very accustomed to dealing with ghostly activity, so he just pulled the covers over his head and went to sleep.

As unbelievable as Ron Schroeder's experiences may appear, they are backed up by the testimony of others who have visited Lot #284.

Mike Kasprzak, a fellow musician, relates a bizarre vision he and others witnessed in the early 1990s:

"It was like a black shadow, a silhouette. Everyone saw it for an instant; then it was gone!"

Crash site of Flight 191, no traces of tragedy today.

On another visit as he was sitting on the couch, Mike recounts, "I felt somebody touch me on the back, and I got the shivers; all my hairs stood straight up. There was no one behind me, or no one nearby."

Today, more than two decades after the tragedy, the site no longer looks like a blackened pit from hell. Bulldozers have leveled the terrain, the burned, dead trees have been replaced by the living, and the grass is verdant once again. But despite the fact that the physical wounds on the land have been healed, the psychic scars run deep.

The historical importance of this site is ignored. The lost lives of those who died here go unrecognized. There is no historical marker or sign from any governmental agency to note the significance of this spot.

Only the ghosts remain.

46 CRASH SITE FLIGHT 191

Location:	Eastern edge of the Des Plaines Mobile Home Park, 500 West Touhy, Des Plaines.
Type of occurrences:	Numerous reports of ghostly activity ranging from ghost lights to phantom footsteps to apparitions.
Characteristics:	All activity revolves around area of jet crash and ties in with sudden death trauma of victims who may not know they are dead.
Status:	Seems ongoing.

GHOSTS STILL ON THE JOB

Victims Still Haunt Job Site

The Allstate Arena is owned and operated by the Village of Rosemont. This multi-use stadium opened in 1980 and rapidly became one of the premier entertainment and sports facilities in the Midwest. It seats 17,500 for sports events and almost 20,000 for rock concerts. It is home to the De Paul University Blue Demons, the Chicago Wolves hockey team, ice shows, circuses, pro wrestling, demolition derbies, and many other events. It also has a tradition of hauntings.

Originally named the Rosemont Horizon, this massive complex began its existence with tragedy, a roof collapse killed construction workers. But this accident could not stop progress. The entertainment center was finished and soon proved wildly successful for the village and surrounding area. Its prime location near O'Hare Airport and the constantly growing northwest suburban population boom fueled its popularity.

The many thousands of its attendees, however, had no idea that the building harbored unsettled spirits.

During various entertainment venues, there is no talk of ghosts. There is far too much in the way of distraction, noise, and excitement. Yet, late at night, when all have gone except for a handful of security, a different mood grips the complex. In the wee hours before dawn, there is time to listen, ponder, and perhaps experience the supernatural become reality.

Jerilyn Harsha, who now operates her own towing business, worked as a bartender at the Horizon for thirteen years from 1983 to 1995. "I never heard anything ghostly myself," she said. "But I was never there late at night. These things would happen long after the events were over." From her conversations with members of the security staff, she was impressed with their sincerity and openness when relating their own personal after hours experiences. Jerilyn became one of the converted.

"When they were building the Rosemont, three guys fell when the roof gave," Jerilyn recalled. "Everybody here always talked about it. Some of our guards told me they could hear hammering at night.

"There is an underground walkway from the Rosemont to the Skyline Room, and some people from security claimed that they could hear chains and footsteps down there."

Walking the beat through the property at night also could be unnerving. "One guard told me how he would make the rounds and heard the sounds of someone walking behind him," Jerilyn remembers

The ghost stories even spooked one officer so much that he was afraid to be alone in the building. "One auxiliary policeman had to have his desk in the vestibule; he wouldn't have it in the building, he was so scared," Jerilyn recalls.

Reports of ghosts were made only by the handful of security who worked very late, but these accounts became the topic of conversation with all the employees, day or night. The convictions of the small number of firsthand witnesses were enough to convince most of the employees there that something paranormal was indeed going on.

Corporate sponsorship came to the Rosemont Horizon in 1999. Allstate Insurance became a corporate backer, and the name of the Horizon was officially changed to the Allstate

Allstate Arena

Arena. A $20-million-dollar renovation program was embarked upon that included a completely new facade of the building, new signage, expansion of lobbies, and a reconfiguration of the lower level seating from squared contours to an arena-bowl.

All of these changes are material, however. As far as the ghosts are concerned, there is probably no change in sight. Many believe the facility will remain haunted for a long time to come.

47 ALLSTATE ARENA (FORMERLY ROSEMONT HORIZON)

Location:	6920 North Mannheim Road, Rosemont.
Type of occurrence:	Auditory experiences involving hammering sounds and phantom footsteps.
Characteristics:	Hauntings are believed related to the deaths of workmen when original construction was taking place and fit sounds and areas connected to tragedy.
Status:	Incidents difficult to document due to bureaucratic apprehensions of Auxiliary Police to go on record, but hauntings widely believed by many.

CUBA ROAD CURIOSITIES
OLD ROAD HAUNTS

Cuba Road is an old rural road that runs east to west between Rand Road and Northwest Highway along the Cuba Marsh Forest Preserve and slices through a large unincorporated tract of land between North Barrington and Barrington Hills. The road is located in Cuba Township, originally Troy Township. The name had to be changed because there was another township with the same name in Illinois. This took place in 1850, around the time the country of Cuba was seeking separation from Spain. Apparently, a top item in the news, local people in the township sympathetic to Cuba's cause initiated the name change.

Indigenous trees and shrubbery line the narrow two-lane road, and particularly at night, its semi-isolated nature seems to make this road more forbidding, thus a perfect place for legends and tall tales.

In the mid 1980s, I once patrolled Cuba Road with some locals. It was a weeknight pushing midnight and the traffic was almost nonexistent. As we drove back and forth a number of times along Cuba Road, it was easy to understand why it had gotten its spooky reputation. The homes that were nearby were set far back on large wooded lots. The only other signs of life were the headlights of cars in the distance. Because of the occasional bend in the road, the cars approaching would sometimes be obscured by the curve. But sometimes, the cars would seem to vanish with no reason where there was no curve or no turn off. The car would literally disappear.

"Scaring yourself silly" driving down the length of Cuba Road by night is still a popular pastime with Barrington area youths. Then there are specific spots along Cuba Road that deserve scrutiny.

Near Cuba and Rainbow Road, there once stood a house. Nature has reclaimed the area. The house has a will of its own, however. Possibly by fire, it was destroyed many years ago. Debris from the house was still visible in the early 1980s, on what is now an area nature has reclaimed. On rainy, overcast days or stormy nights one can see a house here: an apparition, a ghostly house where once the real physical house had existed.

White Cemetery dates back before the Mexican War. This tiny burial ground stands at Old Barrington Road and Cuba Road. Perhaps because it is the only cemetery along this roadway, it has attracted a number of legends, those of ghostly forms and vanishing cars. Yet, it seems there is more here than just folklore.

Today, Raphel Kamner is a recruiter in the computer field. But he still remembers vividly his experience in the mid-1980s when he was a student at Fremd High School in Palatine. Raph and his friends set out one night for some innocent joyriding along Cuba Road. Even though cruising along Cuba Road was a popular pastime, and White Cemetery was a landmark he was familiar with, Raph was unprepared for what would happen.

"It was about 2:00 a.m., and there were no other cars on the road. There was a chain link fence at White Cemetery and a gate," he recalled. "We were doing our usual cruise, and every time we went by the gate, it would be in a different position."

*White Cemetery sign
faces Cuba Road.*

"We had driven by about eight times, and we decided to stop and get out of the car and look. It was a straight road, not hilly at all. I pulled over, and we noticed another car coming in the distance. Knowing we shouldn't be there, we decided to leave, quickly. As I started to pull out, I saw the car in my rear view mirror. It was coming so fast I waited, because I was worried that we would crash.

"Moments later, I checked in the mirror again, and there was nothing there. I couldn't believe it. When I first saw the car, it was a half block away. But it was as close as fifty feet away when it vanished."

Raph's story is characteristic of the occurrences along Cuba Road.

If traditional ghost stories are to survive into the new millennium, it will be because of locations like Cuba Road. And, as long as some stretches of road remain dimly lit and secluded wooded tracts of land stay preserved, and there are brooding mansions purposely hidden from view and isolated country cemeteries dotting the landscape, our imaginations will do the rest.

48 CUBA ROAD

Locations:	Cuba Road between Rand Road and Northwest Highway, from Lake Zurich to Barrington Hills.
Type of occurrences:	Disappearing cars, a vanishing house, and more.
Characteristics:	An area of high strangeness where various "twilight zone" experiences are reported.
Status:	Actual experiences are few, but the area has strong folkloric tradition.

The House With No Corners

The Stickney Mansion

George and Sylvia Stickney came to Bull Valley northwest of Chicago just after the last of the local Indian tribes had left for reservations in Kansas. The Stickneys were the first non-Native Americans to settle in the area. In December of 1835, Stickney erected a primitive cabin.

Originally from New York, home of the Fox Sisters and birthplace of modern spiritualism, the Stickneys were early adherents to spiritualist practices such as séances. Their whole life revolved around these beliefs.

The Stickneys built their two-story house in 1849. The quaint yellow brick mansion stands out along the road, a throwback in time, surrounded by rolling acres of picturesque countryside. It is historically important as the first brick house in the area, but its architectural style would be its main claim to fame. The mansion was built oddly square, rounded at the corners on the outside, and inside, all of the corners of the rooms and ceilings were rounded also.

In certain parts of the world, round barns and houses are common, but for northern Illinois this was quite the novelty, and in the area the house would always be called "the house with no corners."

There was a peculiar arrangement of rooms inside. On the second floor, there was a large room, a hall or assembly that extended clear across the house with a rounded ceiling and rounded corners. Dances were held here on Saturday nights. On the first floor, frequent séances hosted by Sylvia were held in a parlor room. There are no known records of the success rate she may have had with contacting the spirit world here, but in pre-Civil War McHenry County, this was one of the few forms of entertainment available.

It was thought that Sylvia was more of a spiritualist than her husband and that it was she who convinced him there should be no sharp angles. Although local folklore is that corners were shunned because it was thought evil could dwell there, the original reasons were merely to stay in good rapport with the spirit world. When the free-flowing spirits were asked to join in the séance circle, no matter where they landed in the room, they would simple bump off the surface.

Despite the Stickneys' attempts to live in harmony with the spirits, they were plagued with misfortune. The loss of seven of her children could have prompted Sylvia to contact the spiritual world. There are no records of why the children died.

After they had gotten older, the Stickneys moved to a smaller home a few miles away. Maybe they realized that the fabled house with no corners had in some way contributed to their bad luck in this life.

Another popular legend regarding this house claims that George Stickney died here, found in a room where one corner had mistakenly been built with a 90-degree angle. This is not the case, as George had moved away and died elsewhere.

Stickney Mansion, "the house with no corners"

The mansion has had several owners and tenants. The only original rooms left are the two front parlors. However, even with a succession of new occupants, the building continues to be referred to as the Stickney Mansion or the Stickney House.

Vague tales of the property being haunted began to resurface in the 1970s. Vandalism occurred and cult activities were blamed.

A tapping on the shoulder, a cold spot, an eerie sound, or objects found out of place: All of the above manifestations, have been reported by those who have been in the house over the years.

Possibly one explanation could be that the psychic unrest is fueled by the mansion's spiritualist connections.

Today the Stickney Mansion is home to the Bull Valley Village Hall. The village acquired the property in 1985, and a few years later offices opened here.

Police Chief Norbert Sauers has taken an active interest in the preservation and history of the Stickney House. The offices of the police department are on the first floor. He has researched the history of this 150-year-old building. The séances were probably held in what is now his office. Sauers hopes that full-scale preservation of the building can be accomplished. There is now a nonprofit organization to oversee restoration.

This mysterious "house with no corners," from the early days of pioneer Illinois, is an interesting landmark to see. But is the Stickney House truly haunted, or just singled out because of its curious past?

49 THE STICKNEY MANSION

Location:	1904 Cherry Valley Road, Bull Valley. Centered in the triangle of McHenry, Woodstock, and Crystal Lake.
Type of occurrences:	Traditional "haunted house" tales based on the unusual spiritualist beliefs of the original owners.
Characteristics:	House was built according to belief that all corners should be rounded to achieve psychic goals.
Status:	Tradition strong as ever.

BALCONY SEAT FOR A GHOST

ELVIRA, THE RESIDENT GHOST

Woodstock is a beautiful old-fashioned community in the far northwest suburbs. Early settlers who migrated here during the mid-1800s named Woodstock after their hometown in Vermont. It was selected as an "All American City of 1964." New home subdivisions have spread out into the farmland. While developing commerce and industry, Woodstock has nurtured culture and preserved the best of the past. Vintage buildings in the Town Square surround the park where a memorial stands of a lone civil war soldier on eternal sentry duty, and also a bandstand and charming gazebo.

Although its main claim to fame is being the home of Chester Gould, creator of the long running comic strip lawman, Dick Tracy, locals will also boast of their local ghost, Elvira, who holds court at the Woodstock Opera House. For over 100 years, a beautiful actress has been believed to haunt the theater where she tragically died of a broken heart.

The Woodstock Opera House was built in 1889, originally to house City Hall and other municipal functions. Its architectural design, "steamboat Gothic," and its imposing size, four stories topped by a tall belfry, cause it to stand out and dominate the town square. The building was designed and constructed by Smith Hoag.

The first production at the Opera House was on September 2, 1892, when "Margery Saw" was performed to a packed house. Over the years the reputation of the Opera House grew, and it became McHenry County's entertainment hub. Shows varied from vaudeville to minstrel to dramatic. With the demise of the traveling circuits, the Opera House adapted by luring actors from Chicago's Goodman School and other universities.

Shakespearean productions held here in the 1930s included young actor Orson Welles. Before achieving superstar success, Paul Newman, Tom Bosley, Betsy Palmer, and Geraldine Page all played here. Elvira, the ghostly actress, has seen them all come and go.

Just as her last name has been lost to history, so the exact manner of Elvira's death is also mysterious. The legend claims that shortly after the theater opened, our protagonist either lost a major role she desperately wanted, or was jilted by her boyfriend. Elvira then chose the dramatic ultimate exit of suicide, by either hanging herself in the building's belfry or leaping to her death.

No matter how she died, she did succeed at becoming a permanent member of the cast, albeit in a spirit role. Over the years, many have claimed to have experienced the presence of Elvira, including some famous names from stage and screen.

Comedian Shelly Berman's experience is probably the best known Elvira tale. During the 1940s, Berman was appearing here in a production and was just finishing a rehearsal. Suddenly, a number of seats in the empty balcony loudly sprang into an upright position, all by themselves. The sequence appeared to be triggered by an aisle seat, and the superstitious stage crew opted for Elvira as the culprit.

From 1975 to 1977, a two-year, half-million-dollar restoration project took place. The restoration architect, John Vincent Anderson, supervised the meticulously detailed renovation

Woodstock Opera House stands in the Town Square

of the theater's woodwork, lighting fixtures, floors, stained glass, and other furnishings. Upon completion, the building was re-christened the Woodstock Opera House Community Center.

Part of the fund-raising to finance the grand old theater involved those who donated $50. For that contribution, a patron could have a seat marked with a plaque bearing his or her name. A group of grammar school students paid for a plaque in Elvira's name. Seat DD113 is now her official seat.

The "Elvira seat" is the most popular seat in the house during theatrical productions. It is occupied almost every show by someone who is savvy to the legend. One could say it is occupied every show, if you are a believer in ghosts.

A most graphic characterization portrayed Elvira as "diaphanous, flowing and tall." This was according Esther Wanieck, a play director, quoted in a 1979 *Chicago Sun Times* interview. Wanieck described how Elvira dramatically vented audible responses. "She sighs—in approval, in disapproval, in boredom, in frustration or in happiness." She concluded, "She's something you sense, not something you see. There has never been a doubt in my mind that there's a special spirit in that opera house."

John Scharress, a technical director at the Opera House, confirmed there have been many observations and recounted a sighting by a stagehand. He prefaced that the stagehand was trustworthy and truthful.

"He was shutting down the house after a Saturday night show," Scharress related. "He had just turned off the lights and had come down a spiral staircase when he came face to face with a dark outline. Something scared him bad. He did not stick around to find out what it was. He was out of there!"

Never described as evil, Elvira's melancholy mood may, however, be contagious for certain aspiring actresses. The story goes that a strange compulsion overtakes the young actress, and she is seen climbing the stairs toward the belfry. Reaching the window ledge, the young woman glances to the ground below in a trancelike daze. On the verge of jumping, she is pulled back from the precipice by a fellow actor who notices her bizarre behavior and averts disaster in the nick of time. For some unknown reason, these young actresses seem to be driven to reenact Elvira's last moments.

These days, Elvira is quiet. Maybe she is just biding her time, waiting to re-enter the limelight in another theatrical appearance. No recent outbursts have been noted, but she certainly has obtained in death what so many actors strive for in life: immortal fame.

This theater has been in continuous use since its doors first opened in 1890. Elvira holds the record for the longest stage career in American theatrical history.

Save that aisle seat in the balcony, please.

50 WOODSTOCK OPERA HOUSE

Location:	121 Van Buren Street, Woodstock.
Type of occurrence:	A traditional haunting in a theater by poltergeist activity and rare visual appearance.
Characteristics:	Especially during rehearsals, noises are common and certain seats in the balcony are tampered with. A presence is "felt" and at least once seen visually.
Status:	Has been dormant, but inclined to be whimsical so could surprise.

Roadstop Poltergeists

Hauntings at a Former Speakeasy

If there were a prize for the restaurant hardest to find in Chicagoland, this is the place. Al Capone's Hideaway and Speakeasy is located on a bend of the Fox River in Valley View, three and a half miles north of St. Charles. The area is heavily wooded, and the secondary roads leading to it are convoluted and poorly marked. Today, it is hard to locate, but during the 1920s, this isolation was heavy insurance that beer and whisky could flow and interference from the law was almost nil.

The popular restaurant began as Reitmayer's Beer Garden, opening in 1917. After Prohibition became the law of the land in 1919, beer was no problem, since Czech born James Reitmayer made his own in a hidden cellar behind a chicken coop. The elaborate copper tubing system that carried the beer into the restaurant still exists today.

As beer distribution became big business with organized crime, Reitmayer was coerced into buying his product from a big city distributor. Competition was fierce; one week, Capone's boys would be at the restaurant drinking and pitching their brand; next, it would be the sales force of the Bugs Moran outfit. A rival bar just down the road was owned by Moran. Reitmayer stopped brewing his own beer and bought from Capone.

Local gangsters and the law were not the only encumbrances a bar owner had to fear. There were also rowdy customers. Reitmayer's was known as a mecca for rough and tumble railroad men. On Sundays, crowds were the largest, as customers came from even greater distances to sample the hospitality.

Since December of 1973, the speakeasy has been owned by Bill and Claudia Brooks. It was called the Hideaway Lounge when they bought it, and they kept that name, but expanded it to Al Capone's Hideaway and Steakhouse in the mid-1990s when interest in Capone and the gangster era resurfaced.

"Al Capone's" was an appropriate name for the business as Bill Brooks explains, "Capone did not own it, but he controlled it. Beer and liquor had to be bought from him."

Today, the restaurant still has the rustic look and feel, and it boasts fine cigars, wines, and beers, all bearing the "Speakeasy" brand. The barroom brawls and raids by federal agents are a thing of the past. The patronage at the steakhouse is now more refined.

Relics of the past are uncovered here whenever any renovation takes place. When an addition to the dining room was added in the 1970s, they accidentally uncovered the area of the old stills. Bill Brooks remembers "pulling out copper tubing and concrete." The cabins that were once used for overnight visitors or illicit trysts are unfortunately gone now, demolished to make way for a larger parking lot.

The most permanent appurtenance of the restaurant may well be its ghosts. Various hauntings have continued here for a number of years. The Brooks family and staff are among the witnesses.

Owner Claudia Brooks' mother, Annamae Mosher, worked in the kitchen and as a hostess at the restaurant for a number of years. Annamae had never heard any rumors of the place being haunted, though after being there, she became convinced that it was, based on her personal observations. The hauntings never frightened Annamae, as she never considered them threatening, but they could be pesky.

Annamae discovered there was quite a bit of psychic action surrounding a swinging door that stood between the bar area and the dining room. For a number of weeks, Annamae observed how "it would go back and forth as if someone was walking through. I noticed for some reason, the door went back and forth every time I gave out the call, 'everybody upstairs,' for the waitresses to go to their stations." Curious, Annamae would repeat those exact words at other times and check for a reaction. The doors moved. Maybe, it was her imagination, she thought. Wanting further verification, Annamae told others about her discovery. "I had my son, who is the chef, watch," she recalled. Eventually, Annamae convinced her entire family and the staff that something supernatural was going on.

Besides the main floor activity, the second floor is also a hotbed of activity. "You can feel the ghosts on the second floor," Annamae says. "When my daughter lived on the third floor,

AL CAPONE'S HIDEAWAY & STEAKHOUSE

Authentic 20's Speakeasy   40 miles West of Chicago

SPEAKEASY PHILOSOPHY
from quotes by Al Capone
"Whatever else they may say, my booze has been good and my games have been on the square. Public service has been my motto."

"The country wanted booze and I organized it. Why should I be called a public enemy?"

"I've been spending the best years of my life as a public benefactor. I've given people the light pleasures, shown them a good time. All I get is abuse."

"When I sell liquor, they call it bootlegging. When my patrons serve it on silver trays on Lake Shore Drive, they call it hospitality."

Now Featuring the Speakeasy™ Cigar Co.

www.speakeasycigarco.com • info@speakeasycigarco.com

CHEFS AT YOUR SERVICE
Michael Mosher *alias "Chops"*
Ray Heaberlin *alias "Mousse"*.

YOUR HOSTS
W. G. Brooks, Jr. *alias "Sticks"*
Claudia Brooks *alias "Madame"*
Bill Brooks III *alias "Speakeasy Bill"*

1-847-741-1244

35W337 Riverside Drive
St. Charles, IL 60174

Distinctive business card, complete with "bullet holes," for Al Capone's Hideaway and Steakhouse.

we would go quickly up the stairs past the second floor because we knew they were there." Waitresses who worked the second floor were also in agreement that there were hauntings. It was more than just vibes that haunted the second floor; there were incidents involving poltergeist tricks, particularly involving one table.

The place settings commonly looked as if they had been messed with, but the one corner table near a window seemed to give the wait staff all sorts of trouble. "This table would always act up. I would find a napkin off the table, as if it had been thrown on the floor," Annamae remembers. It was only at this particular spot; no other tables were so afflicted.

Employees are the vast majority of witnesses. Since it gets very noisy and hectic when the restaurant is open, most poltergeist antics would be drowned out by normal business hour's hustle. Some patrons have picked up on the auras, however. Annamae said there was one regular customer who told her, "There are beings here, but they are not mean."

The flavor of the notorious Prohibition Era survives at Al Capone's Hideaway. The exciting atmosphere of the genuine speakeasy is preserved and continues to flourish as a popular restaurant, serving the new generations of Metro Chicagoans. But it is also a final resting-place for a few spirits of long ago who call this old roadhouse "home."

51 Al Capone's Hideaway and Steakhouse

Location:	35W337 Riverside Drive, St. Charles.
Type of occurrences:	Poltergeist activity in dining areas on first and second floors.
Characteristics:	Swinging doors move by themselves and table settings are disturbed. Some activity can be triggered by certain verbal cues.
Status:	Less active than previously.

SUBURBAN CHICAGO SOUTH AND SOUTHWEST

SUBURBAN CHICAGO SOUTH AND SOUTHWEST

Emily
The Campus Ghost
Murder Victim Haunts Community College

Emily M. Keseg was in her freshman year at Morton College in Cicero in the fall of 1969. An eighteen-year-old business administration major, Emily was a resident of neighboring Berwyn. She came from a typical middle-class background. Her father was an electrician, and she lived at the family home, a three-flat on Maple Avenue. She is remembered as a quiet, above average student.

Emily's classes were held at the Morton East High School building at 2433 South Austin. On Friday, October 17, Emily was dropped off at school by her father for morning classes at 8:30 a.m. Later that day, Emily met her estranged boyfriend and they argued over a ring he had given her and wanted returned.

With classes over for the week, Emily met a girlfriend at 6:00 p.m. at her Cicero home and made plans for Friday night. Calling her parents at 8:00 p.m., Emily told them she was going out for pizza with friends and not to expect her back until midnight.

According to accounts, Emily and three friends partied at a local pizzeria until after 1:00 a.m. As they left, Emily asked the driver to take her past her boyfriend's house on the 3800 block of Central Avenue. She saw him sitting in a parked car in front of his house and was dropped off so she could talk to him.

At this point, the mystery of Emily begins to deepen. Both the boyfriend and his parents claimed that they never saw Emily that night.

The last witness believed to have seen Emily alive was a twenty-one-year-old motorist who saw a young woman walking west on 35th Street near 56th Court at 2:20 a.m. He stated that he offered the woman a ride but she refused. If accurate, this report is the last sighting of Emily alive.

Sometime between 5:00 and 6:00 a.m. Saturday morning, a Cicero woman heard moaning coming from an alley near 59th Avenue and 35th Street. When her son returned from his paper route, the woman sent him to investigate. He found a bloody dollar bill and a wig in the alley. Two telephone repairmen soon found bloody clothes and Emily's student I.D. Police were notified and a full-fledged search began at 8:00 a.m.

The police search came to an end just before 1:30 p.m. that Saturday. The naked body of Emily Keseg was discovered lying face down in a field near 55th Avenue and 38th Street. The cause of death was determined to be strangulation. Emily's face and head were savagely beaten and there was a deep hole in the base of her skull. She had been dead about ten to twelve hours at the time her body was found. Sadly, her body was later identified by her father at nearby MacNeal Memorial Hospital.

The chronology of witness reports does not fit the medical time of death, and the locations of reports are blocks apart. This case has many loose ends. Despite continuous police work and intensive canvassing of the neighborhood, the case remained unsolved.

Money did not seem to be a motive, as Emily did not have more than a couple of dollars with her at the time of her murder. Police speculated that she might have spurned the un-

Morton College

wanted advances of an assailant while walking home that morning. The severity of her wounds, directed at her face and head, seemed to indicate a crime of passion, but due to a lack of any other firm evidence, no one was ever proposed for indictment.

The murder of Emily continues to be one of the area's most baffling mysteries.

Although Morton College was founded in 1924, it was not until 1972 that funds were voted to establish a separate campus. For almost fifty years, classes were held at Morton East High School and in community churches and storefronts. The bond referendum allowed a much-needed campus to be constructed on previously undeveloped land near the Stevenson Expressway. Ground breaking was in December of 1973, and the campus was officially dedicated on November 23, 1975.

But the new college was not even finished before ghostly activity was being reported. A workman on the roof claimed that he saw girl dressed in white walking along the edge. When he yelled at her she seemed to just jump off the roof. When he ran to the edge and looked down there was no one there.

Another roof incident involved small stones being tossed or falling off the roof. The custodians who witnessed this investigated and found no one human explanation possible. On other occasions a ghostly image of a girl has been seen along the roof.

Campus elevators are frequently known to move from floor to floor and the elevator doors open and close when there is no one inside. In the B and C buildings, doors to rooms have slammed shut by themselves. Throughout Building D strange sounds are often heard.

Ironically, the body of the Morton student from the days when the school had no permanent campus would be discovered at the site where the new campus would later be built.

Many college and university campuses around the country have local ghost stories. Older academic buildings and particularly theaters, often acquire colorful reputations for paranormal activity, usually minor poltergeist disturbances. These tales are usually traditional with no historical incident or facts to back up the legend. Morton College, a comprehensive community college campus in west suburban Cicero, is an exception.

Perhaps the most haunted parts of Morton College are the library and the theater. Often the theater is plagued by electrical disturbances such as lights dimming or going out and problems with the public address system. I have lectured at the theater on a number of occasions, and it never fails that my lectures on ghost lore are interfered with during the opening remarks. When I politely but firmly had to ask, "Emily, cut it out and please let me continue," things seem to go back to normal, at least for a while.

The ghost of Emily seems to have found a home to her liking at Morton College. Emily is a permanent undergraduate here, at least until she graduates to another realm. Perhaps the solution to her murder will free her or maybe just the passage of time. In the meantime she is the best known student on campus.

52 Morton College

Location:	3800 South Central, Cicero
Type of occurrence:	Mainly poltergeist activity, some rare apparition reports.
Characteristics:	Site of a 1969 unsolved murder, now a campus, is still haunted by the victim.
Status:	Ongoing.

RESTLESS GANGSTER

FRANK NITTI HAUNTS AREA OF HIS SUICIDE

Frank Nitti (Nitto was the preferred family spelling) was a quiet and intensely private man. A man of mystery, he was often relegated to footnotes in histories of gangland Chicago. However, Frank "The Enforcer" Nitti became a household name to Baby Boomers thanks to the Robert Stack's TV series, "The Untouchables."

What is known about him is that he was more bookkeeper and accountant than a stereotypical outlaw. Very low key, he still rose to the number-two position in the Chicago outfit, just beneath Al Capone. Nitti was of small stature but had a very strong will. He maintained discipline in the Capone ranks and wielded tremendous power, not so much the "brains" of the outfit, but as its chief troubleshooter. Originally a barber and a fence for stolen goods, he was a chain-smoker and nondrinker except for an occasional glass of wine.

Unlike other gangland contemporaries, Nitti never used an assumed name. A paper trail led investigators right to Nitti after a check was discovered endorsed in his name. This slip-up sent Nitti to the federal prison in Leavenworth.

After Nitti was released in March of 1932, he took over the Chicago operations. Capone was in federal custody on tax-evasion charges, and after his transfer to Alcatraz, he could no longer do the hands-on decision making.

Nitti was completely in control now, but it was a different world. With the election of Roosevelt in 1932, prohibition was on the way out. The once easy-money of beer and liquor running had to be supplemented by other business ventures. Muscling into legitimate business territory was now a top priority as well as a necessity.

The Federal Government found another chance to put Nitti back in prison, when they learned of a Hollywood extortion scheme. Nitti decided to cheat the Feds out of their plans. On March 19, 1943, Nitti loaded a gun and placed it in his pocket. Leaving his beautiful home in Riverside, he began a last stroll through his neighborhood, walking along the Illinois Central railroad tracks that ran just west of Harlem Avenue around Cermak Avenue. A gunshot was heard. Nearby railroad workers heard the sound and spotted a man, gun in hand.

Nitti had missed with his first shot. As the witnesses watched in horror, Nitti calmly raised the gun to his head and fired again. This wound was fatal. Frank Nitti was forever beyond the reach of the IRS and the Justice Department.

Frank Nitti was laid to rest in Section 32 of Mount Carmel Cemetery, not far from his predecessor Al Capone. He is buried next to his wife, Anna, who tragically died at the young age of thirty-eight. The standing stone is quite conservative for this cemetery, known for very flamboyant artistic expressions.

The inscription on the stone may give us a clue as to Nitti's philosophical view of the world: "There is no life except by death."

Mark LaVelle is a long-time Nitti researcher and a member of the Merry Gangsters Literary Society. Mark often speaks of Nitti with a mixture of admiration and sympathy. Of all the Chicago area gangsters he has studied, "Nitti is the one I feel the closest to," LaVelle says.

Frank Nitti area of suicide

Mark has often walked the railroad tracks at the Nitti death spot. Mark and others claim that there is a strong emotional feeling that can be encountered at the suicide location. LaVelle says, "this psychic residue has caused me to feel uneasy; I can feel the turmoil."

Local teacher and professional storyteller Joanne Matousek collects local ghost stories. With an advanced degree in storytelling, Joanne has been developing curriculum programs based on local folklore for area schools. In her fieldwork, she has found a widespread belief

Frank Nitti (Nitto) gravemarker

that a ghost, apparently Nitti, has been seen walking west along Cermak Road (22nd Street), just west of the railroad tracks near the death location.

"Periodically, he is seen walking the tracks," Matousek reports.

In September of 1993, Sharon Macek, an employee of a local car dealership, called me inquiring about a shadowy, silhouette figure that she had seen while driving home at night.

"Is there a ghost on Cermak, just west of Harlem Avenue?" she asked me. Sharon was totally unaware of the Nitti connection until I told her the significance of the area. She had seen the figure on a number of evenings. The image was always in the same area, always walking westbound.

There has long been folklore in the Near West Suburbs about Frank Nitti's ghost haunting the area, walking around the location near his suicide. The tradition is backed up by an occasional sighting of a lone figure, shadowy and remote. The key to identifying this specter as Nitti, lies not only in the proximity to the death site, but also, in the direction it takes. Starting at the railroad tracks at Cermak, the figure heads westerly, in the direction of Mount Carmel Cemetery located in Hillside, apparently to his grave.

Frank Nitti continues to be a vibrant part of Chicagoland's ghostlore.

53 Ghost of Frank Nitti

Location:	Along Cermak Road (Twenty-second Street) just west of Harlem Avenue, and also along nearby railroad tracks, North Riverside/ Forest Park.
Type of occurrence:	Apparition seen on rare occasions, unsettling feelings near exact death spot.
Characteristics:	Hazy, shadowy figure seen walking. Psychological feelings seem to manifest when at location. Much local belief in presence of Nitti's ghost.
Status:	Continuing.

GHOSTLY LIONS AND TIGERS AND BEARS, ETC...

Circus Train Wreck Dead At "Showmen's Rest"

In the summer of 1918, the Hagenbeck-Wallace Circus, one of the nation's largest, was touring throughout the Midwest. Ads for that season promised "60 Aerialists, 60 Acrobats, 60 Riders and 50 Clowns." Three special trains carried the circus, which included 22 tents, 1,000 employees, and almost 400 animals making up the menagerie.

It was not a great time for circuses, however. A World War was in progress, and governmental restrictions on railroad use caused logistical problems and bureaucratic nightmares. Despite all this, the show did go on.

After playing Michigan City, Indiana, the circus packed up for its next stop in Hammond, Indiana. As the circus train roared through the night, the exhausted group caught up on sleep in their berths and bunks in the sleeping cars. The next day, July 22, would herald their return to Hammond and a grand parade through the center of town.

Just minutes before 4:00 a.m. on the edge of Hammond, Indiana, the circus train was slammed from behind by a speeding troop train. This section of the circus train consisted of the sleeping cars. Cars were telescoped together or jackknifed off the tracks. Explosions soon rocked the scene. Many of the sleeping passengers never woke up. Those who survived were jarred into consciousness in a jumble of debris. Many found themselves trapped, pinned down or unable to free themselves due to broken bones. By now the wooden cars were just so much dry kindling, and fires began to spread, started by the broken gas lanterns.

Pitiful cries and screams were heard: "Shoot me!"—"Kill me!"—"Don't let me be burned alive!"

A. K. Sargent, the engineer of the troop train, had fallen asleep at the throttle and plowed through the rear cars of the circus train. He would admit, "I was dozing." He claimed he had been taking patent medicine pills and his main defense was being overworked by the railroad for the war effort. His later manslaughter trial produced a hung jury.

Stories abound of this tragedy. A graphic account of the wreck was published years later in *Reader's Digest* (September 1945). Chicago journalist Ben Hecht described being on the site and watching a circus performer named Hercules Navarro shoot his wife in a mercy killing. Hecht, notorious for his exaggeration and overimagination, may not even have been there at the time. All the characters he named in his article were found to be fictitious.

We will never have a complete count of the fatalities that day. Accurate lists of how many were traveling with the circus or their names were not kept. The last sleeping car contained the roustabouts, temporary employees who were hired for day labor. Bodies were ground into gristle and flesh was burned beyond recognition. A charred man's head was found beneath the locomotive's cowcatcher after the fires were out. Along the tracks were dismembered body parts.

Warren A. Reeder, Jr., of the Hammond Historical Society, carefully researched the wreck and believed that the death toll was eighty-six. This figure is higher than other published estimates, but probably more accurate.

Showmen's Rest

There was no circus parade in Hammond on that summer day.

The Showmen's League of America, founded by Buffalo Bill Cody, is still headquartered in Chicago. In early 1918 this benevolent organization purchased a large plot in Forest Park's Woodlawn Cemetery to be used as a final resting place for their members. On June 27, just five days after the train wreck, this plot was the scene of the mass burial.

Fifty-six were buried at the same time, only thirteen of these identified. They were buried with dignity, each in a separate coffin, and each to have an individual headstone. Most of the stones were inscribed with "Unknown." Other stones include "Baldy" and "4 Horse Driver."

Since those first burials, hundreds of other circus and carnival showmen have gone to their rest here. Standing silent vigil are five stone circus elephants who have their trunks symbolically pointed down in mourning for their fellow showmen.

Motorists driving down Cermak Road between Harlem and Des Plaines Avenues in the Near West Suburbs have often smiled as they past along Woodlawn Cemetery. Their attention is caught by granite elephants, five in number, that stand guard over "Showmen's Rest," one of just a handful of circus and carnival cemetery plots in the US. Some area residents know that the plot began after a tragic circus train wreck. And some have heard that the location is haunted late at night by ghostly animal cries.

The mystery of the circus animal cries at "Showmen's Rest" would eventually be solved in 1975 by North Riverside Police Officer John O'Rourke.

Law enforcement officers are some of my best witnesses.

O'Rourke joined the North Riverside Police Department in 1969, fresh out of the Marines. For years he was known as the flat-top haircut, no nonsense cop on the force. O'Rourke was not the kind of a person to believe in ghost stories, but he did love a true mystery. His interest in the oft-repeated local tale appealed to his "just the facts" attitude, and that is what he set out to do, gather the facts. On his many midnight shifts as a rookie cop, he made it a point to visit the circus plot. "When I first came on the police department in 1969, I heard from various people in the area that they had heard the sounds of animals coming from the cemetery where the elephant markers stand," John recalled.

"Well, I kept stopping by, but I never heard anything. At different times I would get out and walk, especially when I would work the midnight to eight shift. I would walk around there with a flashlight but never heard anything until one hot, humid July, early in the morning about 3:30 a.m.," John said.

"All of a sudden I heard lions roaring coming from the area of the graves and for a moment I wanted to run. Then I realized that the sounds were not coming from the graves, but from off in the distance, from Brookfield Zoo."

O'Rourke had just found a natural explanation for one of the West Suburb's best known legends.

Brookfield Zoo is about a mile and a half from Showmen's Rest. At night, when sounds can carry and the winds are just right, the conditions can cause the animal sounds to be heard in the quiet cemetery. It doesn't take much imagination to view elephant shaped stones in the moonlight, hear the distinctive sounds of circus animals around you, and panic, believing that the train wreck animals are haunting the site.

Although John O'Rourke has now made the rank of sergeant with close to thirty years on the force, his interest in the legendary Showmen's Rest continues. Despite his many visits to the cemetery during the night, he never heard the sounds again. Apparently, the weather and other factors have to be just right.

The ironic postscript to this non-ghost story is that no animals actually died in that train wreck so many years ago. The animal cars were at the front of the train and were unscathed by the disaster. No animals died that day, so no animals can be expected to haunt.

54 WOODLAWN CEMETERY (SHOWMEN'S REST SECTION)

Location:	7600 West Cermak Road, Forest Park.
Type of occurrence:	Ghostly exotic animal sounds were heard.
Characteristics:	After dark, usually quite late, the distinct sounds of circus animals (elephants, big cats, etc.) were traditionally heard around the graves of victims of a 1918 circus train wreck.
Status:	Sporadic but ongoing.

FLAPPER GHOST

West Suburban Hitchhiking Ghost

North Riverside's Melody Mill Ballroom was a popular location for ballroom dancing from the 1920s until the mid 1980s. The red and brown brick building with striped canopy entrance was topped by a miniature windmill, its trademark. The nationally known bands performed here in its heyday, including Big Tiny Hill's orchestra. Hill had a hit 78 RPM record with "Moonlight on the Melody Mill."

The old suburban ballroom had another claim to fame, a ghost known simply as "the flapper." No one seems to remember her name, but a lovely girl who was a regular here in the Roaring Twenties died young. Around twenty-one when she died, the girl, some believed, was stricken by appendicitis and died of peritonitis. Buried in the nearby Jewish Waldheim Cemetery on Harlem Avenue, she was only a short walk or ride away from her beloved Melody Mill.

Our flapper sported the style of the day. Copying silent and early talkie film star Colleen Moore, the original "flapper," our suburban fan also had bobbed hair and wore short skirts with fringes. A brunette like Moore, she was said to resemble the movie star closely.

Some months after her death, strange things started happening. Sorely missed, the flapper began to appear regularly at the dances at Melody Mill. She was seen again and again across the crowded dance floor.

Some young men actually claimed to have met a beautiful brunette at the Melody Mill and to have offered her a ride home. On that ride, she disappeared.

Folklore journals record these legends of the late Twenties and early Thirties. They start out the same with the girl giving directions to the driver to head east on Cermak Road, then north on Harlem. As they are passing by Jewish Waldheim Cemetery (now renamed Waldheim Cemetery) at 1800 South Harlem, the passenger asks for the driver to stop.

One man claimed that the girl told him that she lived in the caretaker's house (now gone) in the cemetery. He watched her head to the building, but then run around its side. Curious, the man followed, only to see the flapper heading back into the cemetery and then vanishing amidst the graves.

Another man who was told the caretaker's house story decided to return in daytime and ask about the girl. He then found out that no such girl lived there.

These legends were the most popular around 1933 and 1934, the Chicago Century of Progress years. Accounts are very rare now, but some spectacular sightings have been made in more modern times.

By coincidence, John O'Rourke, the "just the facts" policeman of the North Riverside Police Department who didn't believe in ghosts, had another dramatic encounter. This time with the Melody Mill ghost.

"It was in the late 1970s. I was just going on midnight to eight shift," John recalled. "There was a slight drizzle and the Melody Mill was just letting out. A woman was walking down the street by herself, so I pulled up along side of her and asked her where she was going."

The woman told John that she was walking home. He offered her a ride since it looked as though more inclement weather was on the way. She directed John east on Cermak Road.

Colleen Moore, the Hollywood "Flapper"

"I asked her questions, and she always changed the subject," John recalled. "She just talked about how she loved to dance and how much she enjoyed the Melody Mill."

When they turned onto Harlem Avenue at Cermak, the woman suddenly said, "Stop!" "It was across from Rizza Ford (then Allegro Ford) where she got out. An eighteen wheeler was passing and backfired. I turned my head away for an instant and when I looked back, she was gone."

John could not believe she had disappeared so fast. "I went up to the apartment entrances but there were no wet footprints," John said. "I checked the buildings all around."

John could not remember anything distinctive about the woman's attire. "It was just a dress, no ballroom gown," he remembered. He described her hair as probably to the shoulder. It was very odd that John, a trained observer, could not recall the details as to the mystery woman's dress and appearance. It was as if he was not in control.

Was the police officer's ride that night our ghostly dancer? John O'Rourke has been asking himself that very question for over twenty years.

A different sort of sighting was made by Deborah Brosseau around 1980 while Deb and four others were sitting on the front porch of a friend's house on Lathrop Avenue, just down the street from Woodlawn and Waldheim Cemeteries.

It was the end of a pleasant summer day just turning to dusk. "We were trying to figure out what to do that night when this hazy, opaque figure came floating down the sidewalk," Deb recalled. "The whole image was one color, dimensional, but milky gray, not white."

The figure was a woman in long, out-of-date dress. "The dress looked strapless, straight cut, had fringes and was one piece to about the knees," Deb continued. "Her hair was wavy, close to her head. There was something on her head, a hat or headband."

"We all saw it. There was just stunned silence. I got up from the porch and watched it move at a walking pace. It passed over Cermak and went into the cemetery. It just sort of evaporated."

The figure was last seen disappearing in a cemetery that is adjacent to Jewish Waldheim. Was she headed back to her grave?

Melody Mill Ballroom

Deb and her friends just decided to go home at that point. "We didn't even talk about it. Everybody just went home," she remembered. Years later, now in radio and theatrical sales, Deborah Brosseau still wonders about that night.

Modern times finally caught up with the Melody Mill by the 1980s. The big band sound was not drawing the crowds of long ago and attendance continued to slip. The longtime landmark closed and then was demolished in 1985. Built on the spot is a new Village Commons Building dedicated in 1987.

Within a week of the demolition of the ballroom, I received a call from my friend Sergeant John O'Rourke with a curious story. A couple of days after the building was debris, a phone call came into the police headquarters. A man claimed that he could not sleep because the music was playing too loud at the Melody Mill, and would the police do something about it.

John told me what a laughing matter the story was at the station. How could there be loud band music when there wasn't even a ballroom anymore? I didn't think it was necessarily funny, however.

I was eventually proven right; it was merely the first report in a steady stream. Since that first phone call, many residents have claimed that on certain nights the strains of the big band sounds of long ago can again be heard by those who live near the ballroom site.

Village Commons today on site of earlier ballroom

I have done many programs for the recreation department of North Riverside over the years. Shortly before they were to move offices into the new facility, I received a phone call from event planner Viola Jansky. "Do you think that we will be haunted?" Viola asked me.

I thought of the reports of ghostly music and told Viola, "Probably."

Since settling down in the new building, Viola and other city employees have noticed odd things from time to time. "When anything goes wrong here, we blame it on the ghost!" she says.

For many, it is comforting to think that our dance-loving spirit still has somewhere to go, even if it is only a phantom dancehall with ghostly music.

55 MELODY MILL BALLROOM

Location:	2401 South Des Plaines Avenue, North Riverside (Ballroom now replaced by Village Commons).
Type of occurrences:	Encounters with vanishing hitchhiker and ghostly big band music in area where ballroom formerly stood.
Characteristics:	Yet another hitchhiking ghost, this one brunette, in the "flapper" attire of the 1920s. Her favorite haunt, the Melody Mill Ballroom, was torn down in the mid-1980s, but ghostly big band music is still encountered here.
Status:	Ghost is seldom encountered, but psychic music is heard on semi-regular basis.

THE BLEEDING STOP SIGN

BLOOD MATERIALIZES AT ACCIDENT SITE

It is late at night. You are driving down a winding road, following alongside the path of a meandering river nestled in the Forest Preserve. The street is dimly lit with old-fashioned street lamps, and the surrounding homes are obscure, guarded by many matured trees and massive hedges. This secluded area seems far removed from Metro Chicago.

Suddenly up ahead, a stop sign is reflected in your headlights. You are going a bit fast for conditions, but some pumping on your breaks brings you to an abrupt stop. Your eyes focus on the stop sign. There is something not quite right. There are streaks of red liquid oozing down its face.

The stop sign is dripping blood!

The legend of the bleeding stop sign of Riverside has been a popular teenage myth for decades. For those who grew up in the Lyons, Riverside, North Riverside, and Brookfield area, particularly in the '60s and '70s, the belief that on certain nights this stop sign actually could bleed was widespread. As the tale circulated, teens would drive out to the site at late night just to check the surface of the sign for any telltale blood. Only the bravest would touch the sign with a fingertip and taste.

The scenic drive along the Des Plaines River in Riverside has long been a popular stretch for cruising. Drag racing formerly took place here, and the geography and lay of the land has spelled trouble for many motorists over the years.

"The road curls and loops with the river; if you're not careful, you'll crash into a tree," says Karl Sundstrom, a local teacher and Civil War memorabilia dealer. He remembers vividly the drag racing of the sixties. A close friend's brother was killed in a July 1967 crash here.

Retired Riverside police office Don Zika knows the location of the bleeding stop sign very well. Until his retirement in 1995, he served thirty-five years with the Riverside Police Department and was at the scene of "numerous accidents, many serious" at this location.

"It's a very precarious area for driving, " ex-officer Zika says. "It's very dark; it's a winding street and meanders through a wooded area. It lends itself to accidents if you are going too fast."

By now, it is impossible to date the origin of the legend. If one particular accident lends itself to the creation of this belief, no one can say at this time. Just about everyone locally knows the dangerous nature of this site and gives it respect, even if they don't believe the stop sign can "bleed."

Can an ordinary, secular object such as a stop sign "bleed" like religious statues and icons reportedly have done over the centuries? Is this some sort of "miracle" of the post-industrial world in keeping with our fast times and national love affair with the automobile?

The true believer may claim that many years ago the stop sign did produce blood through psychic means. At this time, there is no real evidence to support these paranormal claims.

Bleeding Stop Sign

Never the less, this classic supernatural legend owes its life to some very vivid imaginations, or maybe a dab of condiment on the side. It is obvious to those who visit the sign today that some local pranksters have squirted ketchup on the sign trying to fool the gullible.

56 THE BLEEDING STOP SIGN

Location:	Riverside Drive at Olmsted Road, Riverside
Type of occurrence:	Alleged materialization of blood at the site of serious accidents.
Characteristics:	A stop sign at a dangerous intersection is thought to have the ability of oozing blood at certain times.
Status:	Tradition still current in area.

BOOK LOVER GHOST
AVID READER AFTER DEATH

La Grange Road, running through the heart of the southwest suburban community of La Grange, is lined with dozens of beautiful older homes. Just south of the Burlington Railroad, at Cossitt Avenue and La Grange Road, there is one building, a modern library, built in 1969, that breaks the momentum of the classic architecture. The library that stands here was built on the site of an older home, one that was doomed to tragedy.

The La Grange Library has been thought to be haunted from at least the mid-1970s. The stories have remained constant over the years and there are no extra embellishments. It is by no means scary. In fact, the basic tale is sweet and somewhat melancholy.

According to local tradition, a family home had previously stood on this location. One night, a fire tragically destroyed the home and took the lives of a mother and her two young children. The mother had read each night to the children, and one of them, a little girl, was particularly fond of one title, said to be the classic *Little Women*. When the library was built upon the site of the house fire years later, this ghostly bookworm was truly in heaven. Late at night, when mortals had locked up for the day, this ghost would read her favorites in the children's section. On many a morning, the first librarian on duty would find a book strangely out of place on the floor. It was always the childhood favorite that would appeal to a young girl, a book the dead girl read over and over again, *Little Women*.

Joann Matousek has a Master's degree in Urban Folklore. A teacher and professional storyteller, she lives in La Grange Park and since 1977 has been interested in the library haunting. She has been able to confirm the basics of the legend with local contacts.

Joann had been coming to the library for a while before learning about its haunted reputation. "I had a mime theater that performed there," Joann said, "and I took a course there." The reluctance to admit to the ghost puzzled her. She found the community to be very conservative and hesitant to discuss the ghost openly, but her persistent digging paid off.

The tragedy was confirmed. "Years ago, there was a fire," Joann learned, "and a mother and two children were killed."

The ghostly activity eventually followed, Joann discovered: "One book specifically would fall off the shelf every night. It was always the same book and was believed to be the same title the mother was reading to her two children the night they died."

Additional psychic events were discovered involving the children's section.

"The children's section is down in the basement," Joann described, "and at that time they had a storytelling pit. The kids would talk about cold spots there."

The youngsters describing traditional psychic cold spots impressed Joann very much because these were children who had not even known about the little girl ghost. "These were neighborhood children who didn't know about the book story," said Joann.

Joann herself had an experience at the La Grange Public Library that could only be described as supernatural intervention.

La Grange Public Library

"In October about 1990," Joann recalled, "there was a 'Burlington rapist' who committed a number a of attacks along that train route. The library was only about three blocks from the tracks."

Joann said, "I went with my children to the library to bring back some books and I left the kids in the car. I was walking from the parking lot to the building and I was pushed back by a whirling light."

Thinking she was having some sort of stroke, Joann made it back to her car and spoke to her son Patrick. "I told him that if I pull the car over or pass out he was to go and call 911. I drove around the corner toward the hospital, but then everything cleared up," Joann continued.

"When I went to school the next day where I was teaching, I told a nun about it. She told me it sounded like a guardian angel."

"A few days later she came up to me and gave me a newspaper article. The rapist was hiding behind the fence next to the library where I had parked with my little girls."

"He was caught within an hour of my visit, right there!"

The strange phenomenon that Joann witnessed may or not have been connected with the La Grange Library. It may indeed have been some sort of Guardian Angel or spirit as the nun pointed out. But for the past three decades, the hauntings inside this library building are accepted by many in the community, even if not discussed openly.

57 LA GRANGE PUBLIC LIBRARY

Location: 10 West Cossitt Avenue, La Grange.

Type of occurrence: Mysterious activity in library after hours centers upon children's books section. Whirling light in parking lot.

Characteristics: Movement of a book by entity and cold spots plague one area of library.

Status: Current belief is strong.

Ghostly Gutter Balls

The Past Repeats at a Former Bowling Alley

In the fall of 1989, Mike and Pat Alonzi purchased an impressive brick and stone restaurant in west suburban Brookfield. The building has a sturdy feel with its large stone fireplace, a long bar and huge dining room. Built in 1936, formerly a bowling alley, then a restaurant called the Chalet, it was renamed Alonzi's Villa by the new owners.

Preparing for their first Christmas at the restaurant, the Alonzis' daughter, Trisha, was upstairs in a storage room unpacking holiday decorations. The stillness of the room was broken by the voice of a small girl saying, "Hello, there." Startled, Trisha turned around only to find herself alone. She ran down the stairs in fright and told the rest of her family what had just happened. This was not the only incident that has been reported at Alonzi's Villa.

Duchess, the Alonzi family's German shepherd really enjoyed playing upstairs and usually headed right for the stairwell to the second floor of the restaurant. The sounds of Duchess upstairs, running back and forth, could be heard plainly by those on the first floor. It often sounded as though the dog was playing with someone or something.

Working at the bar one night, the Alonzis' son Eddie ran upstairs to a storage room for some supplies. On the second floor he heard the clear and unmistakable sound of a dog growling. He was certain it wasn't Duchess; she was at home that night.

Pat Alonzi has heard a woman's voice clearly shout out her name, "Pat!" when there is no one else around. This name-calling has also been reported by a number of the wait staff. This happens often just before opening when there are no customers present and when only staff members are present. The kitchen area and near the stairwell are favorite areas for the voices.

On many nights, the sounds of footsteps are heard on the second floor when no one is there. There are also visions of dark shadows on the walls.

"I have seen black shadows go by," Pat said. "It didn't scare me. I just talked back when things like this happened: I said, 'Okay, so watch me!'"

Pat's husband, Mike, doesn't seem to have the psychic ability that runs through the rest of his family. Although he has never had an experience here, he still trusts his wife's judgment. They both invited Father Mike from St. Barbara's Church to drop by and bless the place, just in case.

I received a phone call from daughter Debbie shortly after the family discovered the hauntings in 1989. "My parents just bought a restaurant and it's haunted!" she excitedly told me.

I visited the restaurant and talked to a number of witnesses; I felt there was credibility to their claims.

Whenever I was in the neighborhood, I stopped by the restaurant. After about one year, I had my only personal experience there, an auditory one. Late one night while in the dining hall, I heard the distinctive sound of a bowling ball rolling down an alley and striking pins. I heard this again and again. Pat Alonzi confirmed that a number of customers had remarked about the sounds of bowling taking place. I knew that earlier in this building's history there was a bowling alley in this very room, but first, I had to rule out other possibilities.

Alonzi's Villa

Just across the street from the building, the Burlington train makes its commuter stops, so I suspected the rumbling sounds were probably caused by a train. In checking the sounds against the train schedule, I found no connection. Trains were not producing the sounds.

Local Elvis impersonator Rick Saucedo has performed at Alonzi's a number of times. While using the upstairs as his dressing room, Saucedo has personally experienced cold and warm spots on the second floor. Pat remembers his astonishment as he showed her his discovery. "Saucedo," she said, "put out his hand and described the aura, 'Pat, it's warm here...and it's cold over here.'"

Saucedo was convinced that the place was haunted. On later appearances, he brought a doll for the ghost he believed to be a little girl and a bone for the ghost dog.

"He brought a holy candle the last time he came and lit it," Pat recounts.

Pat Alonzi set about trying to discover why the restaurant was haunted. She researched the history of the place at the local library and questioned people in the neighborhood. Pat thinks that the roots of today's haunts could stretch back into the Depression Era. She found that just prior to World War II, there was a club here called the Candlelight Lounge. It was known locally as, what Pat calls, a "hot spot," and rumors were that the second floor was used for prostitution.

She feels that the little girl ghost was the child of one of the women who had worked here. Perhaps the little girl was left alone for long periods of time, maybe alone with a dog.

But regardless of how they began, Pat Alonzi and her family are not afraid of the hauntings they share with the restaurant.

"Whatever they are, whoever they are, they are pleasant," Pat concludes.

58 Alonzi's Villa

Location:	8828 Brookfield Road, Brookfield.
Type of occurrences:	Phantom voices and sounds.
Characteristics:	Distinct voice phenomena and even the sounds of bowling in the area where bowling alleys were years ago.
Status:	Sporadic but ongoing.

FLAMES THAT WILL NOT DIE

BURIAL SITE OF THE OUR LADY OF ANGELS SCHOOL FIRE VICTIMS

Fifteen hundred students were enrolled at Our Lady of Angels Grammar School on the city's west side for the school year 1958-1959. It was a typical big city, middle-class parish of the Baby Boomer era. The neighborhood was mostly single-family frame dwellings with some two flats mixed in. Most neighbors were Catholic, primarily of Italian, Irish, and German backgrounds. Due to the growth of the parish over the years, the school actually occupied two buildings. The original building was built in 1910 and remodeled in 1951. The second school building was erected in 1953.

On a Monday, December 1, 1958, just after 2:30 p.m., as the last half-hour of school was drawing to a close, smoke began to rise out of the basement of the school. Two first-floor teachers who had smelled the smoke evacuated their classrooms safely. But teachers in other rooms were still unaware. The school janitor spotted the blaze and ran down the hall, yelling at the parish housekeeper to call the Fire Department. The alarm went out at 2:42 p.m.

Tragically the older building was remodeled without eliminating a number of features that would make the fire possible. The 1949 fire codes allowed older school buildings to be remodeled without meeting the specifications demanded for buildings built after that year. There was no sprinkler system. The newer building was not involved in the fire.

Priests, parents, and neighbors were soon assisting the firemen in saving children. The door to the fire escape on the second floor was stuck shut until a priest realized the problem and opened the door from the outside. The assistant pastor, Rev. Charles Hunt, helped firemen raise a ladder.

The heroism displayed that day certainly kept the death toll from being much higher. In only a matter of minutes, fate decided who was to live or die. A fast-thinking teacher rolled her charges down a stairwell from the second floor when they were too panicked to move on their own. One father, Sam Tortorice, ran into the blazing school to his daughter's classroom. He personally saved six students, the last one was his daughter.

As the fire was put out, bodies were recovered and transported to the Cook County Morgue. Some were so badly burned that identification was made by personal items such as a ring, a wristwatch, or a girl's necklace. The most tragic discovery was a classroom where twenty-four students were found dead, sitting patiently at their desks, waiting for a rescue that never came.

The death toll in Our Lady of Angel's fire was ninety-five. Three nuns and ninety-two students died. Only two other school fires in our nation's history claimed more lives.

The scene was numbing to all involved firemen, neighbors, and especially families. A visibly shaken Mayor Richard J. Daley publicly asked citizens to pray for the victims and their families. Flags were to fly at half-mast until the funerals. Catholic Archbishop Albert Meyer performed a memorial mass attended by 5,000 at a local armory.

An official city investigation determined that the fire had started in the basement of the school among some rubbish and newspapers. A cigarette or match was the suspected cause,

Our Lady of Angels Memorial,
names of the victims are etched in stone.

but was it accidental or intentional? The findings appeared to shift the blame from the school or city agencies. The Fire Commissioner at the time, Robert J. Quinn stated, "All the laws were complied with."

In 1961, a series of arson fires in the nearby suburb of Cicero drew authorities to a juvenile suspect. The boy had been a student of Our Lady of Angels at the time of the fire. After a lie detector test, he confessed to starting the deadly blaze when he was only 11 years old.

Forty-two of the victims of the tragedy were buried in Queen of Heaven Cemetery that December. Twenty-five grave markers are clustered together at a corner of Section 18 in front of a low wall inscribed with the names of all the victims. The nuns, priests, and parishioners of the parish erected the monument. Watching over the graves is a spiritual stone image of the Blessed Mother with the invocation, "Our Lady of the Angels, Pray for Us."

Visitors to the sprawling Queen of Heaven Cemetery in west suburban Hillside often drive along the curving roads to view the varied monuments and memorials. The cemetery is not as old as turn-of-the-century Mount Carmel directly across the street, but larger than life statues of saints and a giant rosary gives Queen of Heaven some unique attributes. And sometimes visitors unexpectedly encounter a psychic side to this expanse of stone monuments.

Motorists have reported that, on occasion, they distinctively smell smoke in the air accompanied by a feeling of heat. At first, car problems are suspected, but there are no warning lights on the dash. As the driver scans the area, he or she discovers the paranormal reason. There ahead stands the monument to the 1958 Our Lady of Angels Fire and the mass gravesite of many of its victims.

Is this modest memorial sufficient considering the magnitude of this tragedy?

Even now, four decades after the event, the memories are still fresh to family and friends. Flowers, figurines, and other mementos are still placed here on the graves, especially during the Advent season. The cemetery is the only place to remember, however. There is no plaque or memorial to be found at the actual site of the tragedy.

Perhaps these are the reasons why the psychic flames from this suffering have not yet burned out.

59 Queen of Heaven Cemetery (Section 18)

Location:	1400 South Wolf Road, Hillside.
Type of occurrence:	Psychic scent and sensation.
Characteristics:	Scent of burning building and feeling of heat encountered.
Status:	Sporadic.

SCARFACE IS HAUNTED

The Grave of Al Capone

The St. Valentine's Day Massacre in 1929 was both Al Capone's greatest success and biggest mistake. Capone now totally dominated bootlegging activities in Chicago with the demise of the Moran outfit, but he was marked by law enforcement for eradication. The public at large was outraged at the sheer brutality of the event.

Within the Chicago bootlegging fraternity, everyone knew each other. The players needed this vital information to avoid surprise assassination attempts. Capone certainly had at least a nodding acquaintance with all of Bugs Moran's leadership and enforcers. When gunman James Clark (real name Albert Kachellek) died in the garage that day, he seemed not only to know that Capone was responsible, but determined to do something about it, albeit posthumously.

The fallout from Valentine's Day ironically caused Capone to seek refuge behind bars. He copped a plea to carrying a concealed weapon in Philadelphia and was sentenced to a year in jail. While there, his fellow prisoners reported that Capone could be heard screaming in his cell, "Get away from me, Jimmy!" and "Leave me alone!" The ghost of James Clark had started his revenge.

Upon his release, things continued to worsen for Capone and his business empire. The local police were stepping up their efforts to shut down his liquor distribution, and his tax situation was under close scrutiny by the Feds. By early 1931, two years after the massacre, Capone began talking about "a curse" and "something evil I can't fight."

Never one to place faith in professional psychics before, Capone now sought one out for help. A Chicago clairvoyant, Mrs. Alice Britt, was hired for a number of private consultations. Capone told her that he wanted to "get rid of this thing" that was bothering him. Capone said that he was being harassed by ongoing nightmares in which Clark's face would appear. The threat from Clark was always the same: "I'll send you mad, Capone."

During a séance in February of 1931, at the second anniversary of the slaughter, Mrs. Britt claimed that there was a spirit of a man hovering over Capone. She said he was a "tall, sallow man," and that he was wearing a black, silk scarf wrapped around his neck. Capone instantly recognized Clark. "That's Clark," he said, "he just won't quit bothering me."

The séance may have been successful in making contact with Clark, but it would bring Capone no relief. The only advice that Mrs. Britt could suggest was that Capone might try to change his ways, and then perhaps Clark would leave him alone. Capone could only smile at Mrs. Britt's naive advice. He muttered, "It's a bit late for that."

Not long after the séance, Hymie Cornish, Capone's personal valet, saw the ghost. One morning, Cornish entered the lounge at Capone's apartment and found a tall man standing at the window. The intruder just vanished. Capone's ghost stories now seemed certainly more that just his guilty conscience.

By the end of 1931, Capone's career was in total chaos. He had been sentenced to 11 years for tax evasion and was going away behind bars into Federal custody. His first Federal pen was in Atlanta, and his invisible bunkmate was James Clark.

Capone's headstone

Capone complained that he was regularly harassed by the ghost of Clark, who would hang over his bed. His screams on one night that there was a corpse in his cell forced warders to enter and calm him down. Of course they found nothing.

When Alcatraz opened, Capone was in the first shipment of incorrigibles sent there. Even though he was jailed for a white-collar crime, Capone was soon incarcerated with America's toughest men jailed for murder, kidnapping, and bank robbery.

At Alcatraz, Capone's health grew worse, and the visions of Clark increased. The harsh conditions of Alcatraz coupled with brain disease brought on by syphilis turned Capone into a harmonica-playing introvert. During these years, he claimed the constant companionship of the long-dead James Clark.

In 1939, Capone was released from Alcatraz and allowed to retire quietly to his Palm Island estate in Florida. He lived for eight more years, always under the shadow of his victim, Clark.

Just an hour before he died on January, 1947, he claimed that he could see the image of Clark watching him from the window. The figure, Capone said, was beckoning him to follow. Capone soon did.

Gangster buffs have debated the James Clark ghost story for years. Was it really a ghost that Capone kept encountering? Could it have been just his imagination?

On at least one occasion, Clark's ghost was seen by someone else, Capone's valet. And if it were just his past misdeeds haunting him, why did Capone not find dozens of other "ghosts" stalking him as well? Capone was always clear that only Clark appeared to him, even as his mental capabilities began to wane.

Al Capone was laid to rest at Mount Olivet Cemetery on Chicago's south side. He did not find permanent rest there and was reburied at Mount Carmel Cemetery in suburban Hillside. Even here he seems to rest uneasily. His grave marker was stolen and had to be replaced, and other signs show that circumstances may not be totally peaceful here.

When asked, the workers at Mount Carmel Cemetery refuse to give directions to the grave of Capone. They insist that this is due to family wishes. The secret is impossible to keep, however, and many thousands of people come here annually. Capone's is certainly the single most visited grave here. There are deep grooves cut by car tires into the dirt at the edge of the road, and the grass must be resodded regularly due to the constant tramping of feet. Ironically, Capone's callers outdraw the pious who visit the Roman Catholic cardinals at the nearby Bishops Chapel.

On All Saints Day, Saturday, November 1, 1980, a beautiful autumn afternoon with just a hint of winter in the air and the day after Halloween, I was hosting a full busload of forty-five patrons on my Chicago Supernatural Tour. It was about 3:00 p.m. and halfway through our tour that we visited Mount Carmel Cemetery for the grave of Al Capone. Before arrival, I had prepped the group with various Al Capone history, folklore, and ghost stories.

Entering Mount Carmel through its Roosevelt Road gate, we made a quick right turn and stopped at the Capone family plot. Here stands a large stone that at first glance appears to have no name inscribed upon it. The name "Capone" has been deliberately obscured by hedge growth. Set into the ground directly in front of the tall monument were the individual markers for the members of the family.

We left the bus and headed to the stone reading "Alphonse Capone."

Often there are "gifts" left at the grave of Al. We often find flowers, usually white or red carnations, and sometimes combinations of these colors. There is believed to be symbolism in the color and numbers of the flowers left here, but the exact meanings are known only to the anonymous visitors.

This time a very different item was left at Al's grave. Squarely on top of his resting-place was a case of cans of "Stroh's" beer. A number of people had cameras and wanted a clear shot of the grave. Thinking the cans must be empties, I gave the case a shove with my shoe to get it out of the way. Imagine my surprise when I found that the cans in the case were full and only one can was missing which I found empty and hidden in the hedges a few feet away. From the dew on the case, I felt sure that it must have been sitting there all night long. Thanking Al for the gift, I took the beer home with me that day.

Most likely, it was placed there on Halloween, perhaps by someone who planned to have the beers at Capone's grave on such a supernatural night. Apparently the visitor left in such a hurry that the rest of the beer was still sitting on the grave the next day. If it were a cemetery caretaker who frightened off the trespasser, it seems unlikely a gift of an entire case of beer would be left behind. Despite many inquiries, I never did learn who was responsible for leaving that case of beer.

Perhaps a beer-drinking ritual did summon up the ghost of beer runner Al Capone. Or was it James Clark who showed up, still stalking his killer's grave?

60 MOUNT CARMEL CEMETERY (SECTION 35)

Location: 1400 South Wolf Road, Hillside.
Type of occurrence: Possible haunting at grave that frightened a visitor.
Characteristics: Larger than life character, Al Capone, was prominent in a number
                       of ghost stories due to his often violent career. His grave is still
                       thought to be effected.
Status: Unknown.

The Revolving Tombstone

Ghostly Guardians of a Unique Monument

Mount Carmel in Hillside is a plethora of stone memorials with mausoleums scattered about. Monuments in the old section on the north end of the cemetery are often elaborately carved. Many bear Italian names. Angels and crucifixes abound, as well as, a photo gallery, with photographs of the deceased on almost every grave in the north section. In the more modern section on the south end, the monuments are radically less ostentatious, mostly rectangular stones with just the essential information, usually names and dates of birth and death.

Hidden on a small hill in the old section, surrounded by dozens of the very extraordinary monuments and difficult to find, is the massive Di Salvo family memorial. The monument is comprised of two sections, a sculpture and a base. The sculpture sits atop the sturdy marble base. The pale stone sculpture carved in fabulous detail portrays a family scene in a parlor with dutiful children surrounding their parents.

It looks like one complete monument, but the top, the sculpture portion, can be rotated around totally, at 360 degrees on the marble base. It functions perfectly. It glides so easily a person can swivel the detailed carving around with one hand and minimal pressure. This memorial is unique. There is no such tombstone in Chicagoland that I know of like this. The monument is an artistic and engineering marvel.

The carving itself, an import from Italy, is among the best sculptures in this cemetery. On the sculpture is the name, "Florence 1891," and down on the monument's base is the family name, "Di Salvo," "Angelo 1869-1932" and "Rosa 1872-1927."

Somehow over the years, a ghost story became associated with this monument. Local tradition is, if someone turns the statue around, ghostly hands will right the stone by the next day. The statue refuses to be left in any position other than in its proper alignment.

Ghosts with a mission are quite common in folklore. Even if that mission may seem mundane to those who are the living, motivation is a trait that can continue for decades in certain ghost stories.

As quaint and trivial as this story may seem, there may be some element of truth to it. I have examined the revolving tombstone on dozens of visits to this cemetery over the years. It is one of my favorites. I have rotated the stone many times, but I have always left it in its proper position, never wanting to show any disrespect. In all of my visits, I have never found the statue turned in any other direction. It is always facing the right way.

If the monument always being in its proper position is a mystery, so, too, must be the incredible workmanship that allows the stone to still revolve perfectly after decades. Apparently the Chicago area's extremes of heat and cold were bested by the craftsman who created this stone masterpiece.

I met Di Salvo family descendants a few years ago, and they had no family tradition of this tale. Perhaps the ghostly hands that protect this memorial belong not to anyone buried here, but to an old country stonecutter who designed the work decades ago.

Revolving Tombstone

The famous revolving tombstone of Mount Carmel Cemetery is a good example of a steadfast ghostly commitment.

61 MOUNT CARMEL CEMETERY (SECTION 19)

Location:	1400 South Wolf Road, Hillside.
Type of Occurrence:	Tombstone when turned is righted again by ghosts.
Characteristics:	A unique grave marker with a revolving top section that refuses to be left half rotated.
Status:	Tradition is still current.

The Italian Bride

Grave of Julia Buccola Petta

Mount Carmel Cemetery has a split personality. The southern portion, mainly post-Depression Era, is comprised of modern-looking monuments, plain and geometric in shape for the most part. The older, northern half, however, is a marvelous statue gallery of angels, grieving maidens, allegorical figures, and, in some cases, the deceased themselves sculpted in stone. Attached to many monuments are porcelain photo plaques depicting the person buried here. Devotees of graveyard art often spend hours here in awe.

The one monument that has the most mesmerizing affect on visitors is found just inside the old gates of the Harrison Street entrance. It is a life-sized depiction of a bride holding a bouquet of roses. Dubbed "the Italian Bride" by cemetery goers, it stands quiet guard duty at the grave of Julia Buccola Petta, a woman who in life was obscure, but whose following today is in the thousands.

The statue stands atop a base with an inscription from Julia's mother Filomena Buccola, dedicating this monument to her daughter. Mounted on the base are also two oval photographs. One shows Julia on her wedding day, the image copied by the sculptor for her statue. The other shows a remarkable scene of a dirt-encrusted coffin, just disinterred and opened, displaying Julia's body in a perfect state of preservation. According to the inscription beneath this photo, it was taken six years after death. Julia died on March 17, 1921 at age twenty-nine. Her body was dug up six years later.

Ironically, Filomena has her name displayed in larger letters than the daughter she is honoring. Furthermore, Julia is buried with her mother's family, not her husband's family, and there is no mention of her married name.

Although many thousands of people visit this grave every year, the facts known about Julia are scant. There are many wild legends that Julia died on her wedding day, was shot at the church by a previous suitor, and so forth. But the facts as can be ascertained make this one of Chicagoland's most intriguing supernatural tales.

Julia Petta came originally from the area around Taylor Street on the Near West Side of Chicago. She married, and she and her husband moved further west to a more upscale Italian neighborhood.

Eventually, Julia became pregnant with her first child. As was common in those days, she planned to have the baby at home assisted by a midwife. Complications set in, however, and Julia died of fever while giving birth to a stillborn baby. A single death certificate served for both. Many women died during childbirth in that time.

Because of the Italian tradition that dying in childbirth with your first child was a sort of martyrdom, Julia was buried in white, the martyr's color. Her wedding dress served as a burial gown, including a veil. Her dead infant was tucked along the right side of her body, and the two were laid to rest in the same coffin.

Filomena blamed Julia's husband for the death. She claimed Julia's body and buried it with the Buccola dead at Mount Carmel. But Julia's death and burial was only to become the beginning of a much larger story.

"Italian Bride" Monument

Julia's memory would have been shared only by the few who knew her if it were not for a series of supernatural events. Filomena claimed that she was being contacted by Julia from beyond the grave.

According to surviving family members, Filomena began to dream about her dead daughter. Julia appeared in those vivid dreams begging and pleading for her mother to dig up her grave. The distraught woman suffered these recurring dreams, not knowing what she could do. Finally she went to a priest and asked for his help.

Apparently the priest was convinced that something drastic needed to be done. Permission was granted by the Catholic Church to have the grave opened. In 1927, six years after her burial, the coffin was unearthed, the lid was pried off, and there in the casket was the body of Julia, fresh and lifelike. The infant, however, had turned to bones and dust along her side.

How did the body survive in an untouched condition after so many seasons underground? The body was not specially embalmed. The casket was not airtight or watertight. And why had the baby decayed? Why didn't the decay begun in the casket with the baby spread to Julia's corpse?

As these questions were asked by family and friends, it became clear to them that this must be some sort of miracle. It must be a sign from God. And if God had indeed intervened, then He must he given credit.

A memorial must be created. Monies were collected from family and neighbors to create the imposing monument honoring Julia. Not only is this monument the most distinctive memorial in Mount Carmel, it is, with the possible exception of Al Capone's grave, the most visited. So many visitors come here that grass cannot grow in front of the monument. The constant tread of feet, or the kneeling of the devout, wears the grass down to the soil.

After a Hillside police officer first introduced me to the story of Julia some years ago, I began to visit her grave on my tours. I was soon to learn that there was much more to this story than just Julia's incorrupt body and her mother's psychic dreams. There were ongoing ghost stories, as well.

The ghost of Julia is widely believed to haunt the area at Harrison Street near her grave after dark. The monument of Julia is visible just inside the fence. Around the grave, or sometimes walking along the grass in this area, a young woman in white is seen. She is obviously wearing a wedding gown and veil and walks along oblivious to the few passing cars that take this street after hours.

Skeptics who claim that this must be someone dressing up to play a strange prank are quickly silenced when witnesses report that they have seen the figure walking along in the rain, but her dress and veil somehow remain dry.

Proviso West High School is on Wolf Road, directly across from Mount Carmel. The tale of the Italian Bride is obviously very popular here, and there have been a number of school dances that were disrupted over the years by rumors that "Julia is walking through the cemetery." Attendees have streamed out of the dance hoping for a glimpse of the elusive ghostly bride.

I have also talked with apartment building residents on Harrison who live near Julia's gravesite. They claimed that on certain nights they could hear a mysterious crying or moaning outside their windows. These sounds, like a woman sobbing, can never be traced to a living person. Searching is always futile.

Another psychic discovery was made at the grave of Julia in a few years ago. I was leading a private tour for the Notre Dame Girls High School, and one of the locations to be visited was Julia's grave. There were forty-five people on board, including the bus driver, myself, and students and teachers. Of this number, forty of us smelled a mysterious scent of roses that could not be explained. There were no flowers, growing or cut, in the immediate area. The only "roses" were those carved in stone, held in the arms of the statue. And why did some of our group not smell the scent?

The tour was held on March 19, 1981. Julia had died on March 17, 1921 at the age of twenty-nine and was probably buried on the 19th. We were at the grave almost sixty years to the day of Julia's tragic death.

Was this a special sign due to the anniversary? Had this phenomenon happened to anyone else before? Since that day, the unearthly scent of roses has been noted here a number of times. I have personally experienced the floral scent here at least a dozen times over the years since then.

No matter what form the psychic experience takes at the grave of the Italian Bride, the evidence seems clear that a long dead West Side housewife and mother, Julia Buccola Petta, is still with us.

62 Mount Carmel Cemetery (Section A)

Location:	1400 South Wolf Road, Hillside.
Type of occurrences:	Starting in the 1920's with the miraculous preservation of a body and psychic dreams, today an apparition, ghostly sobbing and moaning, and a mystery scent of roses still occur.
Characteristics:	Grave area of a young woman who died tragically in childbirth gives rise to a number of psychic possibilities.
Status:	Apparition sightings are very rare, auditory and olfactory reports are common.

A GHOST JUST CROSSED THE STREET

Justice Public Library

C an a brand new building be haunted? Of course, it's possible! The ghost may be related to something that happened on that location in earlier years. Or, as in the case of the Justice Public Library, the ghost may have just crossed the street. Death does not cause a change in attitude as this ghost story shows.

The town of Justice's beautiful and much needed new library opened in 1995. Their smaller library just could not keep up with the needs of the community. The new building boasted computers and expanded space for periodicals, reference and circulation books, and a much larger children's section. It was all so modern and very state of the art, but then there was the ghost.

The original Justice Library was widely believed to be haunted. Poltergeist activity was commonplace, and the staff pretty much took it all for granted. No one thought that the ghost would be able to pick up and travel to the new location when the new library opened. They were very wrong.

Adrian Dalwood is the former director of the Justice Public Library. He is a firm believer in the existence of the ghost and has witnessed the results of its poltergeist activity.

In late April and early May 2000, Dalwood reported that "the ghost has been picking up books and piling them at the ends of shelves very neat."

Dalwood further noted that ghost selected books "dealing with cats and biographies, as if it were trying to tell us something. Historical books are also moved."

Just what mortal became the ghost is an object of much speculation with the library staff. Many believe that it was probably a former board member, certainly someone who was very involved in the local library in an ongoing way.

Most of the employees of the library have had an experience with the ghost. They are not fearful and treat the entity as just another member of the staff, although feeling maybe it is a little too preoccupied with filing or sorting the collections.

There are certain characteristics to the ghost reports. Spring seems to bring out the spirit. Activity seems to increase dramatically in April and May. The ghost may also be more active because of personality differences.

Adrian Dalwood was appointed director of the library in 1999. He was also the first male director in that post. Immediately upon taking the position, poltergeist activity increased dramatically. It seems the ghost was in some way pushed into action. Dalwood took no offense at the attention, but found it all rather intriguing.

One after-hours sighting of the ghost was reported to Dalwood by a local man and also a library patron. It appears that this man caught the spirit red handed. He had pulled into the library parking area one evening, needing to make an emergency phone call on his cellular. He noticed movement inside the library. He saw a shadowy figure pulling books off the shelf. No paid staff member was there at that hour, of course. The book-obsessed spirit seemed to be working the stacks. This incident just added to the already strange happenings.

Justice Public Library

Things came to a head in late May, 2000. Adrian Dalwood accepted a library position in Canada and left Justice. He told well-wishers that the new position would allow him to be closer to his son and that the move was for personal reasons. The ghost seemed to be happy to be rid of Adrian, however. There have been no more reports of psychic activity since Dalwood left.

Jane McGuire of the Justice Library thinks that the ghost may have been the spirit of Helen Hyry, who was on the library's board of directors. "I remember her saying that as long as she was on the board there would never, ever, be a male director of the Justice Public Library," Jane recalled.

Was the library trustee, the ghost? Did a male library director infuriate the spirit to such an extent that she unleashed a psychic barrage of objections? As in the case of most ghost stories, only time will tell. Right now, however, things are quiet at night at the Justice Public Library.

63 Justice Public Library

Location:	7641 Oak Grove Avenue, Justice.
Type of occurrence:	Poltergeist manifestations and apparition.
Characteristics:	Ghost feels it has a mission that compels it to continue with an earthbound presence.
Status:	Quiet at moment, but ghost seems to have a cause and may return again.

The Legend of Resurrection Mary

The Hitchhiking Ghost: Part One

According to legend, Resurrection Mary was just Mary back in the 1930s, a beautiful young blonde Polish American girl who loved to attend dances and parties. One night coming home from a dance, she was killed in an automobile accident. She was buried in her family plot at Resurrection Cemetery, buried in her dancing dress with her dancing slippers on her feet.

Apparently, she could not stay at rest. She would come back again and again to attend those same dances and parties. At the end of the evening, she accepts a ride from some unsuspecting young man. It was usually along Archer Avenue on the Southwest Side of Chicago or out in the Southwest Suburbs. She would then vanish in the car, or, at her bewitching hour, she would jump out of the vehicle and disappear before the man's very eyes.

These tales all fit the classic hitchhiking ghost story, and Resurrection Mary belongs to this genre. She is the best known of the hitchhiking ghosts to be found anywhere across the United States or around the world. Resurrection Mary is more than just a ghost story. She is well documented.

Over the years, different people have put forward candidates for the title of Resurrection Mary. There are at least three young women, all of whom died in the early 1930s; all blonde, blue-eyed; all with the first name, Mary; all who lived the same life style that would fit the description: She was someone who liked to go to parties and dances on the Southwest Side; someone who had an early death; and someone who was then buried in Resurrection Cemetery.

Two are women who were involved in automobile accidents and passed on; the third is a young lady who, after getting so rundown from partying, succumbed to an early death from tuberculosis. Any one of these three women could have been the prototype for the ghost of Resurrection Mary.

There is something else we must consider. More than one ghost may be active out here. There have been many stories collected over the years involving Resurrection Mary, and they just don't seem to fit just one girl.

There are too many loose ends. But this mystery could be answered easily if there were more than one ghost involved.

Regardless of who the girl was in life, certainly in death, there is at least one Resurrection Mary still to be found along the roads southwest of Chicago, very often near Resurrection Cemetery.

The best time to see Resurrection Mary, they say, is on a night of a full moon at about 1:30 in the morning, the time the dance halls in the 1930s would have been closing; the time when Resurrection Mary would leave the party and go back home—her home, of course, Resurrection Cemetery.

There are many people who have encountered the ghost of Resurrection Mary over the years, and she has been encountered in various ways. Sometimes she is seen walking along the

Resurrection Cemetery front entrance

cemetery fence; sometimes she is seen at the main gates; and often she has been seen walking barefoot along the road, holding her dancing shoes in her hand.

But how can we be sure that she is not a person pretending to be the ghost? Well, because the manifestations are "out of this world." She walks through fences. She glides through gates. She disappears before your eyes. Witnesses are usually quite adamant about what they have seen. They will claim with certainty they have had an "experience" with a ghost.

I have been collecting Resurrection Mary accounts from individuals going back to my high school days. I first learned about Resurrection Mary on the South Side while attending Gage Park High School back in the '60s. It did not take long before I found people who actually had first hand experiences with the ghost. I tracked them down through their family and friends.

Their stories do follow a pattern. They do show that something very unusual is taking place at Resurrection Cemetery. The earliest account I have dates back to 1939.

A Southwest Side man named Jerry Palus met a beautiful young blonde woman named Mary at a dance. It was at Liberty Grove and Hall back in those pre-World War II days, a very "jumping spot" on the South Side. He danced with this young lady, dance after dance. She did not seem to know anyone else that night, and as the evening wore on, he grew bold enough to ask if she needed a ride home. To his delight, she accepted.

When the dancing ended, they went out to the parking lot to get his car. She already told Jerry that she lived around 47th Street and Damen Avenue, the old Polish-American neighborhood, but first, she wanted a ride down Archer Avenue into the suburbs. Jerry said he would have taken her wherever she wanted to go.

They were soon driving south by southwest along the diagonal road, entering into the Village of Justice. When they entered Justice, Mary stated abruptly, "Pull over to the side of the road." When Jerry did, she said softly, "I must leave you now. You cannot follow me."

She jumped from the car and ran across the street to the cemetery—Resurrection Cemetery. She vanished as she reached the main gates.

He had been swept up in the excitement of the evening, but now he sat silently alone staring into the darkness, stunned and confused over the occurrence. There was something reminiscent about this woman. A chilling sensation began working its way throughout his body. He shivered.

Only then did Jerry realize why the girl he was dancing with that night seemed ice-cold to the touch. He shook his head in disbelief. A recollection that had been buried deeply in the recesses of his psyche now emerged. He saw himself working at a funeral home as a teenager. "My God," Jerry blurted out loud, "could this be. . . ?"

Maybe. Because in a more recent incident in May of 1978, Sean and Jerry Lape were coming home from a family function, driving down Archer Avenue heading back toward Chicago. They were coming up by the side of the main gates of the Resurrection Cemetery. Suddenly, a woman with blonde hair and wearing a flowing white dress darted out in the path of their car. Sean hit the brakes, trying to bring the car to a halt, but he could not stop in time. The car struck the girl.

There was no impact, no sound. Surrealistically, the figure proceeded on through the cemetery fence. The white mist fog then vaporized into the darkness.

All they could do was stare in wonderment at one another. After gaining their composure, they concluded they just had had a close encounter of a ghostly kind. If their assumption was correct, the encounter must have been with Resurrection Mary.

Across the street from Resurrection Cemetery at 7400 South Archer stands Chet's Melody Lounge. The bar opened around 1900, the same time that the cemetery opened. The tavern served hot food and drinks, catering to the needs of the people who were burying their dead.

Currently, it is the only bar for miles along Archer from the edge of Summit to Willow Springs. It does play a part in at least one Resurrection Mary story. In 1973, Chet Prusinski, the owner of Chet's Melody Lounge, remembers a night when a man came into the bar very agitated.

"Where's the blonde?" the man said loudly. No one in the bar could understand what he was talking about. They had not seen anyone enter, no good-looking blonde for sure. The frustrated man began describing what had happened.

He was driving down Archer Avenue, southwest of the cemetery through the forest preserve, when he picked up a very attractive young woman standing by the side of the rode. As they traveled north by northeast, they were soon passing by Resurrection Cemetery. The woman pointed to Chet's Lounge and told him to pull over there. She said she would be right back, that it would only take a moment.

He thought she was too polite to say she was going to the ladies room. He watched from the car as she entered the door of the bar. He waited and waited. She didn't come back. He grew impatient and went inside and angrily asked for the "Blonde."

He was shocked to learn that no such person had ever entered. To placate the man, the bar was searched and the restroom, also. She was not found. Embarrassed and frustrated at that point, the man left.

Left portion of gate showing burn marks

Chet's patrons began to put the story together. Blonde. Blue-eyes. White dress. Disappears. Conclusion: Resurrection Mary.

Every weekend since that night in this old tavern, a bloody mary is left at the end of the bar with the hope of luring the beautiful young blonde woman back. On the jukebox are two songs about the local ghosts, "The Ballad of Resurrection Mary" by Guy Gilbert, written in 1977 and "Resurrection Mary" by Ron Randolph, composed in 1988. Both songs are quite popular, especially in the fall of the year near Halloween.

But the greatest evidence for the existence of Resurrection Mary is actual physical evidence. It was discovered one night by a police sergeant from the Justice Police Department. His name was Pat Homa. On August 10, 1976, he was on a routine patrol in his squad car. It was just after 10:00 p.m., a slow night, when his dispatcher came on the radio with an order to proceed to the main gates of Resurrection Cemetery.

He was told that a phone call had just been placed to the police department. The message: A blonde in a white dress was locked inside the cemetery and roaming around. His first thought was that this was a hoax.

Resurrection Cemetery lies across the street from the police department. The police are often the butt of a practical joke of this sort. Sergeant Homa was a responsible cop, so he went to check on the story.

He arrived at the main entrance of the cemetery, got out of his squad car, walked up to the massive main gates, and began shining his flashlight back and forth among the tombstones. He saw no one inside. He was about to turn and leave, but his attention was captured by two bars on the left side gate. The bronze bars were bent apart. On the green patina of the bars, there were scorch marks: definitive finger and palm prints.

The sergeant could not believe his eyes. If this were some kind of a hoax, it was a very elaborate and a very expensive one. It looked for all the world as though two hands with supernatural force had gripped and bent and squeezed these impressions into the bars, while, at the same time, discharging a strange superhuman combustion that seared the metal.

The bronze bars, although they were hollow, were certainly stronger than anything that could be bent by sheer human strength—no more than one can bend a penny by hand. The handprints burned into the metal made it more mysterious.

After weeks of searching and researching, the sergeant came to the conclusion the bars could have been bent only by a paranormal happening.

Perhaps it was the ghost so often rumored to have been seen at that very spot, none other than Resurrection Mary.

I learned about the account of the handprints on the cemetery gates through a teacher whose brother was on the Justice Fire Department. I tracked down the sergeant for an interview and photographed the bars. As word about this discovery leaked out into the community, I watched as the crowds began to come in greater and greater numbers on a daily basis to check out this wonder for themselves.

I knew the cemetery officials were not happy with all the attention, and by the time Spring of 1977 had rolled around, I contacted the Catholic Cemetery Board offering to buy those bars for my private collection. I wrote at the suggestion of a friend who was an archivist with the archdiocese. They sent a curt letter back that the bars were not for sale under any circumstances.

Cemetery employees blow-torched the bars, but it did nothing to the marks that were squeezed into the bronze, nor did it straighten them. Burning them black just made the marks more visible from a greater distance. The crowds continued to come in larger numbers.

The cemetery reacted again. In October 1977 the bars disappeared. They were sawed out and sent away to a mill to be straightened out. They finally came back home again in December 1978, straight. The handprints were now obliterated.

The bars found here today are the original bars welded back into place. They stand there with abnormal discoloration, painted an obscene kelly green. The mysterious handprints of 1976 are now gone.

Extreme measures were taken by cemetery officials to suppress, to cover up, and to destroy the evidence, but what the cemetery could not do was to confiscate all the photographs that had been taken. Photographs, color slides, even a video tape exists, showing that at one time some unique marks had been on two bars of the front gate that stands guard at Resurrection Cemetery.

Paradoxically, the Catholic Cemeteries of Chicago do not believe in this evidence for life after death. But, for the unwashed masses, the only answer is that Resurrection Mary bent them.

Of course, Resurrection Mary did not have to bend the bars to exit. Being a ghost, she could glide through the bars anytime. She has been able to do that in all the years she has been seen in the cemetery. For that reason, people believe by bending those bars, she signified to the world that she does haunt the area around the cemetery.

Who was Resurrection Mary in life? Why did she come back? These are all hotly debated topics, and there is no consensus of opinion as to exactly who the girl was in life who became the ghost haunting the arena. One reason might be that Resurrection Cemetery is so large, one of the largest throughout the Midwest. There are around 200,000 graves found here. With so many dead, the odds certainly are for multiple ghosts. Not just one.

There is also ghostly activity reported to be haunting the Resurrection Mausoleum. The mausoleum made it into the *Guinness Book of World Records* because it boasted the largest amount of stained glass windows in the world; 23,000 square feet of stained glass are wrapped around the building.

Perhaps the building should have been in the Guinness Book for a few more reasons. At night, there are strange occurrences. The alarm system goes off for no reason; taped organ music begins to play; but more unusual, behind the stain glass panels, lights go one and off randomly, creating a kaleidoscope of unusual patterns. The building has been rewired twice according to my sources, but there are still inexplicable happenings.

Why? The old real estate adage of "location, location, location" may well hold the answer, since the mausoleum is right in the heart of the Resurrection Cemetery.

Maybe Resurrection Mary is roaming the mausoleum when she is not hitchhiking on Archer Avenue or perhaps a cadre of ghostly friends could be the culprits.

64 Resurrection Cemetery

Location:	7201 South Archer Avenue, 71st to 79th Streets on Archer Avenue, Justice.
Type of occurrence:	Sightings of a young blonde woman in a white or pale party dress.
Characteristics:	Originally, the ghost was met at a dance or party, given a ride "home," only to disappear at Resurrection Cemetery. Now, seen walking along road, standing near the main gates, or running in front of traffic. Vision now seen for a few minutes or less.
Status:	Annual report or reports with sporadic epidemics, usually after midnight and often at a full moon. Season of year not relevant.

BALLROOM GHOST
THE HITCHHIKING GHOST: PART TWO

While many would-be ghost hunters are drawn to Resurrection Cemetery for their Resurrection Mary expeditions, they should also include the Willowbrook Ballroom a few minutes down the road, south by southwest of the haunted graveyard. The ballroom is said to be visited by Mary herself, perhaps the very place in which she has had many happy times. The elusive hitchhiking ghost has been haunting this popular dancehall and nearby for as long as she has stalked the area close to her grave.

The Verderbar family began operating a beer hall at this location in 1920. In 1929, the structure burned down, and they constructed a large elaborate ballroom on the site. This ballroom was originally called the Oh Henry, but the name was later changed to the Willowbrook.

During the 1930s and through World War II, the big band sound raised the roof as big name touring bands performed for large audiences.

Times and musical tastes have changed. The big band sound is still popular here, at least on certain nights, but country music, oldies, and even salsa nights are now on the venue. Wedding receptions and private and corporate events fill in additional bookings. The Willowbrook Ballroom is the last of the old-time ballrooms left in the Chicagoland area, since all others have been torn down or converted to other use.

In 1998, after almost eight decades, the Verderbar family decided to sell the Willowbrook. Pat Verderbar Williams sold the property to Birute and Gedas Jodwalis. Many of the regulars who come to Willowbrook would breathe a collective sigh of relief when they learned that their favorite big band sound would stay. That's the draw, at least for one, a celebrated ghost.

At Willowbrook, Resurrection Mary has a friendly safe haven on those stormy nights when she roams Archer Avenue. Her shapely silhouette has been encountered on the dance floor numerous times since the 1930s, if claims by both employees and guests are to be believed. They say she is elusive and shy, but a regular visitor to the main ballroom.

The most common reports are sightings of a beautiful blonde in a white party dress somewhere across the ballroom floor, dancing. Bartenders and waitresses have spotted her from a distance, but then she is gone. Her remarkable looks will cause some employees to check at the entrance desk, but the answer is always the same, "No one who looks like that paid admission."

Customers too are well aware of the legendary ghost who haunts the Willowbrook. They have been counted among the witnesses, and some actually admit to attending dances here deliberately looking for her.

Resurrection Mary, however, has never been seen by anyone actively seeking her. All known reports that I have investigated have been chance encounters.

One of the best-known Resurrection Mary encounters-of-a-close-kind happened just outside the Willowbrook at the intersection of Flavin and Archer. It was a night one cab driver would never forget.

Just before midnight on a January night in 1979, a few days before the massive snowstorm that paralyzed Chicago and brought in Jane Bryne as mayor, a cab driver picked up a great fare at O'Hare Airport. The traveler wanted a ride to the southwestern suburb of Palos Park. To the cabby, this meant a hefty fare and probably a big tip also.

After dropping off his customer, the cab driver drove off, trying to intercept the interstate system and head back to his regular beat in the northwest suburbs. Not familiar with this part of metropolitan Chicago, he became confused and was soon lost along dark roads that ran through heavily wooded forest preserves.

Passing by the neon sign of a ballroom, he came up to a stoplight with a bus stop. He now saw the first soul on the road for miles standing near an actual World War II artillery piece and monument commemorating the dead. She was a beautiful blonde in a party dress. She must be someone who came from the festivities a few hundred yards down the road. He thought to himself that it was kind of late for a young woman to be alone like that. Strangely, she was wearing no coat for protection on that cold winter night.

The cabby rolled down the window and asked if she needed a ride. Admitting to her that he was lost, the cab driver told the young woman if she would direct him to a fast way back to the expressway he would give her a free ride home. She accepted and got into the back seat of his cab, telling him to proceed "just up the road." She was quiet and non-talkative. Perhaps earlier she had too much to drink, the driver thought. When they had traveled a little over a mile, this unusually quiet girl blurted out, "This is the place."

Pulling the cab over onto the gravel easement, he turned to look into the backseat. The woman was gone. There was no way the woman could have gotten out. Where was she? As he perused his surroundings, to his right was a cemetery. She had disappeared as they were driving past Resurrection Cemetery. A chill passed through the cab driver's body. He just realized that his passenger was a ghost.

Willowbrook Ballroom

The next day, the cab driver was so disturbed by this incident he called in sick for work. He spent hours on the phone, calling the Willowbrook, calling the police department, calling the cemetery, and calling anyone he thought might be able to give him some answers. He called the local newspapers.

The *Suburban Trib* was a popular newspaper published in Hinsdale at that time. A columnist named Bill Geist happened to take the cab driver's call and was intrigued enough to set up a meeting. "Ralph," as he called himself, told Geist that he would meet him at a local restaurant for an interview, but would not give his real name. The interview was given only on the promise of complete anonymity.

When Geist met with the cab driver, he was very impressed with the man's sincerity. Calling me for added background on Resurrection Mary, Geist published two long columns in his newspaper. Later that year, he sold an article to the monthly *U.S. Catholic* (August 1979).

Bill told me personally he did not believe in ghosts, "but I am inclined to believe in the Resurrection Mary story." In other words, the testimony of that harried cabby who had a late-night encounter with a ghost was a very persuasive argument in convincing a hard-bitten and naturally skeptical newsman.

The columns that Geist wrote about Resurrection Mary proved to be among the most popular pieces he published while working at the *Suburban Trib*. They may also have been somewhat responsible for Geist's spectacular career moves in print and TV journalism. He became a columnist for *The New York Times*, writing the "About New York" column, and then moved to CBS TV. Geist is now a regular commentator for "Sunday Morning," "CBS Evening News," and "48 Hours."

Perhaps it is an appropriate coincidence that the cab driver related his story to this particular reporter or, perhaps, Geist was destined to write those columns on Resurrection Mary. After all, Bill's last name, "Geist," is German for ghost!

For those who attend dances at Willowbrook Ballroom, there is always the possibility that Mary may return. Sometimes a strange woman is seen on the ballroom floor and thought to be "the one."

65 WILLOWBROOK BALLROOM

Location:	8900 South Archer Avenue, Willow Springs.
Type of occurrences:	Sightings of ghost inside ballroom and on dance floor well known. Ghost also seen outside near ballroom, including one much publicized case in 1979.
Characteristics:	Old-time ballroom continues tradition with music of 1930s era. Ghost is believed drawn here because of the big band sound and ambiance.
Status:	Belief in ghost is strong. Sightings inside ballroom spotty over years, but most feel Mary will return again.

THE LEGEND OF GRAY-HAIRED BABY

WEREWOLF RUN

S acred Heart Cemetery is a small burying ground almost totally hidden by the forest preserves along Kean Avenue. Subdivisions now encroach from the east, but for many years, it was familiar primarily to the patrons of the many horse stables in the area. From sometime in the 1950s, a number of strange legends have grown up in the area involving what many have called the Kean Avenue Werewolf.

The earliest tale about this area concerns a strange manlike creature called "gray baby." According to the legend that began back in the 1950s, a young couple and their small child were motoring through the Forest Preserves. A mishap occurred and their car crashed. The couple was killed on the spot, but miraculously their baby was thrown clear of the wreck and survived, apparently unscathed.

The legend continues that before the child could be rescued, it crawled away into the brush. The child did not die from exposure or wild animal attacks, but was saved and raised by the local wildlife. The baby became a feral wild child and grew a protective coat of gray hair. The wild child continued to live in the area on the edge of civilization. It was sometimes caught in the headlights of passing cars on certain nights, or spotted by picnickers and others, as it foraged for food.

The sporadic sightings, of something humanoid and covered with hair, ensured that the legend of "gray baby" would endure.

There is, of course, no historical record of such a crash or lost child in the area. Nonetheless, the tale is still a popular one in the communities nearby.

In the late 1970s, Chris Sainsbury, a Lyons housewife, had an encounter along Kean Avenue. Sainsbury said that as she drove down the road bordering the forest preserve one night, she was frightened by something large and manlike that ran out in front of her new truck. She almost cleared the beast-like creature, but clipped it with the mirror on the truck's passenger side. The entire mirror and its brace were broken or yanked off. She stopped and gained her composure and rather bravely decided to investigate, but she found no physical evidence such as blood or traces of hair. There are many deer in the area, but Sainsbury insisted that the creature was large and upright like a man, and was certainly not a bear. Because the incident happened during a full moon, she often referred to the beast as her "werewolf."

Longtime equestrian Terrie Blazek has ridden the horse trails of the area since the 1970s. She boards her quarterhorse mare, Reebid, at a local stable. She has owned Reebid for 20 years and has had two encounters riding near Sacred Heart Cemetery.

One weekday afternoon during the summer of 1986, Terrie was riding alone, enjoying the solitude of the forest. Most riders come out after work hours or on the weekends, so that day Terrie had the trails to herself.

"I was interested in investigating a side trail in the area," Terrie remembered, "so we started up the little used path, but Reebid got very upset. She was spooked, jumping and

*Sacred Heart Cemetery where
"Werewolf" is said to run.*

twisting around. She didn't want to be there." Terrie rode her horse back to the stable where she said, "It took quite a while to calm her down."

To this day, Terrie says she cannot explain what happened to make the horse that skittish. Reebid was known as a very obedient, perfectly trained animal that was not even apprehensive of noisy motorcycles being close. Terrie blames something about the cemetery for Reebid's strange behavior.

Another puzzling event happened to Terrie Blazek in the same area. Terrie was riding along the main trail with her friend Jody. The two riders were about 20 feet from the side trail that veers off to the cemetery when they heard an ungodly racket close by coming from the brush.

"It was a rustling, like someone was vigorously shaking one of the large bushes," Terrie explained. "I remarked to Jody, 'Listen to that, it can't be the wind,' and Jody replied, 'It's just somebody messing around.' When we rode closer, it was still shaking. But then it stopped." The horses had instinctively picked up the rustling sound before the riders did and seemed to sense "something" was there.

Jody insisted on dismounting and walking into the brush to check. As Terrie held Jody's horse, she searched the brush for a few minutes, but found nothing.

Terrie Blazek believes that her experiences are directly tied to the proximity of Sacred Heart Cemetery. She first heard werewolf stories in the area beginning about 1973. It was a popular belief that a werewolf was buried in one corner of the graveyard.

"There was an old, illegible stone in the cemetery that was away from the other graves," Terrie clearly recalls. "It stood near the northern side of the fence. Eventually, it fell over and now it is gone."

"In the late '70s," Terrie continued, "the fence was bent down toward the ground, with the post and chain link on the side of the cemetery near this lone grave." Terrie added amazed, "The force necessary was beyond human strength. Rumor was this was so the werewolf could get in and out. Eventually the old fence was replaced in the 1990s."

Werewolf? Feral child? Bigfoot? The mystery of the hairy humanoid that stalks the area of Sacred Heart Cemetery and the surrounding forest preserve continues to this day. Bigfoot has been reported on the outskirts of urban areas, but the full moon and the established werewolf traditions of this area point to a more supernatural explanation for the beast in the woods.

There have been no creature reports coming from this area since the gravestone disappeared and the fence was replaced. Has the werewolf been laid to final rest, or is he just dormant, waiting for the proper time or phase of the moon to make his return?

66 WEREWOLF RUN

Location:	Sacred Heart Cemetery (and nearby woods), about 101st Street and Kean Avenue, Palos Hills.
Type of occurrences:	Riders on horse trails observe "something" in the woods; motorists spot creature on road, etc.
Characteristics:	Witnesses believe something large and hairy or "werewolf" type is in area around an old cemetery.
Status:	Sporadic. Though currently dormant, perhaps not for long.

PHANTOM HORSES, GHOSTLY RIDERS

An Equestrian Haunting on Old Horse Path

Yellow caution signs still mark the old horse crossing on 95th Street near Kean Avenue that edges along the southern portion of the Cook County Forest Preserves. The signs are not really needed anymore because most of the local horse stables that were once numerous in the area and catered to weekend riders are now buried beneath spreading subdivisions. The reputation of the crossing as "too dangerous" is well established among current riders. The living seldom cross the road at this spot these days, yet, phantom horses and riders have been seen doing so by some, and the legend has iegs.

One March night in 1979, Dennis James and his fiancée Sandy were traveling eastbound along 95th Street through this area, back to Chicago. They had just dined at a local restaurant and enjoyed a pleasant enough evening, but the young couple was eager to finish their ride home on such a cold and foggy night.

Their headlights were battling the low lying fog cover as the couple approached Kean Avenue. Suddenly, Sandy screamed out, "Watch out for the horses!"

Before they knew it, the couple was almost on top of a number of horses, some with riders, crossing the road. Dennis began breaking, and he and Sandy braced for a possible collision. Then it was all over. The images were gone.

Shortly after this encounter, Sandy decided to contact me. Sandy recalled how she had seen at least three hazy fog-enshrouded horses and riders "gliding" across the road crossing at 95th Street. Their motion was definitely not natural. The horses' hooves did not seem to touch the ground.

"Everything was funny," Sandy remarked perplexed. "Everything was like in slow motion. The look of the horsemen was also weird. The images seemed to have a sheen or glow." Recalling the last fleeting moments she watched the images disappear into the thicket, Sandy said, "I saw the back end of a light brown horse. There was no rider." She added emphatically. "To this day, I remember the glistening."

Both Dennis and Sandy would be forever impacted by the incident. They knew it was something otherworldly.

Sandy, at the time a teacher, had previously been one of my students when I taught at Lourdes High School. I knew that she and her husband-to-be, a local businessman, were credible witnesses and their report was worth further investigation.

One could see that if a driver were coming too fast, he or she would not be able to stop in time to avoid an accident. There is somewhat of a blind spot when coming over the elevation near the crossing area.

It did not take long to establish that this location was the scene of at least one confirmed car-rider accident involving the death of both horse and equestrian. Local horse owner Rita Riordan was a close friend of the victim. Rita provided me with much information on the history of the area. She told me that over the years, there were many accidents at that crossing

Haunted horse crossing

where cars have hit the horses and their riders. Several horses had to be destroyed because of their injuries.

She also told me that years ago, a local stable located a block from the crossing had a large number of horses. Due to the stable owner's inability to take proper care of the animals, the horses had to be put down, an act that drew angry outcries from area horse and animal lovers.

There might be one circumstance or a combination of circumstances that account for the presence of the phantom horses and ghostly riders. Perhaps the reason for the sightings can be traced to the horse-vehicular accidents that occurred at the crossing over the years. An accident that caused the death of a rider and his horse is another possibility. Another strong argument can be made that the hauntings are connected to the slaughtered animal souls, who have returned. Their destiny is to instinctively trot along the old horse path, eternally.

Another unexplainable aspect of the local legends involves the yellow diamond horse crossing signs put up at both sides of 95th Street. When first erected, these much-needed signs were free of nearby shrubbery and overhanging trees. Although the greenery grew close to the signs, they were never even partially obscured. Otherwise, the signs would have been useless.

The ends of the branches and twigs near the signs were broken or snapped off as if by hand. Pedestrians would be few and far between and would have no motivation. Riders thought it odd that the twigs and leaves were not trimmed with sharp cuts as would be done by road maintenance. Those who saw the evidence believed the crossing signs were being protected by ghostly hands to ensure that no one else would ever die at this spot.

In the fraternity of south suburban horse owners and riders, the legends of 95th and Kean are well established. Eyewitness accounts may be lacking in recent years, but the traditions are firm.

67 EQUESTRIAN HAUNTING ON OLD HORSE PATH

Location: 95th Street and Kean Avenue, Hickory Hills.
Type of occurrence: Apparitions.
Characteristics: Location of accident where a horse and rider were killed is haunted by phantom forms.
Status: Probably still active, but infrequent.

GRAVE OF THE MIRACLE CHILD

Mary Alice Quinn

Born to an average South Side Irish-American, middle-class family in 1920, little Mary Alice Quinn was destined for tragedy and greatness. One of three children of Daniel and Alice Quinn, Mary Alice was diagnosed with a heart condition that would take her life at an early age. Yet despite her weak condition, Mary Alice showed a spirit and inner strength that was an inspiration to all who would come into contact with her.

Due to poor health, Mary Alice would spend much of her time in bed and at rest. When she did attend classes at the local Catholic school, she was often pulled there in a little red wagon. She was still able to graduate grammar school early, allowed to skip grades because of her quick mind.

Early in life Mary Alice developed a devotion to St. Therese of Lisieux known as "the Little Flower." This saint was canonized by Rome in 1925 and had a very strong following with American Catholics. Fr. Charles Coughlin, the popular "Radio Priest," promoted her message on the airwaves during the '20s and '30s and built the Shrine of the Little Flower in Royal Oak, Michigan, with donations solicited on his national radio network.

St. Therese's motto was, "I will let fall from heaven a shower of roses." Mary Alice vigorously prayed to her, asking her intercession, and roses would later play an important part in her saga as well. Mary Alice often told those around her that she did not mind dying young as she could then come back like St. Therese and help the sick. Those who heard the devout little girl's wishes could not guess at just how prophetic those words would become.

Mary Alice's health finally gave away in 1935. She died at the tender age of 14. Even as her body was being given an Irish wake at the Drumm Funeral Home, accounts of the supernatural began to circulate.

A sick nun at Mary Alice's school claimed she was visited by an apparition of the dead girl and cured. Some who came to view Mary Alice's body saw what appeared to be a mysterious veil over her face. The "veil of grace" is a supernatural manifestation that is known in rare cases involving very saintly people.

Although a few reports of apparitions of Mary Alice would become known to the Quinn family, gradually they would be replaced by a different manifestation of the young girl's intervention, a psychic scent of roses. The inspiration of "the Little Flower" had led Mary Alice to become the "Chicago Miracle Child."

For years Daniel and Alice Quinn had hoped that the numerous reported supernatural healings and related phenomena would attract the attention of the Catholic Church and that their daughter might be beatified and eventually canonized a saint. They would distribute literature and holy cards and assisted in providing documentation for the few articles that were published about Mary Alice in Catholic periodicals.

Sadly there was no interest forthcoming from Chicago's Roman Catholic bureaucracy, but a grassroots following for Mary Alice continued to expand among the faithful. The place

Family plot of Mary Alice Quinn, the Chicago Miracle Child

for pilgrimage for those seeking Mary Alice's aid would be her grave at Holy Sepulchre Cemetery in south suburban Worth.

My personal connection to the Mary Alice Quinn story dates back to my undergraduate days at De Paul University. On a hot Sunday afternoon during the summer of 1968 I visited the family of Mary Alice in a quiet south suburb. Jill Reilly, a cousin of the family, arranged the meeting and traveled with me. It would prove to be a memorable few hours. As a college student with a deep interest in the paranormal, I was about to have my first brush with something unexplainable.

Mary Alice's parents, Daniel and Alice, were living with their daughter Patricia and her family in a conservative suburban home. Patricia Kelly was a gracious hostess, recounting many tales of Mary Alice and showing me around her home.

On the second floor was a small room called the "Mary Alice Room." Here were photographs and a painting of Mary Alice on the walls, a trunk of clothing on the floor, and a dresser set. The clothes over the years would be cut into tiny squares and stapled to small photos to make keepsake relics for devotees.

As I moved around the room taking in all the memorabilia of a girl dead for over thirty years, Mrs. Kelly brought up the subject of testimonial letters. "If you'll excuse me, I'll get some and be right back," she said.

I was absorbed in my surroundings and paid little attention to her leaving, but a few seconds later I began to almost choke on an overwhelming scent of roses. In order to catch my breath, I instinctively made for the door and stepped out of the room into the hallway. As soon as I cleared the door jam, the heavy scent of flowers was gone and I could breath again.

Stepping back into the room, there was no more floral scent. Again and again, I stepped back and forth through the door wondering where the odor could have gone. There could be no way that a scent so strong could leave without some lingering smell. I even looked behind pictures on the wall and behind furniture for a spray or nozzle devise, and found nothing out of the ordinary. There were no flowers alive or dead in that room.

As all this was taking place, I began to suspect Mrs. Kelly as the culprit. I presumed that when she returned the topic of a rose scent would be brought up by her. When she came back a few minutes later, however, no mention was made of roses and I was soon going through her collection of old letters.

At the end of the day as I drove Jill home, the conversation in the car turned to the scent of roses. Jill brought it up first, asking me what I thought. We both had shared the experience of a strong scent of roses that came out of nowhere and was then gone. Although I had heard about such psychic scents before, it took a firsthand experience to convince me of its importance and power. I had been actively collecting data on local supernatural tales for a few years by this time, but that was my first personal experience.

A few years later I would again have an experience with Mary Alice's rose scent. I was visiting Holy Sepulchre Cemetery to pay respects at Mary Alice's grave for the first time. Although I knew the Quinn plot was in Section 7, finding one grave marker amidst hundreds was still a task. As I drove along the quiet roads I once again encountered the extremely strong scent of fresh roses. Pulling over to the side of the road I spotted the Quinn headstone a mere 50 feet from my car. Mary Alice must have shown me the way.

Since that day at the grave, I have encountered the mystic rose scent at Mary Alice's last resting place many times. I have visited there in all seasons. Snow may be on the ground or it can be the hottest day of summer, but no natural explanation is in order. At most, there are only one or two dead roses nearby, not nearly enough to account for the sometimes overwhelming scent.

From my various experiences, I have noted unusual properties of the scent. It can sometimes be localized—you can walk right into it, stepping back and forth into an "odor zone." You can smell the scent better when you close your eyes. And perhaps the most intriguing fact: when you smell the scent in a group, not all will have the experience, sometimes few, sometimes most, but never all.

Those who visit the grave also have the chance to bring the psychic scent home with them. An ancient Irish custom involves taking a pinch of dirt from the grave of a holy person or warrior as a relic. Those who have taken soil from the grave of Mary Alice have later had a psychic scent occur in the area of their home or apartment where the soil was kept. In some cases the soil was "dormant" for years then a strong explosion of floral scent would erupt. The scent, as usual, does not last very long when activated.

For Irish-Americans, particularly in the Chicagoland area, Mary Alice Quinn will forever be known as the "miracle child." Although the Roman Catholic Church has not bestowed beatification or sainthood upon her, as far as the common people are concerned she is "saintly" even if not an official "saint." And that is good enough for them.

68 HOLY SEPULCHRE CEMETERY (SECTION 7)

Location:	6001 111th Street, Worth.
Type of occurrence:	Originally an apparition sometimes preceded by or accompanied with a psychic scent of roses, now just a psychic scent alone that happens primarily at her grave.
Characteristics:	A religion-based return from the dead theme, a helpful spirit.
Status:	Cemetery incidents of psychic scent are ongoing and fairly common.

MUSIC FROM BEYOND
THE WHITE MAUSOLEUM

F airmont Hills is one of the most beautifully landscaped cemeteries in the Chicagoland area. It borders on two sides of the southern Cook County Forest Preserves, and its low hills are the beginning of the Sag Ridge. This nondenominational cemetery holds 130 acres and some 22,500 graves. The first burials here date back to 1909.

Just south of this cemetery is Maple Lake, a popular picnic and recreation area, which is the destination of many motorists driving along Archer Avenue. As they pass by, they are often captivated by a unique family mausoleum perched on a low hill a short distance into the cemetery. Sometimes, curiosity lures them in for a closer look.

The cemetery office can provide no historical information on the White family members who are buried here, but local traditions assert that they were prominent and wealthy. A Cook County Police officer friend told me that decades ago there were reported sightings of a ghost near the crypt, but he had no additional details.

The ghost may no longer be seen haunting this spot, but an equally interesting phenomenon is now active. The White crypt is the source of otherworldly music.

Today, Valerie Behling is a successful businesswoman, but in the spring of 1982, she was a high school senior at Shepard High School in Palos Heights. Shortly before graduation, she was to have a very close brush with the supernatural.

Valerie's grandfather is buried in Fairmont Hills, and the family visits his grave regularly. One beautiful Sunday afternoon, Valerie, along with her older sister, Diane Ricchiutto, and niece, Denise Ricchiutto, set out for the cemetery. On this day, however, the entrance on Willow Springs Road that they ordinarily used was closed. They drove to the opposite side of the cemetery to enter from Archer Avenue.

The White mausoleum soon caught Valerie's attention, and she begged her sister to stop so that she could walk up and get a close look. "I had never seen a mausoleum before," Valerie remembered, "and my niece, Denise, and I wanted to see this one."

Valerie and Denise scrambled up the incline to the crypt and began to peer inside. According to Valerie, "All of a sudden, faint but quite clear, a harpsichord began playing. It was not a particular song that I knew, just a harpsichord."

Valerie noticed her niece's eyes were wide open in astonishment. "Are you hearing what I'm hearing?" she asked. All Denise could do was nod a silent, yes.

Valerie's sister came to check moments later. As soon as she got close, the mysterious music stopped. Excitedly, the girls explained to Diane what had just happened.

Valerie did her best to analyze what had happened. The music had lasted about thirty seconds and both Valerie and Denise had heard the same odd sounds. The notes only began as the girls began looking into the crypt. The sounds abruptly stopped when Diane approached, as if the music was meant only for the two girls and no others. "I don't know if it was the presence of my sister there that stopped it or what," Valerie said pensively.

"It was a perfectly clear day, not windy," Valerie recalled. "So it wasn't something that traveled on the wind."

White Mausoleum

As the realization set in that something quite unusual had just taken place, a chill crawled up the backs of Valerie and Denise. "Okay, we're leaving!" Valerie declared hurriedly. The three were soon driving away.

Almost twenty years later, the family still talks about that afternoon in the cemetery. "We still go to the cemetery, but we always use the other entrance," Valerie admits.

Others have had experiences with this musical tomb over the years, but although we can document its reality, its reason is still unknown.

69 White Family Mausoleum

Fairmont	Willow Hills Memorial Park Cemetery
Location:	9100 South Archer Avenue, Willow Springs.
Type of occurrence:	Strange, otherworldly music emanates from old crypt.
Characteristics:	Described as "harpsichord-type" music; short duration; may confront curious cemetery visitors who come too close to the distinctive crypt.
Status:	Firsthand accounts very rare, but location is well known in local folklore.

THE MAPLE LAKE GHOST LIGHT

FOREST PRESERVE HAUNTING

Maple Lake is a manmade lake situated at the swampy north end of the Sag Ridge. It is on the edge of Willow Springs, a part of the forest preserve belt that follows the Des Plaines River. By day, it is a pleasant recreational area for rowing, fishing and picnicking; but at night, when the sun goes down, it is a place for ghost hunting. On the far side of the lake, on sporadic occasions, a ghostly red ball of light appears. Those who have seen it and tried to explain it, call this enigma a "ghost light."

This light, perhaps one could use as an example, skull-sized, is viewed from the parking lot and overlook on 95th Street. All other roads into the area are closed after dark and this is the only vantage point unless you trudge into the woods on foot. The light is consistently observed in the same fashion. When it does appear, it sits on the opposite shore facing you, across the very center of the lake and rests just at the edge of the shore. At times, it casts a thin sanguineous reflection onto the surface of the water. The light never moves from its location from the water's edge. It is not swamp gas or "will-of-the-wisp" methane gas, which would move in wind.

Ghost lights have been reported at many sites around the United States, particularly the Midwest. Red is a more rare color for a ghost light; they are usually described as white or yellowish. Traditions for their meaning will vary by region. In the Southwest these lights are said to indicate a hidden treasure, often left by outlaws or pirates. The color of the light and its size will signify the value and type of treasure buried.

In many folktales, a ghost light is caused by a headless person returning to the once fatal scene, lantern in hand, looking for his or her missing, decapitated head.

Historically speaking, there may easily have been any number of incidents that could have taken place around Maple Lake that contribute to the headless ghost scenario. During Native American times, the entire ridge was populated with villages and campsites. An early scalping or beheading party may have set the ghost light in motion. Back in the 1830s, there were many industrial accidents resulting in mangled bodies during the construction of the nearby Illinois and Michigan Canal. Finally, in more recent times, during the Prohibition Era gangland wars, nearby Archer was the route for many nefarious one-way rides, ending with a few well-placed slugs into a head.

Any of these possibilities could have created the necessary ingredients for a ghost light haunting, according to folklore. All we know for certain is that there is something out there on certain nights.

I have heard stories about the fabled ghost light of Maple Lake for many years. I had come here numerous times during my high school and college years, but after a decade of looking, I finally saw the light for the first time one night in 1979.

My sighting took place while running one of my bus tours. I was doing a private party for my friend John Sheahan's Irish bar, the Old Southside Pub. The bus was full and I was setting the scene, recounting the tales of the mystery light as we approached the lake. Pulling into the overlook to view the site, screams rang through the bus as we saw the light glowing across the lake.

Panic began to break out on the bus. Two men jumped up and tried to push past me. Drawing their revolvers, they muttered that they wanted to shoot out the light. They were Chicago police. It took a couple of minutes of explaining to calm them down and get them seated. By this time this scenario was over, the strange light was gone.

After this initial sighting, I then knew, within a range of about 100 feet, where the light emanated. I made notes using the silhouettes of trees for points of reference and prepared to search in daylight. Walking that portion of shoreline a few days later, I found that there was nothing unnatural about the spot, or anything natural for that matter, that could cause the appearance of a red light.

I saw the light twice more within a year, and always at the same location. Each time, I was with a tour bus and on those sightings it was only visible for about thirty to forty seconds before disappearing. Then came a hiatus of a number of years.

In 1986, Sheila Houck from Indiana, a member of Spiritual Frontiers was visiting friends in Chicago. Knowing her avid interest in the subject, I offered to take her on a private tour to various haunted sites, including Maple Lake. We drove to the lake arriving about 10:00 p.m. As we got to the overlook, much to our surprise, the red light was there in the distance, bright and burning away. We sat fixated on the sight for a half-hour that night, which is an astonishingly long time. All the while, I cursed to myself for not having binoculars. It was exactly at the place that I had previously seen it, nestled on the far shore of the lake.

Ghost lights are thought to be caused by supernatural forces, but sometimes a natural explanation can be found. In my travels, I have exposed some cherished paranormal beliefs.

View of Maple Lake. The ghost light appears on the far shore across the lake.

"Moody's Light" is a famous ghost light east of Francisville, Indiana, not far from St. Joseph's College. It has been the scene of many an impromptu ghost hunt by local students. Armed with baseball bats and six packs, they caravan at night to an old oak tree and wait for the light to appear in the field beyond.

Investigating the site one weekend, I arrived well before dark. Finding the exact spot was easy, the beer cans and other party trash on the site gave it away. Setting up a telescope and checking with detailed county maps, I soon had a theory. As night approached and headlights of cars came on, I was sure. The mystery light was actually just an optical illusion caused by car lights across the farm field. In the distance, cars came down a low hill and then turned right or left. The pulsating yellowish light was in reality the headlights of numerous cars. Human eyesight could only perceive one light, but aided by optics like a telescope, the true cause of the "ghost light" was found.

In yet another field trip, I found a similar site near Elgin. Students from Northern Illinois University in De Kalb took me to their personal "ghost light." Once again a natural cause could be found. This light, observed down a stretch of railroad tracks, was actually caused by the brilliant lights of a ball field turned on for night games far in the distance. It took knowledge of the lay of the land and good maps to lay to rest this supernatural chestnut.

Although I have been able to find non-supernatural causes for other so-called ghost lights around the Midwest, the Maple lake light still baffles me. There seems to be no simple answer. It is not red taillights or a red stop light since the next road south of 95th Street is 107th Street, a mile and a half away, and below the horizon.

Would a coordinated expedition with searchers equipped with radios or cell phones work? The light's unpredictable schedule, and its usual short span of brilliance make this not very likely.

The Maple Lake light has been the stuff of teen legends since at least the early 1960s and probably much earlier. It is still as mysterious today as it was when the first sighting was made decades ago. As ghost lights go, this one in Metro Chicago, has real staying power.

70 Maple Lake

Location:	South shore of Maple Lake, 95th Street, just east of Archer Avenue, Willow Springs.
Type of occurrence:	Mystery red ball of light appears on far shore of lake, directly across from parking area.
Characteristics:	A typical "ghost light," a mystery ball of light, appears in an area where nothing natural can explain it. The light stays in one spot.
Status:	Light is seen from time to time, but follows no pattern yet discovered. Obviously only seen after sundown.

Monks' Castle

St. James-Sag Church and Graveyard

S t. James-Sag was the second Catholic Church founded in the Chicago area. In 1833, Father St. Cyr founded St. Mary's Catholic Church in Chicago, in 1833 or 1834 (records no longer exist), he established St. James at what is now Archer Avenue and Route 83. The area was being settled by Irish immigrants, mainly from Munster and Connaght. Many planned to find work digging the Illinois and Michigan Canal that would run through the area. When finished, the I & M Canal linked the Great Lakes waterways with the Mississippi system and became a gigantic spur to Chicago's economic success and importance.

The first church was a simple log cabin construction built on the highest point of the Sag Ridge. In 1850, it was replaced by a limestone building that is still in use. St. James-Sag is the oldest church building of any denomination in constant use in Metro Chicago.

The first Irish settlers were a superstitious lot and noticed the mysterious ruins on top of the ridge. Log palisades were discovered, apparently dating back to the 1690s when the French had a lookout post here. The Native American presence dates back much further, and archaeological digs over the years proved there were many campsites and villages located in the area.

Today, St. James-Sag Church is still an imposing sight. A pale yellow stone church stands at the top of the hill, just yards from a newer stone rectory. The church stands guard over hundreds of graves, many marked by weathered tombstones with the family's name and where in Ireland they hailed from. The graves go back to the early "canal years" of the 1830s and 1840s. There is even a grave from 1818, the year that Illinois became a state.

The scene could be an Irish country graveyard, rather than anything in urban Chicagoland. It looks like the stuff of legends and has proven to be so.

Around the 1890s, there were tales of a phantom horse-drawn carriage haunting the church entrance. This legend seems totally forgotten in the decades that came later, but a persistent story of phantom monks remains. The church on the hill, fortress-like, combined with ghostly monk reports, have inspired local teens to dub this venerable site "Monks' Castle."

St. James-Sag is part of the Archdiocese of Chicago. The priests assigned here over the years are locally trained, graduates of the Archdiocesan seminaries. Since they are not members of religious orders like the Franciscans or Dominicans, they do not wear "monk-like" robes. Yet, over the years, there have been many reports of strange figures roaming the wooded areas around the church and graveyard at night. They are always described as wearing robes with hoods up, concealing their faces in shadow.

These figures are encountered in groups of threes or multiples of threes. Three, six, nine, or twelve are usual. The robes are a dark gray or dark brown color.

Although the reports are consistent, over the past thirty years and more, it is tempting to write them off as simply teenage legends. But reports from local police make the sightings feasible. They are out on the front lines in the community.

Police are great witnesses when they encounter the unknown. Trained observers, they are also natural skeptics. The agency that patrols the area around St. James is the Cook County Police.

I have many friends on the various police forces around Chicagoland. They not only offer me information on a regular basis regarding anything strange or unusual, but I am often called as a consultant to help them out. "Officially," they do not believe in ghosts and the supernatural, but privately it's a different matter.

Toward the end of November 1977, I was called by a good friend, Herb Roberts, of the Cook County Police. He wanted to tell me about an encounter he had at St. James a few days earlier. This would confirm years of teenage accounts.

Just a few hours after midnight, the morning after Thanksgiving, he was making his rounds in a one-man squad. As Roberts pulled up in front of St. James Sag's massive front gates that had been locked for the night, he noticed some figures moving about inside. They were dressed in monks' robes, and it looked to him as if there must be nine all together.

Roberts knew that they did not belong in the cemetery and may even have been members of a cult. He yelled at them to come toward him, they were under arrest for trespassing. The figures ignored him, heading away from him, up the hill, towards the church and rectory.

At this point, Roberts grabbed the shotgun from his squad and ran around the gate into the graveyard in pursuit. He ran after the figures. He almost caught up with them, he thought, but as he reached the church, they were gone. The figures actually seemed to vanish before his eyes.

Unable to believe what he had just seen, he searched the area further. He stopped to listen for twigs breaking or brush rustling, or any sign his quarry was still around. After much searching, he went back to the squad to write up a report.

The paperwork that Roberts filed that night merely stated that he had chased trespassers on the church and cemetery grounds. He would not write that he believed he had chased ghosts, concerned a psychiatric review might be ordered by his superiors. But that is what he personally believed. I still have a copy of Roberts' police report from this incident.

The question remains, of course, what are these figures and what do they represent? Perhaps, it is the west country Irish origins of those who settled here that holds the answer. In rural parts of Ireland where superstitions run deep, a belief in otherworld denizens is strong. Along with the banshee, the ghost that predicts a death by its wailing, there are many other types of ancestral spirits.

Hooded figures, much like our popular conception of the grim reaper or the angel of death, have been believed in since pre-Christian times. From the Celtic portions of western Britain and throughout all of Ireland, these forlorn emissaries of the dead are encountered in graveyards, usually in groups of three. Could the first Irish settlers in this brave new world have carried these traditional guardian spirits with them? Well-known legends tell that banshees, the predictors of death, have traveled with the Irish Diaspora to all parts of the world, so why not other spirits as well?

For decades, a lesser known, but equally intriguing phenomena has also been taking place at the graveyard.

A pastor at St. James-Sag in the early 1960s, Father Ploszynski confided to certain friends that he could look out the rectory window at night and watch the graves heaving up and down as if they were breathing. Those who heard the priest believed that perhaps the solitude of living alone at the rectory in the woods might be too much and that maybe he needed a

St. James-Sag Church and Graveyard

change of assignment. I learned about this unusual claim when a teacher at De Paul University, a friend of the priest, mentioned it in class.

Some years later, I met a Chicago Police Officer named Kate James. In conversation, James brought up that as a girl, she used to spend time at St. James because her aunt was a cook and caretaker for the priest. While the aunt was busy preparing dinner inside the rectory, Kate amused herself playing in the graveyard around the tombstones.

Kate said, "The graves looked as though they were breathing up and down." She would frantically run inside to tell her aunt. Kate's aunt told her to forget about it, that it was only her imagination.

For years, Kate suppressed those memories until she met me and volunteered her account. She realized that her youthful adventure in the graveyard had been real.

"Breathing graves" have been referenced in Middle Eastern folklore. Rather than something scary, the belief is quite pious. In that part of the world, if graves are observed heaving up and down, the belief is that holy people are buried there and that their souls are underground, alive and breathing, waiting for the resurrection of the dead and the last judgment.

Well over a century of legend and folklore make St. James-Sag one of the most haunted spots in the area. New discoveries are certain to be made here as the hauntings evolve with the new millennium.

71 St. James-Sag Church and Graveyard

Location: 107th and Archer, Lemont.

Type of occurrences: Encounters with phantom monks and the graves "breathing" up and
                           down are the most recent manifestations.

Characteristics: Very old church and graveyard are the perfect setting for a number
                           of visual and auditory psychic encounters.

Status: Currently quiet, but the long tradition of hauntings here means
                           things will probably start up again.

Ghost Car of German Church Road

Haunted Grimes Crime Scene

A series of three baffling child murder cases that happened in the mid-1950s, panicked Chicagoans. The Schuessler-Peterson case, the Judith May Anderson case, and the murders of Barbara and Patricia Grimes all taught a generation of children to be fearful. "Don't talk to strangers," and "Don't take rides from strangers," were the mantras we became very familiar with. The fact that all these cases remained unsolved for years made matters all the worse. Except for the Schuessler-Peterson case, which was declared solved in recent years, the killer or killers are still loose.

Barbara and Patricia Grimes lived in the south side neighborhood of Brighton Park. The teenagers were great fans of a new singer named Elvis Presley, whose first movie, "Love Me Tender," was playing at the local Brighton Theater. On December 28, 1956, they left home to see the movie one more time. They never came home.

For over three weeks, a massive police search was underway to find the missing girls. The girls' mother refused to believe that her daughters were missing voluntarily, but police were not as convinced. It was not just local news; it spread nationally. From Memphis, Elvis Presley himself issued a plea to the missing teens: "If you are good Presley fans, you will go home and ease your mother's worries."

But pleading was too late: The girls were already dead. On January 22, 1957, a construction worker driving down German Church Road spotted two naked figures in a culvert within only five feet of the road. The bodies laid out on the cold winter ground, proved to be the missing Grimes sisters. They were found close to a stream with the seemly name of Devil's Creek, by the banks of Devil's Hill.

The case was botched from the beginning. The preservation of the crime scene, the gathering of evidence, and the autopsies were all flawed. How were they murdered? Were they strangled by brute force? Were they sexually attacked by a deviate predator? When did the girls die? Were they held and tortured for days? Where were they killed? Were they murdered somewhere else and dumped into the culvert? Were they still alive and pushed out of a car, then died of exposure? Why were their bodies at the German Church Road site, miles away from their home? Were they killed nearby?

Thousands of people were questioned, and it was said that at least 2,000 people were strongly interrogated. Authorities from all the law enforcement agencies were involved. The investigation went on for several years. The unsolved questions of the Grimes case were talked about for years. The aftermath of the case was as bizarre and full of mysteries as the actual murders. Conjecture runs the gamut, and all these questions remain unanswered. In the case of the Grimes sisters, lack of closure meant psychic unrest.

Teaching at Lourdes High School in the 1972–1973 school year, I began to collect stories about the "Grimes Girls House." The house, at that time in ruins, was a ranch house that stood on a hill overlooking the location of the infamous crime find, the culvert on German Church

Ectoplasm at ruins of house.

Photo by Joe Sanchez

Road. Supposedly, the owners had deserted the house after the Grimes girls' bodies were found in that culvert next to their driveway. The occupants left in such a hurry that their possessions were still there in the vacant house, waiting for curiosity seekers to find.

Visiting the spot with some of my students, I did find the ruins of a large home and evidence to back up this fascinating story. There were pieces of furniture, children's toys and appliances strewn about, and food in the kitchen. There was even a 1956 Buick convertible in the garage, sitting on four flat tires and reeking of mildew.

Something strange had certainly taken place here. The property owners refused to grant any interviews over the years, and the mystery of the abandoned house with contents intact from 1957 may never be solved.

There is a well-documented haunting at this site, however. It has been described as the psychic re-enactment of the dumping of the bodies, over and over again. A ghost car, long and black, comes down German Church Road. It stops at the guardrails next to Devil's Creek, a door is opened and then something is flung out. The car door shuts and the car pulls away into the night. For years this haunting, sometimes with variations, has been witnessed at the gruesome scene.

A typical sighting of the ghost car was made on Halloween night of 1982. Six couples decided to try their luck at this well-known haunted site. Jim and Debbie Serpico still vividly recall that night. They did find what they were looking for. Their story was featured in my video "The Ghosts of Chicago."

The visitors parked their cars a short distance up 83rd Street in a church parking lot. They walked west towards the wooded lot and started up the overgrown trail. A metal cable had been strung across the road to block cars from entering and the 12 stepped over the obstruction and continued.

We got up to the ruined house," said Debbie "and we were deciding if we wanted to go inside or not. Then we saw a car coming up the driveway with no lights."

Jim added, "The car didn't seem to make any noise, and it seemed like it was blacked out. We thought we were being shagged out by the local police, or someone was joyriding up to the house, but when we walked back out, we came to the cable, and it was still strung across two trees and hadn't been moved."

When the group got back to the road they saw a Cook County police officer sitting on the hood of his car watching them come out. He told them that they were trespassing, and that they shouldn't be on the property.

Jim asked the cop if he had seen the black car racing up the path and why those people were allowed on the land if his group wasn't. "The officer replied that there was no car. He had been there over fifteen minutes or more, and no one had come through except our group," Jim said.

Such reports of a ghost or vanishing car are made from time to time, but are relatively rare. Far more common are the claims that the sounds of the mystery car are heard with no visible car nearby.

The car sounds have been described as a car racing, screeching to a halt, doors opening then slamming shut, and the car then pealing away. The sounds are believed to represent a psychic audio replay of the dumping of the bodies in 1957.

The explanation given by skeptics for these sounds is that they are merely

Culvert where the bodies were found.

the sounds of nearby Santa Fe Speedway. Yes, the car sounds are real, but the overactive imagination of those who know something about the history of this spot does the rest. The only problem with this theory is that the sounds are often heard in the dead of winter, near the anniversaries of the murders, and the discovery of the bodies, and, of course, at a time when the speedway is closed for the season.

One racing car sound story came my way from a Cook Country policeman friend who patrolled this area in the 1970s. He was on County Line Road around the corner from German Church Road when he heard a car racing towards him. Rather than round the corner, he waited for the car to reach him so he could put on his flashing lights and nab the driver for speeding.

Suddenly the car sounds stopped. Puzzled, the officer rounded the corner and found no car in sight. At that time, there were no driveways that the car could have turned into. Not surprisingly, the police officer privately chalked the incident up to an encounter with the infamous vanishing car of German Church Road. No written report was filed.

Photographic evidence also indicates that this site is haunted. Joe Sanchez visited the site in the summer of 1985 with his 110 Instamatic. All his photos of the vacant house and surroundings were normal, except for one print. The one shot of the barred entrance to the garage, produced enigmatic shapes and swirls of white fog. Examination of the film and cam-

German Church Road

era showed that the unusual imagery, not visible to Joe's eyes, was nonetheless caught in the photograph.

In 1998, new home construction changed the site. A development called Bridal Path now stands where a lone ranch house and acres of trees once stood. The final question must be, what will happen to the ghostly manifestations? With the Grimes case still unsolved, many are betting on the supernatural.

72 THE GRIMES GIRLS

Location:	German Church Road (83rd Street) just east of County Line Road (where creek bends towards road), Burr Ridge.
Type of occurrences:	Rare sightings of a ghost car and, more common, car noises with no real or visible car in immediate area.
Characteristics:	Events reported are believed to be caused by a psychic re-enactment of the dumping of the victims' bodies here decades ago. The case is still unsolved so the psychic events will continue until there is closure.
Status:	No recent sightings of car, but sounds seem to still be ongoing.

THE SOUL OF A PET

HINSDALE ANIMAL CEMETERY

Metro Chicago's first animal cemetery is the Hinsdale Animal Cemetery, opened in 1926. Originally founded in once unincorporated Hinsdale, suburban sprawl has now caught up with this seven acre, 20,000-grave cemetery for beloved pets. The Remkus family has owned and operated this cemetery since 1950.

Dogs, cats, horses, even birds and other exotic pets have been laid to rest here. Besides family pets, there have been championship breeds, hero dogs, and seeing eye dogs interred, all with dignity and appropriate headstones and markers. On many of the markers, photographs of the pets are displayed. Pinwheels, reflectors, and other ornaments on the graves show the unbroken bond of affection owners have for their pets.

One unique marker has both a pet's photo and a portrait of Elvis Presley. This site is the last resting-place of "Tippy, the Elvis Dog," a well-known performer around Chicago for many years.

Tippy was a basset hound that became a part of Elvis impersonator Mike Keating's musical show. Tippy would come out on stage when Mike sang the Elvis classic, "Hound Dog," and to the delight of the audience, would howl right along. But Tippy was more that just a fixture in Keating's tribute show; the dog had actually met and sang with Elvis at one time.

One night while still a puppy, Tippy was in the car with Keating family members outside an Elvis performance. A limo pulled alongside their car. They could see Elvis at the limo window pointing to the real "hound dog." He rolled down his window and began to croon to Tippy. The basset hound began "singing" his melodious response.

From that time on, Tippy was bestowed the title, "the Elvis dog. " That became the moniker for which the public knew him when he performed on stages with Mike around the Midwest for many years. When Tippy eventually died, the performer was laid to rest at the Hinsdale Animal Cemetery.

When performing in the area, Mike Keating would stop by the cemetery in the early hours before dawn and visit his old partner and faithful sidekick. There were no fences, so Tippy's grave was easy to visit late at night.

It was Mike who discovered the ghost hound at Hinsdale Animal Cemetery. On a number of those visits, an eerie sound would carry through the cemetery, a ghostly howling. It certainly wasn't the voice of Tippy that Mike knew so well, although it was a definite hound's baying with otherworldly qualities. Mike did take the time to investigate the possible origins of the sound, but never came up with a "living" source. As the sounds continued for years, the likelihood of a living hound being responsible became more remote.

Mike Keating told me he believed the sounds to definitely be of a ghostly origin. Even though it might not be Tippy's voice, it was reassuring to Mike that even animals can survive death. Perhaps Tippy is performing again with Elvis somewhere tonight.

Hinsdale Animal Cemetery

73 Hinsdale Animal Cemetery

Location:	6400 South Bentley Avenue, Clarendon Hills.
Type of occurrence:	Auditory: sounds of a hound baying
Characteristics:	Late night baying of a dog in animal cemetery area
Status:	Was ongoing, but no recent reports.

GHOST IS NOT ON THE MENU

THE HAUNTED COUNTRY HOUSE RESTAURANT

In 1974, David and Patrick Regnery purchased a country store with a bar and grill in the western suburb of Clarendon Hills. The old wooden building dated back to the early 1900s and had been a roadhouse in the days when this part of the area was undeveloped.

After an extensive remodeling that modernized the building, yet still kept a cozy, rustic look, the Country House Restaurant opened in the early winter of 1975. Little by little, incidents happened that perhaps individually could be explained away, but as they continued and seemed to intensify, the new owners began to wonder if the building might be haunted.

During the mid-1970s, I appeared as a guest on many radio talk shows at nearby WTAQ Radio. Since the Country House advertised on the station, I often wound up at the restaurant with the radio hosts after the programs to take advantage of the station's trade agreement. I became a good friend of the Regnerys and was able to keep tabs on the ghostly occurrences as they developed.

David Regnery told me how at first he heard noises, sounds that could be heard plainly, like someone walking around upstairs or coming down the staircase. When he investigated these phantom footsteps, there was never anyone there. In the beginning, David thought that maybe these sounds were caused by old boards or timbers in the heart of the building creaking and groaning through stress or temperature changes. But once he learned about the apparition, David became a confirmed believer.

One night, David was greeting and carding people at the front door when a customer came in with his date. "What kind of place are you running here, David?" the man asked. He insisted that he plainly saw a mysterious woman in a white dress looking out of a top floor window, facing the parking lot. She was seductively beckoning with her hand to come inside.

Regnery knew that this was the window to a storage room and that it was always locked. He ran upstairs to check, but when he let himself into the room with his key (the only key to that room), there was no one there and nothing was disturbed.

The woman in white was eventually seen by others, not only looking out onto the parking lot, but also on the other side of the building, facing traffic driving down 55th Street. It became a common practice for local people, especially families with children, to "watch for the ghost" as they drove past the restaurant at night.

Although David Regnery admits he has never seen the woman in white, he has observed unusual activity at the restaurant. While in the restaurant during remodeling the building, both he and the carpenter saw the wooden shutters on the windows on the north side of the bar suddenly open by themselves. Sunlight instantly flooded the room. There was no explanation as to how a series of shutters, unattached to each other, could have accidentally opened. To this day those shutters are often in need of repair, being mysteriously moved and broken on a regular basis.

While at his desk in his upstairs office after hours, David has been interrupted by ghostly visitors. Usually the restaurant is closed and all doors are locked when the sounds of people entering and going to the bar are plainly heard. The footsteps and muffled voices seem to indicate a number of people are downstairs, but when David goes down to check, all is quiet. This has happened to him a number of times.

The ghostly customers have been encountered in the morning prior to opening, as well as late at night. Manager Lis Grogan has opened the building at 9:00 a.m. many times. She has often heard the sounds of clinking glasses in the bar area when she is the only one in the building.

Her scariest experience took place while she was taking a family upstairs to show them the haunted area. Lis was discussing the legends when suddenly a loud thump on the wall was heard and a piece of paneling popped out. No one was on the other side of the wall, and a great amount of effort would have been necessary to do this type of damage.

Stomping sounds, like heavy footsteps, or heavy dragging sounds have been heard many times by those on the ground floor, usually over the dining area. I have witnessed such loud noises three times.

On Father's Day night in June of 1986, I was at the Country House with a video crew working on a documentary about its ghosts. It was after hours and I was in the middle of interviewing David Regnery when everyone heard three heavy stomps coming from what seemed the west-end of the building's second floor. A police officer friend, Bill Karmia of Berwyn, who was assisting ran to check it out, but no one was there and nothing had fallen. Only a handful of people, video crew and restaurant staff, were on the premises, so we went outside to the equipment truck to play back the sound track that was recording when the sounds were heard.

The stomping sounds had not been picked up. They were either beyond the range of our microphones or perhaps beyond its capabilities.

Later that morning at about 4:00 a.m., everyone had gone home except David, two managers, and myself. The thumps returned again, once again three in number.

David instantly said, "Oh that's only the coffee machine going on. It makes noise like that all night long." At that point the coffee machine did go on, but making a totally different sort of sound.

"Well, I hoped it was the coffee machine," David quipped. We four realized the ghost was back again.

Later in 1986 on All Souls' Day, November 2, the day always thought to be very good for receiving communications from the dead, the Country House ghost was particularly active. I arrived at about 10:30 p.m. at the restaurant with a tour bus. We entered and tried to find room amidst the weekend crowd. Those who were in the dining area pointed out that there were strange sounds coming from the second story of something heavy being dragged about.

Well, it was the Halloween season, so I naturally suspected that some of the staff were playing a prank on us. I sneaked up the stairwell in an attempt to catch someone in the capricious act, but there was no one there.

Twice more, I ran up the stairs in an attempt to catch someone, but the room was always empty. When my friends pointed out, that from below, they could hear both me walking around and the dragging sounds, I realized that only a paranormal explanation would suffice.

In true poltergeist tradition, mischievous psychic activity does occur at the Country House, along with the phantom footsteps and the apparition. Anything electrical can and often is, tampered with. Lights on the same circuit have impossibly flashed on and off, one at

Country House Restaurant. View from parking lot.
Ghostly woman was first seen looking out second floor
window.

a time. A jukebox was so uncontrollable with antics, like playing by itself or playing songs no one selected that it had to be replaced by a modern CD version. The restaurant has a state of the art computer system, but there have been glitches that mystified the programmer.

A number of the employees have seen the adding machine, a manual push-button type, begin operating by itself at different times.

If you want to have an experience at the Country House, try to be seated at table number 13. Strange noises seem to plague this spot; one is the annoying crying of a baby. A peculiar scent of perfume also materializes in this area.

Perhaps the most meddlesome activity here is when the ghost calls your name over the public address system. On busy nights, customers leave their name for a table and wait in the bar area. Some come to the hostess stand claiming that their name has been called, but actually they are still far down on the list. This has occurred with uncommon names too, so there is no chance of hearing a similar name and being mistaken.

With all the psychic action, it is amazing that only one employee is known to have quit in fear of the hauntings. That does not mean that employees are keen to stay late or be alone here. The last person to live here found that claims of the paranormal were not over exaggerated.

In the early '80s, a local police officer friend of David Regnery asked if he could temporarily stay in an upstairs room. He needed a place to crash until he could find a permanent abode. David told him he could use an upstairs room.

The police officer had a number of scary experiences. He was aroused in the middle of the night by the loud noises, which seemed to be someone on the main floor then he heard someone walking up the stairs. Each time he drew his revolver and investigated, but each time he found no one else present. Eventually, he just learned to sleep through the intrusions.

Just who is the Country House ghost and why is she earthbound? These are questions that are often asked at the restaurant. There may be one incident from long ago that could explain at least some of the hauntings.

One night in 1982, I attended the wedding reception for a professional psychic friend of mine at a Downers Grove Moose Lodge. The band had finished playing, and since the night was still young, some of us conferred on places nearby where we could continue to party. "Let's go to the Country House," I suggested.

A short while later, I was at the restaurant with well-known local psychic Evelyn Paglini and psychic astrologer Barbara Gessler. I realized the potential I had in front of me. "This place is supposedly haunted," I told my friends. "Do you feel anything?"

The two women closed their eyes and began to meditate. Soon Evelyn began describing an incident that happened in the late 1950s. As Paglini talked, Gessler added other details. Basically, the tale is that of a young blond woman, about twenty-one-years-of-age, who was in love with a bartender here. The secret lovers got into a furious row at the bar one night, and the woman left the place very upset. Jumping into her car, she drove away into the darkness and committed suicide nearby.

When David Regnery heard of these revelations, he was intrigued. He had never heard that story before and decided to look into it by calling the previous owner. Richard Montanelli had owned the location during the '50s and he confirmed that an incident very close to that described by the psychics had taken place. There was an argument and a woman had left very agitated. She died in a car wreck a short distance from the bar, and it seemed to have been a deliberate crash.

Could the anger and rage that led to this woman's death decades ago still fuel her psychic presence after all this time? Is unfinished business or even remorse over her sudden end the motivation for decades of hauntings? One thing is certain, the Country House ghost is not only widely believed in; it is constantly claiming new converts after they have their personal brushes with this tragic spirit.

The Country House Restaurant in Clarendon Hills is both Du Page County's most charming restaurant and perhaps its most haunted.

74 The Country House Restaurant

Location:	241 West 55th Street, Clarendon Hills.
Type of occurrences:	Ranges from an apparition to electrical disturbances, psychic perfume, phantom footsteps and other poltergeist activity.
Characteristics:	Most happenings are believed to be tied to a young woman's death in the Fifties.
Status:	Continuing.

SECRETS OF PEABODY'S TOMB

Mayslake Mansion and Estate

Growing up on the South Side of Chicago in the 1960s, one of the most scary, popular, adolescent stories was the legend of Peabody's Tomb. For many, as soon as you were old enough to get your driver's license and some vehicular freedom, you would drive into the wilds of Oak Brook in search of Peabody's Tomb. It was almost a rite of passage.

Parking your car adjacent to a large forested estate, you then made your way on foot to a large crypt near a brooding mansion. Entering the crypt, you would find a large glass case filled with liquid. Bubbling around inside was a corpse, the body of Peabody.

Now the real trial began. You must get back off the property and to your car without being captured by the monks who guarded the land. Robed men would chase you down with German Shepherds, and if you were captured you, were held prisoner all night. The penance was being forced to kneel on rice, salt, or pebbles and to pray through the remaining hours of the night. At dawn, you would be allowed to leave and go home.

For a very bizarre legend this persistent tale does contain some kernels of truth. There really was a man named Peabody who lived here and there was a sort of body. But let us begin with the beginning.

Francis Stuyvesant Peabody (1859-1922) was a robber baron of the first order. A coal magnate, through various backroom wheeling and dealing, he became a millionaire many times over and never got his hands dirty with soot. Peabody parlayed his coal company into a number of interlocking operations, gaining a stranglehold on coal production in the area. His ties with Samuel Insull allowed him to become the coal provider to Commonwealth Edison, along with other companies. By his thirty-fifth birthday, Peabody was raking in some ten million dollars per year.

A major player in Democratic politics, Peabody was even considered for the Democratic vice-presidential spot in 1912. Perhaps not wishing to take a pay cut, Peabody turned Woodrow Wilson down, but did work on the election campaign and later with the Bureau of Mines.

With his fabulous riches, this local King Midas decided to build himself a magnificent mansion where he could hold court and throw lavish parties. The grounds of the estate were to be extensive, large enough for holding fox hunts and other outdoor events. Peabody would call this utopia Mayslake in honor of his first and deceased wife, Mae Henderson.

Some 900 acres were purchased in Du Page County, and construction began on the big house. From 1919 to 1921, the work went on, based on plans by architect Benjamin Henry Marshall. The thirty-nine-room Tudor Revival house contained numerous fireplaces (after all, he got coal for free), expensive wood paneling, heraldic ornamentation, oversized bathrooms, secret tunnels, and hidden passages.

Peabody may have had great wealth, but he could not purchase peace of mind. He felt that one day there would be a workers' revolution in America and that he might be lynched by his employees. To cheat such a fate he planned to escape from the house via the passageways and tunnels. He would later find more practical uses for them.

Ironically, the multimillionaire never had much of a chance to enjoy his personal wonderland. A year after the mansion was completed, and with the grounds still being developed, Peabody died.

The death of Peabody came in a way he probably never envisioned. On August 22, 1922, while hosting a fox hunt, Peabody fell from his horse within sight of the mansion and died on the spot. Heart attack or fall, it made no big difference; death overtook Peabody. His son found him on the ground, while his horse loyally stood guard.

The sudden end of Peabody brought down the curtains on the Great Gatsby, Roaring Twenties, party atmosphere at Mayslake. A chance encounter between Francis' son Jack and a Franciscan priest while on a train journey led to the sale of the entire estate in 1924 to the Franciscan Order of St. Louis. Only one piece of unfinished business was left. Francis Peabody's gravesite on the estate was marked by a magnificent stone building, the Portiuncula Chapel, a replica of the famous Franciscan landmark in Italy.

Peabody's widow and son moved away, with the senior Peabody elaborately honored. He would certainly be remembered differently by some in the area, however.

The Franciscans had grand plans for their new acquisition. The mansion was turned into a home for religious retreats and a 100-room wing was added to accommodate overnight visitors. The St. Joseph Franciscan Seminary was built on land west of the estate house.

Years later, the Franciscans sold off parts of the estate. A spiritual drought occurred, and the seminary closed due to lack of entrants. By 1991, Mayslake was shut down and its eventual fate was in question.

It was during the 1950s and '60s that Mayslake was in full swing as a retreat house. Catholics from all over the Chicago area came for reflection and meditation. Many thousands attended seminars there, including me. The Franciscans gave tours of the property and talked about the Peabody connection. One of their favorite tricks was to disappear and to reappear as they told of the secret passages.

When the retreats were over, the groups dispersed and, once back in their neighborhoods talked about the mysterious Peabody whose mansion was honeycombed with secret rooms and other wonders. The legend of Peabody was becoming firmly established.

And what of the stories of Peabody's body preserved in a vat of formaldehyde? Oddly enough, there really was a body owned by the Franciscans, but it was not Francis Peabody.

The Poor Clare Sisters of Italy had a long history of unearthing the remains of martyrs from the catacombs of Rome. These bones were then painstakingly reassembled in a wax manikin and dressed in period style clothing. These life-sized figures were then sealed in glass cases, a large reliquary, and sent around the world to various religious organizations and churches.

The Franciscans of Chicagoland were given the bones of St. Innocent, an early martyr for his faith. It was this glass case, on display in their chapel, that inspired wild tales of a tank of liquid containing Peabody's corpse. St. Innocent's reliquary was even depicted on picture postcards sold by the priests.

The strange legends did have some grounding in truth. Yes, there was a man named Peabody, an eccentric, somewhat paranoid millionaire. And yes, there was also a massive chapel that could be taken for a mausoleum. Finally, there was a body in a glass case on the grounds, albeit not Peabody. Generations of teens were deluding themselves on wild goose chases.

In November of 1992, the Mayslake Estate was purchased by the Forest Preserve District of Du Page County by referendum. The 90 remaining acres of Peabody's original holding was saved from development and the buildings were conserved. But with new ownership came the need to carefully protect the property.

When Du Page County received ownership of Mayslake, a ranger moved into the mansion to protect it. Sally Beaumont lived on the grounds and had a number of unsettling experiences that seemed to verify that someone else from the Peabody estate's past was haunting. It was not Peabody, but a lonely little boy.

This was a new ghost story, previously unreported at Mayslake.

Sally described to me

Chapel erroneously called "Peabody's Tomb" over the years.

spending the night in one wing of the big house and hearing a ball bouncing just outside her door. It was almost a childish sort of game taking place, but of course, there was no one there. This happened a number of times.

Later there would be additional confirmation from the fiancée of Joe Pinter, a curator who moved into the property after Beaumont was reassigned. Looking out of the window from a top floor, she saw a small boy, maybe eight or nine years of age, with a mop of dark, curly hair. This child was seen a few times, and it was presumed that he was one and the same with the ball player.

Speculation as to the identity of the mystery boy eventually pointed to a possible illicit love. One of Peabody's celebrated secret passageways leads to an upper floor and the servants' quarters. The servants lived in Spartan conditions: a common area with mattresses for sleeping and a communal washroom and shower. Adjacent to this area, however, is a mystery room, a private room furnished with a large cedarwood closet.

The "special room" makes no sense on its surface, unless someone was being "kept" there away from all the other prying eyes of the estate. It is believed by some that Peabody kept a female servant there, a mistress who bore him a boy. Either by childhood illness or accident, the tragic product of this union died young and still haunts the mansion.

Peabody is still a name to remember throughout the Du Page County area, even though he has been dead over three-quarters of a century. His legacy is one of much mystery and folktales, but the truth here is far stranger than fiction.

75 MAYSLAKE

Location: 31st Street and Route 83, Oak Brook.
Type of occurrence: Scary teenage legend loosely based and facts and newly discovered ghost story.
Characteristics: Secluded million-dollar mansion on large estate is the setting for a number of strange legends, some of what have a factual basis.
Status: Legends still current. Ghost seems to be permanent fixture.

COLD SHOULDER
FROM A SAINT

STATUE OF ST. JOSEPH

After the Franciscan Fathers acquired the massive Mayslake estate of Francis Peabody in 1924, they embarked upon a number of construction programs. A retreat house was added onto the original mansion, and the St. Joseph Franciscan Seminary was built west of the mansion.

The seminary building, set in a semi-wooded area, had a charmed Old World look of brown brick, slate roof, and bell tower. Because the seminary chapel was open for Sunday services, it was a well-known landmark in the Oak Brook area. Worshippers would come from miles away to hear mass in the European-style chapel of dark wood festooned with traditional statues and religious paintings. I remember coming here on many a Sunday for what was known as one of the fastest masses in the area.

The entrance to the seminary was St. Joseph's Drive off Midwest Road. Standing here atop a tall brick pedestal to greet visitors, was a life-sized statue of St. Joseph holding the Christ child. The statue was like an old friend welcoming everyone to the seminary property bearing his name.

Initially a successful venture, the seminary's enrollment began to decline rapidly in the 1970s. The Franciscans were faced with no alternative than to shut down.

After closing, the large seminary building became a real estate white elephant. An attempt was made to convert the huge building into condominiums, but the venture failed. Eventually in 1993, the wrecking ball came to visit, and the magnificent old building came down in a heap of rubble. In fact, the only reminders that a seminary was once located here were the street name and the abandoned statue.

Real estate developers were eager to divide the valuable Oak Brook land, and before long, new magnificent homes were built in the area. St. Joseph's Drive still remained and the statue of St. Joseph continued to stand on silent lookout duty.

Just before the demolition of the seminary building and the development of new subdivisions, a curious event took place.

It was the spring of 1993, and I was driving down Midwest Road and preparing silently to acknowledge my old friend, the statue of St. Joseph, once again. I did a double take. I saw that he was no longer in his standard position facing the road to greet visitors. His back was turned to the flow of traffic.

Completely baffled, I did a U-turn a short distance down Midwest Road and returned to St. Joseph Drive. After parking my car, I walked up to the statue to take a closer look. The statue was facing away from the road almost completely turned around. This was no mean feat since the statue stood on a solid brick and concrete pedestal and was cast in cement.

I immediately searched the ground around the base of the statue for tell-tall signs of a bulldozer or at least a truck. The sod was undisturbed and could not have regrown in this short amount of time. And, there were no signs of replacement. So any intentional repositioning of the statue was not the answer.

At first, I suspected that the statue had come loose from its perch on the pedestal. I pushed on it. Try as I would, I could not budge the statue. The statue was firmly in place, and there was no sign of recent cement work. It was so fixed that even if the local football team had joined forces to shove the statue, they would have not been able to move it.

Since I traveled this road on a regular basis, usually every week or so, I knew that the statue's rotation was relatively recent. Questioning friends in the area did not supply any answers. It was quite the local mystery.

Bleeding crucifixes, weeping Marian icons, and other such alleged religious miracles have definitely been on the rise in recent years. St. Joseph images have, for the most part, been inactive, but there is a curious real estate custom that may hold the answer.

Statue of St. Joseph as it looks today from road with back turned to traffic.

Realtors need sales for survival. Property that does not sell means no commission. One long-standing practice in real estate is to enlist the aid of St. Joseph, patron saint of carpenters, and by a reach, realtors.

If your property just won't sell, a small statue of St. Joseph is placed in a plastic bag and buried on your property, and a plea is made for the intercession of the saint. There are realtors that swear by this custom and claim that a sale is usually imminent after this ritual.

The one necessary follow-up is, however, before you leave the property you sold; you must dig up the statue of St. Joseph and place it in a position of honor in your new home. Failure to do this is a grave slight to St. Joseph and may involve consequences.

Although this may sound totally Roman Catholic, realtors I have talked with claim that this ritual is also popular with other Christian denominations. So prevalent is this custom, realtors sell prepackaged "St. Joseph sales kits" with directions, to customers needing that edge.

When the Franciscans sold off their St. Joseph Seminary land, should they have taken the statue of the patron saint of that school with them? Did St. Joseph feel that he was in some way being slighted after years of service? Symbolically did the life-sized statue stand for the same thing as the small buried versions do?

Maybe there is an even more important question: What will Oak Brook's Saint Joseph do next?

76 Statue of St. Joseph

Location:	St. Joseph's Drive and Midwest Road, Oak Brook.
Type of occurrence:	After neglect, a holy statue seems to have rebelled against its treatment and rotated almost 180 degrees to visibly show its displeasure.
Characteristics:	Religious icon believed to have special properties.
Status:	Only the original incident.

THE GLOWING TOMBSTONE

A MONUMENT BURSTS INTO ORANGE LIGHT

In the early 1980s, a popular evening pastime for many Du Page County youths was to cruise into Naperville and head for the Sts. Peter and Paul Cemetery. Curiosity spurred them to drive along the residential and lightly traveled backside of the cemetery. The payoff was that one tombstone on a hill surrounded by many others seemed to flare up in a blast of orange flame. By the time the driver slammed on the brakes, the show was over.

As an ongoing piece of local folklore, the legend spread through the west suburbs and the glowing tombstone soon attracted a following.

I learned of the legend from Bobbi Raudebaugh, a local nurse. "Did you ever hear about the glowing tombstone?" Bobbi asked me one day. After hearing Bobbi's version of the tale, I couldn't wait for the chance to see the wonder myself.

On a spring night in 1983, I organized an impromptu group of ghost hunters. We met at an Oak Brook Steak'N'Ale restaurant. It was a weeknight and we waited till closing time. Bobbi and her friend, both eyewitnesses, would be able to guide us. At that late hour, we figured we could visit the area in relative obscurity. At 2:00 a.m., with notepads and tape recorders in hand, our party of five headed for the unknown.

We entered Naperville and found ourselves on Old Plank Road. Turning onto Columbia Street, we drove along with the old cemetery on our left, then turned left on North Street. Not far from the corner, suddenly, there it was—a brilliant flash of pale orange light that illuminated one tombstone for just a second or two. We turned around and drove back for a second look, and then a third time. The tombstone glowed each time.

Parking our car, we got out to investigate the site on foot. It was an adrenaline rush. We thought we were really onto something paranormal. One stone stood out, glowing on the hillside. This time, however, the light did not flare and go out as it had when we were driving past. The stone was illuminated by a strange orange aura.

Financial investor Dr. Robert Ritholz was one of my party that night. With an academic background in history and education, he is a shrewd observer and often helps me on cases.

He was the first to discover the obvious reason for this enigmatic light that night, and the answer would turn out to be astonishingly simple.

"When we climbed the wall and walked towards the stone, I noticed that if you stood directly between the tombstone and the light, you would block the glow," Ritholz recalled. "But to the untrained eye, if you are just driving by and not paying attention, it appeared to be continuously glowing," he added.

Just this one shiny, reflective stone was set on an angle that would reflect an orange vapor street light that stood partway down the street. It was a case of a freak topography, perfect positioning of the light source and the stone.

Querying Bobbi and her friend, we learned that the glowing phenomenon was known for about four years and, coincidentally, first reported just about the time that the new street lamps were installed with their distinctive orange hue.

*Glowing tombstone. The shiny surface of the large
stone on the right reflects an eerie glow after dark.*

Collecting ghostlore and folklore for many years, it soon became obvious that at least some tales are based more on wrong observations than reality. Quite a few colorful stories owe much more to imagination and the will to believe than to a genuine paranormal event. One of my more memorable cases was the "glowing tombstone" of Naperville.

Although I take pride in occasionally solving a colorful mystery, there are always more enigmas out there. For every such report that I can find a logical answer to, there are many more still unsolved and perhaps unsolvable.

77 Sts. Peter and Paul Cemetery

Location:	Columbia and North Streets, Naperville.
Type of occurrence:	Tombstone appears to burn with a bright light after dark.
Characteristics:	Nestled amidst many other grave markers on a hill, one stone regularly appears to suddenly illuminate as motorists drive past.
Status:	Ongoing visual occurrence.

ENIGMAS OF BACHELOR GROVE

CHICAGOLAND'S MOST HAUNTED GRAVEYARD

For South Side teenagers from the 1950s until the late '70s, the number one lovers' lane and the most haunted spot around were one and the same, Bachelor Grove Cemetery. Often confused with Bachelor Grove Forest Preserve or Bachelor Grove Road, both further west, this cemetery with the poetic name has been a magnet for the curious and would-be ghost hunters for decades.

Sadly, Bachelor Grove is a terribly defiled graveyard, where most of the original tombstones are missing and those remaining vandalized. The haunted reputation has attracted the unsavory occult elements and grave desecration, and animal sacrifices have even taken place. In an attempt to protect what is left, the Cook County Board in 1977 declared the area closed to the public. It is no longer lawful to come here, but the temptation is too strong for many.

Almost everything about Bachelor Grove Cemetery is mysterious. Even the name Bachelor is the subject of much debate. Despite the persistent legend that the area was settled by a bachelor or bachelors in pre-Civil War days, others opt for Bachelor being a surname of an early settler. Although Bachelor is the spelling commonly used on maps and county signs, it is common to find Bachelors, Bachelor's, or Bachelors' used in writings about this spot.

Before 1977 when a barricade was erected blocking car access to the cemetery, it was possible to drive down an unmarked tree lined asphalt road to the entrance of the old cemetery. Countless adventurous teens and adults made this trip, for many a rite of passage. Once they left the safety of their car, they entered into a world of many ghostly possibilities. In telling their tales later, some were greeted with disbelief. Many of these stories seem at first too strange too accept, but don't be too hasty.

The best known tale of Bachelor Grove is that of the blue ghost light. Generations of teens have visited the cemetery by night in hopes of encountering this will-of-the-wisp. A softball-sized ball of blue light bounces around the graves by night. It seems to have an intelligence of its own and teasingly approaches, then bounds away. One witness I talked to years ago was astonished to see it alight on, but not melt, fresh snow.

There are other famous ghost lights haunting the Midwest, but this is the only one blue in color. Such phenomena are ordinarily white, yellow or sometimes red. Blue is very rare.

Tales of a vanishing farm house have also been connected to Bachelor Grove since the 1970s. I must admit that I am responsible for starting that trend in ghost stories here.

During my undergrad days at De Paul University from 1966 to 1970, I actively collected accounts of Bachelor Grove. A lot of people seemed to have an adventure to relate, and in order to make sense of these tales, I would ask for them to sketch a map of the area and mark-in the landmarks. Usually the maps were fairly similar: the asphalt or gravel road, the cemetery, the creek, and the pond were all in the basically same places. Then they would describe an old wooden farmhouse, but when positioning it on their map, it could be anywhere. Sometimes it was on one side of the creek, sometimes the other. It might be to the left of the road in some accounts, but to the right in others.

Vandalized markers at Bachelor Grove Cemetery

I had been to the Grove many times and never found the celebrated house. My witnesses who claimed to have seen it certainly knew all the other landmarks there. The only thing out of place was the strange house.

Doing guest appearances on late night radio talk shows, I began to mention the vanishing house, and I was regularly contacted by people who had seen the house but didn't know that it really didn't exist. They presumed the house they saw that night was physical, until they learned years later that it was spectral. The disappearing house of Bachelors Grove became a popular late night topic on the air.

Mary Ann Kerbs saw the house one night in the mid-Sixties when visiting the Grove with friends. "On the left was an old house, wooden porch, and wooden stairs coming down," she recalled.

Another witness, Grace Nortman, saw the mystery house in the winter of 1967. While on a double date, they entered the secluded area with their car, parking near the cemetery entrance. "There was a house sixty-five to seventy feet away," Grace recalled. "It was an old farmhouse, two stories high, with a light on inside the first floor. The light was flickering , maybe a TV, and I was fearful that someone would come out with a shotgun." The couples left that night, fearing whoever might be at home in the spooky house.

Both women learned that the house they thought was real was an immaterial one by listening to my radio broadcasts. They had never met each other until I brought them together in 1986 for a reunion at Bachelor Grove. As a segment for my video, "The Ghosts of Chicago," I had the two women independently sketch the house they remembered. Despite the passage of years, the drawings were remarkable similar.

Phantom cars have become a popular type of haunting in the post Word War II era. But how can a car haunt if a car has no soul? Nonetheless, disappearing or phantom cars have been documented, and I have seen such images twice around Bachelor Grove Cemetery.

Road next to Grove plagued by disappearing car reports.

One warm Saturday night early in the summer of 1977, I was showing Bachelor Grove Cemetery to my friend, author Jim Brandon. Jim was in town researching his guidebook, *Weird America*, and wanted to visit the place I had so often told him about.

After encountering no ghosts, just swarms of ravenous mosquitoes, we decided to leave. I began driving west on 143rd Street, heading towards Ridgeland Avenue. We were about to cross a small bridge when I defensively swerved slightly to my left. I was passing a car, dark and medium sized, parked on the shoulder with its lights off. Just as I came up even with it, the car literally vanished. I yelled at Jim, "Hey, did you see that?" but Jim had been facing toward me talking and had not been watching the road, so he had not seen anything.

I hit the brakes and instinctively looked at my watch. It was 10:02 p.m. I tried to explain to Brandon what I had just seen, and both of us tried to come up with a natural explanation. It was not confusion over a reflection in the rear view mirror; there were no other cars on the road. I was not overly tired and had not been drinking.

The entire incident nagged at me for more than a year. I couldn't rationally believe it and only discussed it with a few close friends. Then came my second experience.

It was another Saturday night, September 16, 1978, and I was driving south on Cicero Avenue. Being close, I gave into my urge to drive past Bachelor Grove again. I hadn't been there in a number of months and just decided to take a look. It was almost 11:30 p.m. when I turned west onto Midlothian Turnpike, angling into 143rd Street.

Minutes later, I could see the entrance to Bachelors Grove cemetery coming up on my left and the Rubio Woods on my right. I spotted a car backing into the entrance of Rubio Woods. I could tell by its lights that it was a large car and probably older, an early '70s model.

It blended into the darkness as its lights went out. I naturally presumed that this was a squad car hiding in the shadows to snag a speeder. I had seen police here many times before.

I cut my speed, and as I came closer, I looked for the car. I saw nothing. When I saw a chain blocking the driveway entrance into the woods, a chill ran up my spine. I realized that there was no way someone could have driven in and replaced that chain in those few seconds that had elapsed. No cars were back in the parking lot, none were on the road, and there was nowhere for a car to hide because the entrance to the woods crosses a narrow culvert.

Once again a car had vanished before my eyes. Now I knew that my original experience a year before was real.

These days it is impossible to visit Bachelor Grove Cemetery without finding discarded film wrappers and boxes everywhere. This is certainly the best known site in the Midwest for photographing ghostly images. From Polaroids to Nikons, the psychic safaris have attempted to catch on film evidence of ghosts. At this spot many think they have been successful. Credit for the first reported "ghost" photos taken here goes to Tony Vaci, an Oak Lawn artist, who, by chance, discovered the strange effect this place can have on film. In July of 1974, Tony, his brother, and a cousin were enjoying a walk in the woods.

Tony had just purchased a Polaroid SX70 camera and was eager to try it out. Even before he could frame a scene, his camera fired off by itself. That afternoon Tony's new camera continued to act up.

"I took a number of photos, and the ones that fired by themselves had a 'mist' on them," Tony remembered, "There was no fog or mist present to the human eye at the time. The images were on photos, but not visible to the human eye."

The puzzling Polaroid photos showed a mysterious fogging or mist in different shapes. Most of the shots were taken in the western portion of the cemetery, an area with dense underbrush and trees. That area allowed for greater contrast between the green foliage and the "mist" in the foreground.

Was it bad film or a defective camera? Tony decided to drive to the Polaroid offices in Oak Brook.

"I was there a couple of hours." Tony said. "They took the camera apart and couldn't find anything wrong with it. There was nothing wrong with the film, either. They just couldn't explain it."

Tony began experimenting at Bachelor Grove with more rolls of film. He began to develop a real knack at capturing strange images on film. He contacted me that summer and we collaborated on a number of experiments.

I would buy the film and load it, so Tony never had the chance to tamper with the film. Squeezing a film pack can cause some chemicals to run and leave strange marks on the photos. Tony took photos, and so did I. Whatever was out there was pretty consistent. On almost every trip, we found an area where images popped up, although we had to sometimes shoot a number of normal shots before trapping our quarry.

From 1974 to 1977, Tony amassed a collection of hundreds of Polaroid photos taken here. About 200 have definite images of the phantom mist, some better than others.

Whatever this "stuff" is, it is not cold, wet, or anything that you can feel. In experiments with Tony, I was photographed walking right through it and I could feel nothing. Only the camera could tell.

*Bachelor Grove,
author walking into the
mystery mist unaware of
the manifestation
around him.*

Photo by Tony Vaci

Researcher Dr. Peter Bander, psychic Uri Geller, and many others have been fascinated by the Vaci photos. Although others have taken enigmatic photos at the Grove, Tony Vaci's were not only the first on record, but also the clearest and best defined.

In recent years, photographs taken here cannot touch the Vaci images for quality. Polaroid was always better that standard film for some reason, but then Polaroid changed their lens. The original photos were taken with a camera that had a glass lens. In later models, the lens was plastic, and the classic images were no longer being taken.

In my slide lectures over the years, images of Tony Vaci's Bachelor Grove Polaroids continue to elicit great audience response. I would also guess that Tony's work has inspired thousands of amateur ghost hunters and been responsible for tens of thousands of dollars in film sales. Students seeing these photos have created high school science fair projects on psychic photography.

New photographic discoveries here are probably still waiting. It will just take finding the right combination of film, camera, and photographer to once again unlock photographically more enigmas of Bachelor Grove.

Bachelor Grove Cemetery does not draw the crowds it once did in its golden years of the 1960s and '70s. The efforts of the Cook County Police to patrol and seal off the area have been successful, especially around Halloween time. There is only one thing, however, that the authorities can have no ultimate control over at Bachelor Grove Cemetery—the dead.

BACHELOR GROVE CEMETERY

Location:	Intersection of Midlothian Turnpike and 143rd Street, unincorporated area west of Midlothian.
Type of occurrences:	This old graveyard plays host to visual hauntings including disappearing cars and a vanishing house, nebulous blobs of ectoplasm, a blue ghost light, and more. Catching ghosts on film has been a favorite pastime since 1974.
Characteristics:	This cemetery is so haunted that a range of psychic possibilities await the visitor.
Statue:	Photographic anomalies ongoing. Apparitions sporadic.

GLOSSARY OF TERMS

ALL SAINTS DAY
November 1. The Catholic Church honors its official saints on this day. It is also a day considered special for supernatural activity.

ALL SOULS DAY
November 2. Perhaps even more charged with psychic potential than Halloween, All Souls Day is the Catholic Church's day set aside to remember all the dead, our ancestors, those who have gone before. Many unique supernatural events have occurred on this day.

ANCESTRAL SPIRIT
An ancient spirit that can follow certain families of groups of families to wherever they migrate. These spirits are considered watchers and protectors and often give forewarnings of death or tragedy. Certain royal or historic families claim such connections. The Irish banshee is one example.

APPARITION
A ghost seen visually. It can be solid or semitransparent. It may also be multiple figures or an entire scene.

BACKWARDS HALLOWEEN
October 13. A relatively modern creation. Reversing numbers is a popular occult pastime. The reverse of Halloween's October 31 is October 13. There is no evidence that there is any more potential for this day than any other, unless it happens to fall on a Friday the 13th.

CLARENCE DARROW'S PROMISED RETURN
March 13. Every year, followers and friends of "Attorney for the Damned", Clarence Darrow gather at 10:00 a.m. at a bridge over the Jackson Park Lagoon to await his return from the dead. Darrow died in 1938.

COLD SPOT
A psychic manifestation of extreme cold in a small area or as a "wall of cold" that one can walk through. Because the area is localized, it cannot be explained as natural in origin. It sometimes precedes an apparition.

CURSE
Usually a curse is bad luck caused by a verbal pronouncement. Sometimes a curse is not articulated but caused by owning something connected with a tragedy, especially one involving great evil.

DEVILS NIGHT
October 30. An American creation, this is the eve of Halloween celebrated in Detroit by the burning of garages and other acts of arson.

FENG SHUI
Feng=Wind, Shui=Water. The Chinese science of placement and harmony. This is a holistic approach to achieving balance in your life so physical and psychic problems (including ghosts) don't arise. The five elements, water, wood, fire, earth, and metal, interact in productive sequence to shape and stimulate one's daily life, which leads to harmony, prosperity, and happiness. If this sequence is out of order, it can cause bad events and calamities.

GHOST
The popular term for the returning soul of a dead person. Ghosts can be encountered through any of the five senses or through dreams. Electronically they can be taped, photographed, videotaped, or "measured." They have been believed in since the dawn of time and are still strongly believed in worldwide.

GHOST LIGHT
A ball of light seen at a certain spot with some form or regularity that cannot be explained by conventional means. White or yellow or yellow-orange are by far the most common. Red and blue are scarce.

GHOSTLY MANIFESTATIONS, TYPES OF
Ghosts can be seen (apparitions, ghost lights, etc.) but can also be experienced by the other senses. They can also be heard (phantom footsteps, disembodied screams, unexplained crashes, etc.); smelled (see PSYCHIC SCENT); and felt (tapping on shoulder, invisible cobweb sensation, and chill up spine, etc.). Some ghosts are caught on photographs while remaining invisible to human eyes.

HALLOWEEN
October 31. After sundown this day is traditionally thought to be the beginning of a period of time when the dead roam the earth. This Druidic belief was adopted by Catholic Church who hold November 1 and 2 sacred. "All Hallows Eve," the eve of All Saints Day, became Halloween.

HITCHHIKING GHOST
A popular type of female ghost that can be blonde or brunette or from any ethnic group, but always beautiful, who accepts a ride "home", only to disappear later under mysterious circumstances. Chicago's "Resurrection Mary" is perhaps America's best-known ghostly hitchhiker.

JINX
Bad luck, usually mischievous, caused by a supernatural means, but not as vicious as a curse.

PHANTOM CAR
A rare type of vision in which a car haunts. These cars are usually described as black or dark in color and at locations of murders or cemeteries.

POLTERGEIST
A mischievous ghost from the German term for a pelting ghost, one who throws things. A poltergeist is not seen itself, but affects things by moving them or causing rapping or knocking sounds. Although some types of poltergeist activity can be caused by living people unconsciously, there are haunted places where this activity has taken place for many years and is tied to other manifestations.

PSYCHIC PHOTOGRAPHY
Capturing "ghosts" on film is a popular pastime. Fully formed images are rare, but anomalous streaks of light or fogging on photographs are believed to be caused by ghosts. Certain locations, like Bachelor Grove Cemetery, seem to produce such photos with regularity.

PSYCHIC SCENT
An olfactory experience that is believed to be caused by a ghost. Floral scents or perfume are common. Pipe or cigar scent (without smoke) has also been reported.

SABBAT
There are four major witches' sabbats (Sabbath) throughout the year: Samhain (October 31, Halloween); Imbolc (February 1); Beltane (May 1, May Day); Lughnasadh (August 1). Supernatural happenings seem to occur on these dates.

SIMULACRA
A spontaneous image thought to be caused by nonhuman or supernatural means. From images seen in cloud patterns to ghostly imagery in the shadows and background of photographs, these devilish forms taunt us. Are they "real" or just the product of our imagination? These images are usually faces and sometimes identifiable as known individuals.

SPIRIT
A nonphysical entity that may be of human or nonhuman origin. (Angels or devils are spirits, but never existed in a human body.)

SOUL
The theological term for the surviving, spiritual portion of a human being after death.

TELEKINESIS
Objects moving without apparent cause.

WALPURGISNACHT
April 30. The halfway point to Halloween and the second most evil night in the occultic calendar. Named after St. Walpurgis, after sundown on this day, evil is unleashed. Walpurgisnacht or Walpurgis Night is much better known in Germany and Central Europe than in the U.S.

WEREWOLF
Traditionally a human who can transform himself into a wolf. It may also be a ghost or spirit that manifests itself as a wild beast.

BIBLIOGRAPHY

Besides the sources already mentioned in the text, a number of books have been particularly helpful to me in writing this book. To begin to unravel the twisted history of Chicagoland ghosts, the following sources can provide the searcher with a firm footing in history, geography, literature, politics, crime and other human endeavors that shape these specters.

To understand ghosts, one must get into their heads and find out what was important to them: how they lived in a physical existence and how they died. The social history of Chicagoland from pioneer days to the present is an essential component in tackling Chicago ghost hunting.

Anonymous. *X Marks the Spot: Chicago Gang War in Pictures*, no location: Spot Publishing Company, 1930. A heavily illustrated exposé of Chicago's turf wars during Prohibition. Published before Capone was sent to prison, no wonder the author preferred to remain unknown. It is a great source for addresses of locations.

Bach, Ira J., editor, *Chicago's Famous Buildings*, Third Edition, Chicago: University of Chicago Press, 1980. A superb introduction to many of Chicago's buildings, and its compact size and tight text makes this the perfect volume for day tripping. I knew Ira Bach during his Planning Department days at City Hall.

Busch, Francis X. *Casebook of the Curious and True*, Indianapolis: Bobbs-Merrill Company, 1957. Busch personally knew and interviewed George Streeter. The strange saga of Streeterville from the Captain's point of view is contained in the chapter "To Hell with the Law."

Girardin, G. Russell, with William J. Helmer. *Dillinger: The Untold Story*, Bloomington: Indiana University, 1994. To date this is the definitive Dillinger biography. Girardin obtained information from Dillinger's lawyer, Louis Piquett, that was never before published and probably too "hot" to print until most of the cast of characters were dead. Crime authority Helmer met Girardin years later and greatly expanded upon the vintage Girardin material. This will undoubtedly remain the last word in Dillinger research since all major contemporaries are now dead. Helmer, a founder of the John Dillinger Died for You Society, is a longtime friend and associate.

Heath, Chester H. *Spirit Photographs at Treasure Sites*, New York: Vantage Press, 1976. Author Heath has captured ghost lights and "simulacra" images on photographs at a number of Native American-related sites. This book relates only to Georgia and Cherokee locations but is of use to anyone interested in claims of spirit photography. Treasure hunters have often alleged ghost encounters and now photographic evidence seems to collaborate these reports.

Helmer, William, with Rick Mattix. *Public Enemies: America's Criminal Past 1919-1940*, New York: Facts on File, 1998. From Prohibition to our entry into World War II the bootleggers, gangsters and outlaw bank robbers caught the public's attention. When times were hard, the lawbreakers became folk heroes. Crime may have been national in scope, but Chicago was a major theater of operation. This book is the best so far to document the big picture. Helmer and Mattix are especially good at recording locations that can be visited by the historically minded.

Johnson, Curt, with R. Craig Sautter. *Wicked City Chicago: From Kenna to Capone*, Highland Park, IL: December Press, 1994. The authors dish out a fascinating crime and social history look at Chicago.

Karamanski, Theodore J. *Rally 'Round the Flag: Chicago and the Civil War*, Chicago: Nelson-Hall Publishers, 1993. A definitive and fully documented history of this period with much detail on the Lincoln funeral train.

Lanctot, Barbara. *A Walk Through Graceland Cemetery*, revised edition, Chicago: Chicago Architecture Foundation, 1988. Short but to the point, this is a fine introduction to Graceland Cemetery art and architecture.

Lindberg, Richard. *Return to the Scene of the Crime: A Guide to Infamous Places in Chicago*, Nashville: Cumberland House, 1999. Lindberg is a Chicago author of note and this is his best work to date. For Chicago buffs this work is essential for addresses and locations of nefarious places around the Metro area. To Lindberg's credit, he often disputes the "official" version of a crime. His account of the Kowalski "jump" from the John Hancock is a good example of his diligence.

Longstreet, Stephen. *Chicago: An Intimate Portrait of People, Pleasures, and Power: 1860-1919*, New York: David McKay Company, Inc. 1973. A large, easy reading volume that covers everything its subtitle promises.

McDonald, Forrest. *Insull*, Chicago: University of Chicago Press, 1962. The definitive biography.

Miller, Ross. *American Apocalypse: The Great Fire and the Myth of Chicago*, Chicago: University of Chicago Press, 1990. Ross offers a new reinterpretation of the Chicago Fire and how it changed this city.

Nash, Jay Robert and Ron Offen. *Dillinger: Dead or Alive?* Chicago: Regnery, 1970.

Nash, Jay Robert. *The Dillinger Dossier*, Highland Park, IL: December Press, 1983. These are the primary sources for the "Dillinger's Double" theory. Although this theory has lost steam over the years, Nash's research does serve to point out the many mysteries surrounding Dillinger's time on the run and the possibility that he, or someone, was set up for assassination.

Sautter, R. Craig, and Edward M. Burke. *Inside the Wigwam: Chicago Presidential Conventions 1860-1996,* Chicago: Wild Onion Books, 1996. A wonderful history of Chicago's importance in national political conventions since the days of the Civil War. Co-author Alderman Ed Burke is a fellow classmate of mine from Visitation grammar school.

Sinkevitch, Alice, editor. *AIA Guide to Chicago,* San Diego: Harcourt Brace and Company, 1993. This American Institute of Architects guidebook covers all parts of Metro Chicago. Its many photographs, superb maps and concise text makes it the single most user friendly and essential work of its kind.

Stead, William T. *If Christ Came to Chicago!,* Evanston, Chicago Historical Bookworks, 1990. William T. Stead was a social reformer and a spiritualist who went down to glory on the *Titanic.* After visiting Chicago at the close of the 19th Century, he published a scathing account of what he saw here. This is a reprint of the 1894 edition, a classic of Chicago social history.

Whittington-Egan, Richard, editor. *Weekend Book of Ghosts,* no location: Associated Newspapers Group Ltd., 1975. This is a rare English anthology of "true" ghost stories previously published in London's *Weekend* magazine. (I found my copy in a Limerick City bookstore in 1976.) One of the articles is "The Curse on Al Capone" by Peter Ellis, the account of the haunting of Capone by James Clark. In an attempt to contact Ellis for more information on this tale, I wrote the editor, Richard Whittington-Egan, a well known true-crime and Jack the Ripper expert. According to Whittington-Egan, Ellis just vanished after publication of the article and never surfaced for his fee. This, the only source account of the Clark haunting, is extremely detailed and seems genuine.

Woodyard, Chris. *Haunted Ohio,* Beavercreek, OH: Kestrel Publications, 1991
_____. *Haunted Ohio II,* Beavercreek, OH: Kestrel Publications, 1992.
_____. *Haunted Ohio III,* Beavercreek, OH: Kestrel Publications, 1994. Woodyard's stories range from traditional to historically based. A number of accounts have Chicago connections including Julia Dent Grant's dream premonition of the Chicago Fire. (U.S. Grant was born in southern Ohio.)

THE LAST WORD

"I never met a ghost I didn't like."
(With apologies to Will Rogers.)

Richard T. Crowe

The most interesting thing about a "true" ghost story is that it never really has an ending. The haunting may start up again, and often does.

The tales presented in this volume are far from over. You, dear reader, may have an experience at one of these sites, or you may discover a previously unrecognized haunted spot.

Please keep me in mind and get in touch with me when that day occurs. Statistics show that most people will have a psychic experience during their lifetime. To be forewarned is to be forearmed.

DARE TO VISIT REAL HAUNTED SITES

The Chicago Supernatural Tours: afternoon and evening versions, year round.
The Chicago Supernatural Cruise: summer through Labor Day.
Supernatural Chinatown: lunch/lecture/walking tour, year round.
And out-of-state trips: Voodoo New Orleans;
                           Witchcraft Salem, MA;
                           Haunted Civil War Gettysburg; and more.

Richard Crowe also offers nine different slide lectures.
Both public events and private parties are available.
Call or write for more details.

Richard T. Crowe, Chicagoland Ghost Hunter
P.O. Box 557544
Chicago, IL 60655-7544
(708) 499-0300
http://www.ghosttours.com

This guide was written to document the many supernatural sites and tales around Chicagoland.

It is your duty to use the information properly. Private property must always be respected. Parks, cemeteries, forest preserves as well as churches, museums, restaurants, and bars all have set hours. Check before you visit. Trespassing is a crime, Always be respectful of those who own or manage these sites. Do not be disruptive or attempt to take photographs without permission. Be polite and courteous at all times.

Certain sites may be in high crime areas. Always stay alert and be prepared, The best ghost hunter is the one who is the most observant and least obtrusive. Knowing as much as possible about a site before you visit will greatly enhance your chances for a unique experience.

Good luck and good ghost hunting!

Richard T. Crowe

RICHARD T. CROWE'S SUPERNATURAL TOUR CHRONOLOGY

1973

First Chicago Ghost Tour runs on October 27, sponsored by De Paul University's Geographic Society. The waiting list of over 100 prompted me to hire two coaches myself and hold two more tours in December. The world's first ghost and supernatural travel service is born.

1974

More requests in spring lead to public tours being offered on a regular basis. I am invited to speak at various events and start creating a series of slide lectures. Hillside Shopping Mall hires me for a private tour and both public events and private charters are now available.

1977

A new tour called the Chicago Supernatural Tour (also an afternoon tour) replaces the original package. Bachelor Grove Cemetery is closed to the public, so new and different sites are developed.

1979

After running the tours as a part-time operation for six years, I go full time. I leave my job in the Planning Department of the City of Chicago and become a full-time tour guide, lecturer and ghost hunter.

1980

The nighttime edition of the Chicago Supernatural Tour is launched. Meant to be run in the evening when cemeteries are closed, it features haunted bar and restaurant locations. It becomes far more popular than the afternoon tour.

1981

A three-day weekend package, Haunted and Voodoo New Orleans, is offered including airfare, hotel and walking tours. It becomes an annual event.

1985

Haunted Dillinger Jail Tours are offered to Crown Point, Indiana. The coach tour includes lunch in a restaurant located in the old jail complex and a tour of the building where bank robber John Dillinger escaped in 1934. The tour is discontinued in 1986 due to the restaurant closure and renovation needs of the jail.

The Chicago Supernatural Cruise is offered on the Chicago River and Lake Michigan. In partnership with Mercury the Skyline Cruiselines, I created a tour of local maritime material ranging from haunted buildings on the waterways to ghost ships and lake monsters. This begins the world's only supernatural cruise.

1988

"The Ghosts of Chicago," a 90-minute video is released. This production, narrated and written by Richard T. Crowe, is also an infomercial on television. The first and only video on Chicagoland ghosts, it is still in print.

1989

A three-day package, Salem Witchcraft, is offered to Salem, Massachusetts. Featuring colonial witchcraft sites and a dinner party with a local witch, the tour becomes an annual event, It is usually held yearly at Beltane, Mayday, a witches' holiday.

1997

Supernatural Sunday, a dual event of lunch at the haunted Country House restaurant and a tour of Mayslake, the Peabody estate, runs for a number of months. Zoning problems at Mayslake force it to end. Supernatural Chinatown, a package of lunch in a haunted restaurant, slide talk and walking tour begins. This event becomes very popular with corporate and senior groups, as well as the general public. It is my first tour to concentrate on one neighborhood.

1999

Haunted Gettysburg, a four-day bus tour to Civil War locations, premiers. Offered through the Oak Brook Terrace Park District, this tour is expanded to five days in 2000. It becomes an annual offering.